DECODING PRIVILEGE

This book explores how White students understand the concept of privilege so that educators can more effectively teach students about social power and inequality. Specially, the text examines three elements that influence how White college students understand privilege: Ideas, beliefs, and feelings. As this volume demonstrates, examining all three aspects of students' understanding is critical for educators who wish to effectively educate White students about the nature of social inequality and specific manifestations of privilege. The book concludes with curricular and pedagogical considerations that educators may incorporate into their teaching practice.

D. Scott Tharp is an affiliated faculty member in the MSW Program at DePaul University and a scholar-practitioner and educational interventionist in the areas of social justice education curriculum design, facilitation, and assessment. For more information, visit his website at https://dscotttharp.wixsite.com/portfolio.

DECODING PRIVILEGE

Exploring White College Students' Views on Social Inequality

D. Scott Tharp

Cover image: Getty Images

First published 2022
by Routledge
605 Third Avenue, New York, NY 10158

and by Routledge
4 Park Square, Milton Park, Abingdon, Oxon, OX14 4RN

Routledge is an imprint of the Taylor & Francis Group, an informa business

© 2022 D. Scott Tharp

The right of D. Scott Tharp to be identified as author of this work has been asserted in accordance with sections 77 and 78 of the Copyright, Designs and Patents Act 1988.

All rights reserved. No part of this book may be reprinted or reproduced or utilised in any form or by any electronic, mechanical, or other means, now known or hereafter invented, including photocopying and recording, or in any information storage or retrieval system, without permission in writing from the publishers.

Trademark notice: Product or corporate names may be trademarks or registered trademarks, and are used only for identification and explanation without intent to infringe.

Library of Congress Cataloging-in-Publication Data
A catalog record for this book has been requested

ISBN: 978-0-367-53531-5 (hbk)
ISBN: 978-0-367-53529-2 (pbk)
ISBN: 978-1-003-08237-8 (ebk)

DOI: 10.4324/9781003082378

Typeset in Bembo
by Apex CoVantage, LLC

*To the many formal and informal educators and mentors
in my life who helped me learn and stay accountable through
participation in the Antiracism Discourse. And to my family,
Krista, Leo, and Auggie, whose presence reminds me why
participation in the Antiracism Discourse is
necessary and critical.*

CONTENTS

List of figures		*viii*
Acknowledgments		*x*
Preface		*xii*
	Introduction: Contextualizing White College Students' Views About Privilege	1
1	Exploring How Student Learning Works	22
2	How Social Groups Contextualize Learning About and Our Understanding of Privilege	43
3	Core Ideas About Privilege	67
4	Anchoring Beliefs About Privilege	98
5	Compelling Feelings About Privilege	129
6	An Iron Triangle: How Ideas, Beliefs, and Feelings Collectively Inform Our Understanding About Privilege	170
	Conclusion: What Have We Learned and Where Do We Go?	193
Index		*217*

FIGURES

1.1	Visualizing Information About Privilege Organized Around Social Power	28
1.2	Visualizing Information About Privilege Organized Around Hard Work	29
1.3	Visualizing the Relationship Between Information About Privilege and a Belief in Equality	33
1.4	Visualizing the Relationship Between Information About Privilege and a Belief in Superiority	33
3.1	Visualizing the Relationship Between Race Critical Knowledge Ideas	77
3.2	Visualizing the Relationship Between White Racial Knowledge Ideas	90
6.1	Visual Representation of Ideas, Beliefs, and Feelings Related to a Discourse	172
6.2	Clockwise Visual Representation of How Ideas, Beliefs, and Feelings Reinforce One Another	173
6.3	Counterclockwise Visual Representation of How Ideas, Beliefs, and Feelings Reinforce One Another	173
6.4	Visual Representation of Ideas, Beliefs, and Feelings Related to the Whiteness Discourse	175
6.5	Visual Representation of Specific Ideas, Beliefs, and Feelings Related to the Whiteness Discourse	175
6.6	Clockwise Visual Representation of How White Racial Knowledge, a White Supremacist Ideology, and an Emotionality of Whiteness Reinforce One Another	177

6.7	Counterclockwise Visual Representation of How White Racial Knowledge, a White Supremacist Ideology, and an Emotionality of Whiteness Reinforce One Another	178
6.8	Visual Representation of How Select Ideas, Beliefs, and Feelings Associated With the Whiteness Discourse Reinforce One Another	179
6.9	Visual Representation of Ideas, Beliefs, and Feelings Related to the Antiracism Discourse	181
6.10	Visual Representation of Specific Ideas, Beliefs, and Feelings Related to the Antiracism Discourse	182
6.11	Clockwise Visual Representation of How Race Critical Knowledge, a Race Critical Ideology, and Racial Emotional Resiliency Reinforce One Another	183
6.12	Counterclockwise Visual Representation of How Race Critical Knowledge, a Race Critical Ideology, and Racial Emotional Resiliency Reinforce One Another	184
6.13	Visual Representation of How Select Ideas, Beliefs, and Feelings Associated With the Antiracism Discourse Reinforce One Another	185

ACKNOWLEDGMENTS

This book was a long-term labor of love made possible with support from a community of scholars, professionals, family, and friends. First, I am grateful to the many formal and informal educators and mentors throughout my life who introduced me to the Antiracism Discourse and helped me develop into a scholar-practitioner committed to social justice. Among these individuals, special thanks go to Rev. H. Scott Matheney, Richard Hazley, Dr. Brenda Forester, Roger Moreano, Dr. Michael Spencer, Dr. Beth Glover Reed, and Dr. Diane Goodman. I would not be the person or professional I am today without their dedication to antiracism and patience educating and mentoring White people like myself. Furthermore, my endless gratitude goes to the many colleagues who belong to my National Conference on Race and Ethnicity in American Higher Education (NCORE) community for making this space a place where I have been able to grow over the years.

The original research used for this book would not have been possible without the steadfast support and guidance of Dr. Torica L. Webb, along with additional insight and feedback from Dr. Thomas Philip, Dr. Josh Radinsky, Dr. David Stovall, and Dr. Victoria Trinder. Additional thanks go to Dr. Joe Feagin for generously sharing his time to discuss his research and offering insights on my original analyses related to Whiteness. I am further appreciative to the numerous unnamable professional colleagues and students at Great Lakes College who supported this research and believed in the worthiness of its findings.

I was fortunate to have tremendous support from colleagues and friends through the drafting of these chapters. Special thanks go to Dr. Horace Hall and Dr. Krista Rajanen for being generous with their time to review the entire manuscript and offer thoughtful feedback and encouragement. Additional thanks go to Dr. Diane Goodman, Dr. Charmaine Wijeyesinghe, Erik Hodges, and Matt

Turskey for their feedback on select chapters. Finally, I am appreciative to the many colleges and friends of mine who indulged my constant discussions about the broader topics and ideas presented in this book.

The production of this book was made possible with the support from another wonderful set of individuals. I am grateful for the support from DePaul University's Center for Writing-based Learning, specifically Jen Finstrom and Lexi Jackson, for reviewing and copy editing the early versions of the manuscript. A huge thank you goes to the wonderful team from Routledge for their help turning this manuscript into a book, with special thanks to Matthew Friberg for his early support and belief in this project.

Last, but not least, I want to express my deepest appreciation to my family and friends for their enthusiastic support and encouragement throughout this project. I specifically want to thank my parents, Betsy and Dave, for being my longest supporters. Most of all, thank you to my wife and children, Krista, Leo, and Auggie, for being my eternal motivation for this work and everything I do.

PREFACE

Personalizing Education About Privilege

Early in my career as a social justice educator, I would feel frustrated with students in my classes or workshops who did not seem to get "it." The "it" was an enlightened understanding of privilege as a structural phenomenon that provides benefits to members of social identities based on who they are, not based on anything they have done. I was not alone in my frustration. Many of my colleagues also shared these feelings of frustration. Sometimes we would joke that we wish we could just shake them until the wisdom and knowledge about social justice would permeate their consciousness like a snow globe. Alas, as we all knew, shaking our students was not nor would ever be possible.

What is interesting about my memory of these conversations is that I was one of those unenlightened college students who struggled to get "it." During my high school and early college experience, I was a firm believer that privilege was not what my teachers and peers of color made it out to be. In high school, I participated in a class debate to argue for English as the official language of the United States because I believed that if Spanish-speaking immigrants wanted to live here, they ought to learn "our" language. In a college course discussion about slavery, I recall chastising a Black peer, saying that Black people ought to remember that communities in Africa had slavery systems before the transcontinental slave trade developed. During my first college experiences learning about White privilege, I adamantly said, "I don't have White privilege because I grew up working class." These misinformed and defensive comments reflected my genuinely held ideas, beliefs, and feelings about the world, others, and most of all myself.

It was not until I began my doctoral studies examining social justice education curriculum that I started to wonder *why* college students, particularly students from privileged social groups, had these notions and defended them passionately.

This became my mission: To shed light on why college students reject the concept of privilege and help social justice educators navigate students' resistance in our practice. In particular, I found wisdom from the scholarship in the learning sciences that explores misconceptions and how curriculum and pedagogy can enhance students' knowledge. When preparing my dissertation proposal to study White college students' understanding of privilege, I framed my study around students who had a "correct" versus an "incorrect" view of privilege. However, Dr. Thomas Philip, a particularly gracious member of my committee, invited me to chat with him about my original framing of my topic. In our conversation, he helped me understand the learning sciences literature on conceptual understanding and misconceptions. Instead of viewing misconceptions as wrong, he encouraged me to consider students' notions as rational based on their current contextual understanding. He challenged me to remember that notions of right versus wrong, correct versus incorrect, and good versus bad suggest a belief in a single, universal way of knowing the world, which he knew I did not believe to be true. While I believe that society should embrace social justice, I also believe that truth is contextual from our lived experiences. Therefore, how could I view some students as being wrong when, from their current point of view, their beliefs make perfect sense and are completely rational given their context?

I am forever grateful that Dr. Philip called me in to reconsider my stance and alter my approach to my research. His wise counsel did much more than rectify an incongruence between my methodology and my philosophy. He also helped me remember my own experiences and beliefs about privilege and that they were rational given my context at the time. In essence, he reminded me that how we understand social inequality is directly linked to both how we are socialized and the hegemonic narratives that collectively make our views rational.

Awareness of our own positionality and its influences on our work is important for both social justice education and research. Since this book exists at the intersection of both these disciplines, it is important that I share who I am and how my own experiences with privilege and social justice education shaped my approach to this book. Doing so will provide insight into my passion for this work and highlight an example of my own socialization into Whiteness that I will refer to through the book.

I am a White, able-bodied, heterosexual, cisgender man who grew up in a working-class, culturally Catholic family. The majority of my social identities provide multiple axes of privilege that benefit me in society. However, while growing up, my race and social class were most salient to me for very different reasons across time. To help set the stage for later conversations in this book, I primarily focus on my experiences related to social class and race.

I grew up in a family where being a hard worker was the highest compliment you could receive. My parents modeled this work ethic across my youth. At one point, my mother worked full-time as a clerk at an electric wire company, and my father worked full-time as a custodian for a distribution company while also working part-time jobs at a local fast-food restaurant and gas station.

Concurrently, they would spend some weekends helping my aunt and uncle clean office spaces. My parents' hard work provided for the family; however, we still needed to shop at discount grocery stores and drive used cars given to us from friends and family in exchange for mowing their lawns or making meals for their families. Hard work helped my family stay afloat but did not bring the wealth or comfort normally associated with having privilege.

My racial identity was an unexplored area of my life growing up. I have no memories of my family ever discussing being White. When my peers and I were asked in elementary school to explore our family backgrounds, my family was less familiar with and attached to their ethnicity. While our White racial identity was hardly discussed, race was a familiar theme. My grandfather would sing racially demeaning songs about Black people to my sister and I as children. During extended family parties, conversations among the adults would have multiple racial themes where racial tropes and slurs were commonly used. Common topics involved "Mexicans" bringing down property values by living together with their extended families and "Mexicans" and "Blacks" taking away jobs from hardworking Whites.

Collectively, these two identity-based threads converged to replicate a powerful narrative that Whites were hardworking and thus entitled to good jobs while people of color were not. Social class and race converged when a television manufacturing company that employed multiple members of my extended family closed the local plant and caused my family to lose their jobs. This event happened shortly after the North American Free Trade Agreement (NAFTA) was passed and a new manufacturing plant was opened in Mexico. At family gatherings after this decision was made, the conversation focused on how "those people" were taking "our jobs" that my family worked hard to earn. Notably, I do not recall my family blaming the company leadership, who were undoubtedly White, for making the decision to close the local plant and open a different plant in another country where they could increase their profit margin. Instead, the anger of my family was focused on "cheap Mexican labor" and the individuals who unfairly took their jobs.

These race- and social class-based ideas persisted and were reinforced in my middle and high school experiences. I developed deeper suspicions and mistrust toward people of color in general, and Latinos in particular, while also deepening an elevated sense of self. During middle school, two racialized gangs attempted to harass me (the "Latino gang") or offer me protection (the "White gang"), fueling my deeper mistrust toward people of color. In high school, my advanced placement courses had more White students than students of color, influencing me to believe White people were naturally smarter. For a class assignment, I debated in favor of English being established as the official language of the United States because if "other people" wanted to be in "our" country, they needed to earn that right by learning "our" language. However, I struggled during the college application process as a first-generation college student. When I faced obstacles resulting in incomplete applications or admittance rejections, I never viewed that as an indicator that I did not work hard enough, but instead situated the blame outside of myself. I wholeheartedly believed that I was not getting a fair shake as a working-class person while simultaneously believing that anyone else not experiencing success simply was not working hard enough.

It was not until halfway through my undergraduate college experience that I engaged in any critical examination of my privileged identities as a whole or my White privilege in particular. At first, I remained unaware of and defensive about my privileged positionalities while simultaneously devouring anything I could to understand my marginalized positionalities related to social class and religion as someone who identified as non-Christian. It was my interest in systemic social class inequalities and religious oppression that prompted my desire to add an intercultural studies minor to my degree. At first, I struggled in these courses where race was the focal point when I preferred to focus instead on the social identities where I faced discrimination. However, the faculty who taught these courses alongside conversations with my peers prompted a powerful "waking up" moment by asking me to channel my intense frustration with others who were oblivious to their social class and religion privilege and also consider how my obliviousness and defensiveness to my White privilege impacted others. It was at this moment that something clicked in my mind and heart that prompted me to expand my focus beyond the oppression I experienced to include the oppression that I sustained through my action and inaction.

After initially deciding to question and reject my old ways of thinking and knowing the world, I actively sought out spaces and communities to continue unlearning my internalized dominance and adding new insights and understanding to advance social justice. In my journey to unlearn my internalized dominance, I had to adopt different ideas, beliefs, and behaviors to continually support social justice and prevent sliding back into old cognitive habits. This process has been and remains unending because I lived 20 years of my life actively upholding Whiteness compared to subsequent years of a journey gradually increasing my commitment to antiracism with every thought I have, belief I hold, and action I take. It is easier to learn Whiteness without knowing anything else than it is to actively unlearn Whiteness and learn antiracism as a new way of being. While I have successfully unlearned most of the ideas and beliefs I adopted early in my life, they still reside within me as a permanent part of my consciousness.

During college, I deepened my commitment to social justice by developing relationships with students of color, working with them to advocate for various equity issues on campus, and starting a new student organization committed to multicultural empowerment. I went on to graduate school and eventually received my master's in social work with a focus on community organizing and advocacy from the University of Michigan. During my master's program, I doubled down on my commitment to social justice and unlearning multiple forms of internalized dominance focused on race, gender, and religion in two profound ways. First, I immersed myself in social justice education training and facilitation experiences, including studying intergroup dialogue facilitation, leading intergroup dialogues on campus, and helping implement a social justice orientation experience for incoming graduate students with a small group of peers. Second, I worked part-time at the Sexual Assault Prevention and Awareness Center and was a part-time intern for the Interfaith Council for Peace and Justice. In both of these professional experiences, I worked alongside a diverse group of people (diverse in terms of sex, gender, and sexuality in the former, religion in the latter) in pluralistic coalitions to advance equity in institutional policies and practices. Through these experiences, I was immersed in spaces where I needed to challenge past assumptions and beliefs rooted in Whiteness and other systems of dominance in order to develop authentic, vulnerable relationships with others grounded in mutual understanding, respect, and commitment to justice.

My undergraduate- and master's-level experiences inspired me to become a social justice educator in higher education. I decided to apply my knowledge and skills related to community organization, intergroup dialogue facilitation, and social justice education to create and implement educational interventions for college students, specifically students with privileged identities, as a means to "reeducate" them out of their socialized dominance. My belief was that if higher education institutions can be recalibrated to educate college students around social justice, these students would eventually work across society with an enlightened understanding that would influence policy and practice in favor of equity. I eventually decided to pursue a doctorate in curriculum studies to further my understanding of how to design and assess social justice education curriculum for college students as a means to further my commitment to being effective in my practice.

My collective journey provided me with unique insight from both ends of a path toward social justice. I have a deep understanding and appreciation for the power of being socialized into Whiteness and how it shapes someone's ideas, beliefs, and feelings that show up in education spaces. I am also committed to a continually evolving understanding of social justice that is capable of imagining a different way of knowing reality, developing authentic relationships with others, and being in community with people from different social identities than my own. This bifurcated lens enables me to analyze how White college students learn and unlearn Whiteness coupled with deep empathy for the challenging process this work entails. I hope these insights are valuable to you as you consider the rationality of Whiteness in order to help White students develop a commitment to antiracism.

This is the stance I adopt for this book: Knowing why and how White students understand privilege is necessary to identify and acknowledge their rationality in order to help them evolve in their understanding. Not only does this stance provide insight into educational solutions, but it also generates empathy for our students and humility regarding how powerful the forces of socialization are in our society. I believe it is important for educators to remember that our efforts are part of a larger, structural whole. Therefore, instead of focusing on *individual* students as good or bad, it is critical to remind ourselves that the project of social justice education must be committed to challenging *structures* that replicate privilege through our work with individual students.

INTRODUCTION

Contextualizing White College Students' Views About Privilege

In recent years, colleges and universities across the Unites States have increasingly turned to curricular and cocurricular diversity education experiences to enhance students' development of cultural competence. This attention to the development of students' cultural competence is driven by multiple key factors. National organizations such as the Association of American Colleges and Universities have stated that developing college students' cultural competence needs to be a priority as part of a liberal arts education designed to prepare students for their professional and civic lives.[1] Additionally, the demographic composition of the student body is shifting as the proportion of underrepresented racial groups increases across the country and the racial diversity of students on campus also increases.[2] As a result, a range of diversity education experiences have begun to emerge that are traditionally embedded in academic curriculum or delivered through cocurricular trainings and intergroup dialogue opportunities.[3]

However, the broader social and political context also shapes the need for diversity education, as well as the way college students come to and participate in these diversity education experiences. White supremacist activity remains a growing threat overall, fueled in part by overt racist beliefs and support for White supremacist activity from the Donald Trump presidency and the broader Republican party.[4] White supremacist groups are increasing their recruitment of college students, and the number of hate incidents continues to rise on college campuses.[5] Meanwhile, the growing strength and the presence of the Black Lives Matter movement continue to raise awareness of structural racial inequities, including sustained police violence toward communities of color.[6] This movement has gained traction nationally and among college students in particular.[7] Increased attention to race and racial injustice fuels student protests for real changes and commitments to antiracism.[8] Collectively, the broader national

DOI: 10.4324/9781003082378-1

conversation about race and racism shapes the environment in which diversity education experiences occur.

It is critical for educators who oversee such diversity education experiences to consider how students make sense of social inequality and privilege overall and racism and White privilege in particular. Specifically, it is important to contextualize how the broader social context influences the ways that college students (particularly White college students) make sense of privilege and bring their understanding into educational spaces. To do so requires an exploration of privilege, how Whiteness facilitates a particular understanding of privilege, and how existing ideas, beliefs, and feelings about privilege influence student learning.

Privilege and Oppression

Multiple scholars have discussed privilege in general and White privilege in particular.[9] Most notable is Peggy McIntosh's (1989) frequently cited paper that describes privilege as an invisible backpack granted to individuals because of their social identities. On the basis of this scholarship, I define privilege as the benefits, rights, and access to resources bestowed on individuals based on their social identities at both an individual and institutional level through hegemonic social power. Furthermore, racial privilege in the United States refers to privilege bestowed upon White people.

There are three important aspects to this definition worth making explicit. First, privilege is an *ascribed* status based on social identity, not an *attained* status based on what someone has or has not done. Privilege can be neither asked for nor given back by an individual because it is not distributed on the basis of an individual's wants, actions, or feelings. Second, privilege encapsulates visible and semivisible advantages. Visible advantages refer to things that help us move ahead in life that are relatively easy to identify as helpful. However, semivisible advantages refer to the lack of barriers we face making them hard to notice, yet real. For example, a visible advantage might include a White person being able to talk our way out of a police interaction because we are given the benefit of the doubt that we meant well and are assumed to be lawful. However, a semivisible advantage might include all the times law enforcement officers do not use force in their interactions with White people, which happens 50% less for White people than Black and Latinx people.[10] Third, privilege is both personal *and* structural. We commonly talk about individuals having privilege and how it operates at the individual level. However, these individual experiences are grounded in structural realities where privilege has been normalized in societal values, beliefs, policies, and practices around White superiority in the United States as early as British colonialism.[11] Therefore, racial privilege must be understood as a phenomenon beyond a single White person or group of White people. Privilege is structurally created, systemically replicated, and collectively maintained.

In order to understand the phenomenon of privilege, we must also acknowledge its dialectical cousin – oppression. Oppression is a pervasive system of dominance that operates at the individual, institutional, and cultural levels, creating and maintaining disparate advantages and disadvantages based on social group membership.[12] Oppression is a force of domination and social control that permeates our policies and practices at the institutional level, as well as our thoughts, beliefs, and feelings at an individual level. These institutional and individual forces mutually reinforce one another. Collectively, the system of oppression generates a hegemonic way of knowing and understanding reality that seeks to maintain itself. It is for this reason that Zeus Leonardo (2004) explicitly states that any examination of privilege is incomplete without attending to the forces of social domination that actively manifest privilege as their primary product. In order to explore how White college students understand privilege, it is necessary to examine the hegemonic way of knowing and understanding reality that it influences. Because privilege and oppression are innately tethered to social group memberships, our exploration will be contextualized around race.

Whiteness as a Racialized Lens for Privilege and Oppression

Leonardo (2009) uses the term Whiteness to describe a collective racialized way of knowing and understanding our reality that is grounded in the experience of being White. Whiteness is a lens through which the world is viewed and interpreted. Joe Feagin (2013) explores a similar construct he calls the White racial frame that White people learn and adopt for themselves. The White racial frame entails multiple dimensions that include racial narratives, stereotypes, imagery, emotions, and actions that discriminate against people of color[13] while simultaneously reinforcing a view of White superiority. Both Feagin and Leonardo also describe how this collective racialized lens is not only normative but also generative. By learning and adopting Whiteness as a lens to understand reality, it also works to ensure this reality is replicated at an individual and institutional level. *Whiteness begets Whiteness.* Even though the lens of Whiteness is based on the experiences of White people, it is not a lens exclusive to them. Anyone can – and everyone *does* – learn Whiteness. To better understand how Whiteness operates, it is useful to examine the three legs that prop up Whiteness: White racial knowledge, White supremacy, and White emotionality.

White racial knowledge refers to the specific truths and histories that anchor our understanding of reality. However, this knowledge is centered around the White experience and therefore reflects a particular reality.[14] Roediger (1994) critiqued this type of knowledge as false and oppressive: False because it is socially constructed around a particular racial understanding and oppressive because of the real impact such knowledge has on people of color. Let us consider a range of examples. A common idea is that Black oppression in the United States is by and large based upon chattel slavery that is believed to be a relatively brief event that occurred in the distant past.[15] However, Black chattel slavery was one aspect of the broader systematic and institutional oppression of Black people by White people in power, accounting for 83% of US history.[16] To view slavery as a remnant of the past allows us to dismiss the ripple effect of slavery over time that persists in the present. Such an idea connects to yet another example of White racial knowledge: That the Presidency of Barrack Obama is evidence that racial equality has been achieved in the United States.[17] Despite Obama's election, multiple disparities still exist. The median wealth among Blacks is roughly 10% that of Whites, Black unemployment is at least twice as high relative to Whites, and Blacks are at least twice as likely to be arrested for misdemeanors relative to Whites.[18] To adopt the view that racial equality has been achieved despite evidence to the contrary reinforces a false understanding of reality that makes it easier to dismiss race overall and any racial analysis of reality in particular. These two examples illustrate how White racial knowledge is selective to reinforce and replicate a particular understanding of reality that benefits Whites at the direct expense of people of color.

Just as there are racialized ideas, the way these ideas are used to construct broader beliefs and explanatory frameworks are also equally racialized. White supremacy refers to this racialized ideological dimension of Whiteness. I use Kendall's (2013) definition of White supremacy as an explanatory worldview that positions people of color as inherently inferior to White people.[19] Critical race scholars have explored racialized ideology when examining racial interpretations and narratives, justifications in favor of the racial status quo, "sincere fictions," and most explicitly as a Whiteness ideology.[20] Common explanatory frameworks include, but are not limited to, racial beliefs linked to genetic or biological differences (e.g., eugenics), moral differences (e.g., Whites are more pure and virtuous than others), cultural differences (e.g., laziness stems from Black culture), and sociopolitical values (e.g., rugged individualism).[21] In some cases, Bonilla-Silva (2014) describes how generic attempts to minimize the existence of race and racial explanations also support White supremacy. As such, the explanatory frameworks within White supremacy attempt to be viewed as nonracial in nature or color-blind.[22]

White supremacy works in tandem with White racial knowledge to reinforce each other. Consider the example shared previously that the Obama Presidency is "proof" that racial equality has been achieved. Imagine that someone makes this claim and is presented with the evidence previously mentioned that contradicts their claim. This person might use a culturally based frame to argue that the wealth disparity is due to Blacks being lazier. They might use a moral frame to suggest that the reasons Blacks are arrested more often for misdemeanors are linked to their moral inferiority. Donald Trump has expressed both of these racialized beliefs and many more.[23]

If our thoughts and beliefs are racialized, it stands to reason that our feelings about others and ourselves are also racialized. White emotionality, the third leg of Whiteness, refers to racialized emotions rooted in Whiteness that manifest themselves when engaging race in our lives to perpetuate Whiteness. Because race is connected to social power in society, emotions reveal how our experiences, thoughts, and beliefs related to social power are felt.[24] However, scholars have examined a multitude of emotions on this spectrum of White emotionality. Shame and guilt are among the most commonly explored emotions felt by White people in the context of race as White people wrestle with unearned advantages they are given based on their racial identity.[25] Additionally, White college students experience and express emotions of grief, narcissism, and disgust as they navigate the process of unlearning Whiteness.[26] What is notable about these emotional responses is how none of them contribute to a positive view of oneself and could be considered "negative" emotions. Such negative emotions actually discourage individuals from more deeply exploring these feelings and deconstructing them to examine their source. When these emotions are not examined, the result is twofold. First, these emotions revolve around how White people feel about themselves as individuals in attempts to continue to view themselves as "good" White individuals. Second, by retaining a focus on how individual people feel, these emotions erect barriers from our ability to examine race and racial power in the context of institutions and systems. Taken together, White emotionality obfuscates the collective White racial experience to reduce White accountability for systemic racism by using emotions to redirect energy to how White people feel about themselves as individuals as juxtaposed to feelings about race in general and people of color in particular.[27]

These three legs are both products of, and anchors for, Whiteness as a worldview. What ideas exist and are true, how these ideas sustain our beliefs, and how our feelings related to these ideas and beliefs mutually influence our perspective about others, ourselves, and society. While ideas, beliefs, and feelings can be discussed separately and may be viewed as distinct, they operate as parts of a collective lens. Our ideas and knowledge related to race are cognitive and emotional, creating a strong link between White racial knowledge and White emotionality.[28] Racialized belief systems are often used to support our racialized ideas and knowledge, creating a connection between White supremacy and White racial knowledge.[29] Emotional responses to racial interactions and race as a concept are also linked to racialized explanations and beliefs about others and ourselves, making the final link between White emotionality and White supremacy.[30]

To make the relationship explicit between White racial knowledge, White supremacy, and White emotionality, consider the simple act of conversation about race. One example of White racial knowledge includes the notion that talking about race innately highlights race and creates racial disparities that would not otherwise exist. Therefore, the logic follows that the best thing someone could do is to not talk about race as a path to stop racial disparities in society because if race is not seen, there would be no basis upon which to discriminate against others. This example of White racial knowledge exists with support from a meritocratic belief under the umbrella of White supremacy. A belief in meritocracy supports the view that hard work is a better reason that race to explain differences between people, thus rendering a racial analysis unnecessary. This belief in hard work both reinforces the "fact" that race is unnecessary while also promoting positive feelings toward oneself as "hardworking" relative to people of color who are assumed to thus not be working hard enough. In this way, any challenge to the "fact" that focusing on race is problematic can be deflected with an alternative belief that supports a positive view of oneself. Any challenge to this idea is not only a conceptual argument but also an ideological and emotional one.

Soccer provides a useful analogy for conversations about race and the relationship between White racial knowledge, White supremacy, and White emotionality in this context. In a soccer match, two teams play against each other to kick a ball into the opposing team's net. In the game of soccer, most of the action on the field happens away from the net where the team's goalie is positioned. After both teams go back and forth with each other, eventually they will begin to advance closer to the opposing team's net. When the opposing team's players begin to advance toward the net, the goalie becomes alert and adopts a defensive position. When the ball is kicked toward the net, the goalie moves swiftly to either deflect the ball away or potentially stops the ball in order to throw it back for their team to attempt an offensive play.

Now, let us apply our conversation about Whiteness to this situation. Imagine that the soccer match is a conversation about race between Jack and Jill and that Jack fully embraces Whiteness. For Jack, the soccer ball reflects various beliefs grounded in White Supremacy and the various soccer moves players employ to gain control of the ball reflect multiple aspects of White racial knowledge employed to support these beliefs. Jack may use multiple ideas to advance his beliefs in a conversation. However, should Jill gain control of the conversation and advance her beliefs, Jack's goalie, who embodies White emotionality, becomes alert and ready. The more Jill advances on Jack in their conversation, the more Jack's emotions will continue to heighten in anticipation. Every time Jill asserts a statement intended to persuade Jack, or kicks the ball toward the goalie, Jack may express various emotions intended to stop or deflect the arguments she makes. Expressing shame or guilt could be the equivalent of stopping the ball to temporarily pause the game. Expressing anger or disgust could be the equivalent of the goalie forcefully kicking the ball back into the field of play. Just as the goalie works to defend the net, White emotionality works to protect one's positive sense of themselves. Every attempt to defend the net is ultimately an act to protect Whiteness as a way of seeing and understanding the world, others, and themselves.

Student Learning and Socialization

In order to understand why students' misconceptions about privilege and social inequality are rational, it is necessary to examine how Whiteness is learned. Vygotsky's (1978) sociocultural learning theory describes how individuals are constantly learning about the world through our social interactions. For example, we learn about race when interacting with people from different racial groups by noticing similarities and differences. However, we also learn about race through our social interactions even when race does not seem to be the primary focus. We learn about race when interacting with people from our own racial group, watching television and noticing how race is portrayed, and even in school settings when learning a curriculum that is centered around White people. In these latter examples, we learn about race through what is left unsaid and normalized.

Because learning about social phenomena like privilege is linked to how we view ourselves and others, and interact with people in the world, socialization is a more useful term when thinking about how we learn. Bobbie Harro's (2013b) cycle of socialization provides a thorough explanation for how individuals learn, internalize, and replicate lessons about social identity groups within the context of privilege and oppression. People are born without any knowledge about or awareness of social identity groups and social inequalities. However, through ongoing social interactions with other people and societal institutions (e.g., educational, medical, legal), individuals learn the prevailing views about our social identity groups, different social identity groups, and how these groups relate to one another. People then reproduce and reinforce what they have learned in future social interactions. Because of this cycle, understandings about social identity groups are both internalized and normalized and therefore tap into our desires for emotional security and certainty as well as social affirmation and reward. The result of this socialization process is the further entrenchment of social inequality in society that is reinforced through widespread misconceptions about the existence and cause of these persisting inequities.

When considering how we learn about Whiteness as a broader worldview and racial privilege as one specific concept, the cycle of socialization helps explain how people are socialized to adopt Whiteness. Let us revisit my personal experiences growing up and examine how the cycle of socialization explains this process. Originally, I was born without any consciousness of race or racial privilege. However, during my childhood, I was socialized to adopt a particular understanding of race. While my family did not talk about being White, my relatives did talk about people of color, using negative racial stereotypes and ethnic slurs, which contributed to my early understanding of how people of color were inferior to White people. My uncle, a lighter-skinned Mexican man who openly shared these sentiments in the presence of my family, further reinforced these ideas about people of color and Latinx people in particular. Even though my family did not name Whiteness or discuss the White experience, it was clear that White people were better than people of color because there were never any negative comments about White people made implicitly or explicitly.

The messages shared among my family were similar to those I experienced through my social interactions in institutional contexts. In school, these same messages reinforced in multiple ways. I took advanced courses in middle and high school that were primarily filled with White people, further reinforcing the notion that White people were smarter than people of color without it ever being said aloud. Similarly, my social studies courses primarily focused on White figures and their accomplishments while people of color, specifically Black and indigenous people, were primarily portrayed as uncivilized native peoples or unfortunate and uneducated slaves. On film, television, and the news, White people were always portrayed as the heroes or victims while people of color were always portrayed as the villains.

Collectively, the racial distinction between White people and people of color was clear enough for me to replicate these messages, such as debating in favor of English being the national language of the United States or downplaying structural critiques of racism by claiming African communities participated in slavery first. These stances both reinforced the dominant collective understanding of race while also reaping the rewards of inclusion among my White peers. Given how the cycle of socialization operates to maintain social inequalities while simultaneously obfuscating its existence and causes, it is rational for a White person to internalize and defend White racial knowledge, White supremacy, and White emotionality to maintain their misconstrued sense of self and society.

While this explanation of how we learn about race and Whiteness centers around myself as a White person and the White experience, it is important to clarify that *everyone* is socialized to learn about and adopt Whiteness. As Leonardo (2009) states, Whiteness is grounded in the White experience but is a collective racialized way of knowing and understanding our reality shared by people of color and White people alike even though Whites are more likely to adopt and reproduce Whiteness. For example, consider some results of a 2019 Pew survey on race in the United States:

- 16% of Black people and 42% of White people did not think the legacy of slavery affects Black people today.
- 7% of Black people and 14% of White people thought that being White hurts their ability to get ahead in life.
- 31% of Black people and 45% of White people attribute a lack of good role models as a reason Black people have a harder time getting ahead in life.[31]

If White people were the only people susceptible to learning and replicating Whiteness, White people and Black people would have bipolar results on this survey. However, when we remember that Whiteness is a collective framework all individuals are socialized to adopt, these survey results become intelligible. This point is critical because it prevents us from inaccurately viewing Whiteness as a problem at the level of the individual based on their social identity. Instead, Whiteness is pervasively produced and reproduced at a cultural and institutional level that is reinforced by individuals.

However, just as we all are socialized to internalize Whiteness, these survey results also show that people can unlearn Whiteness and provide hope for achieving the goal of social justice education. Harro's (2013a) cycle of liberation, a model that describes a path toward critical transformation, illustrates how this happens through intrapersonal, interpersonal, and structural stages of development. The start of this cycle begins when we have a "waking up" experience that creates cognitive dissonance with our prior knowledge. Such experiences might include developing relationships with people from different racial groups that challenge notions of White superiority or learning about the history of colonization and its pervasive impact to the present day. These critical experiences create a wedge between our internalized ideas, beliefs, and feelings anchored in Whiteness and the evidence that contradicts a Whiteness worldview. As a result, individuals start a process of intrapersonal development where they reflect on their ideas, beliefs, and feelings and begin the process of unlearning Whiteness. This process does not happen right away or quickly but instead is akin to finding a loose thread on a blanket and slowly pulling it until it unravels. During this process, individuals also seek out additional experiences that help them in their unlearning process (such as learning more about racism and Whiteness) or provide support for practicing new ways of acting that do not reinforce Whiteness (such as making new friends with those who share a critical analysis of Whiteness and engaging in dialogues about race and racism). From these new experiences, individuals continue unlearning Whiteness and begin to adopt new ideas, beliefs, and feelings that are grounded in social justice and equity.

After developing themselves intrapersonally, they shift to building community and coalitions as part of their interpersonal development. In this stage, individuals lean into their relationships to continue examining and questioning reality that reveals different ways of knowing and being in the world. A key part of this stage is the realization that all people are harmed by Whiteness, albeit in starkly different ways, and should be equally invested in dismantling the social structures that replicate Whiteness and the harm it causes. These interpersonal efforts make way for advocacy for structural changes that create socially just changes and efforts to maintain these gains. This is a key stage because it makes explicit that changes in individuals' hearts and minds alone are insufficient and require changing our social institutions that reinforce and replicate Whiteness.

Increased mainstream attention toward police brutality and violence against communities of color within the United States provides an example of how some folks are "waking up" and questioning the role and impact of police in our communities. Seeing the stark differences in how police forces responded to protests in the spring of 2020 has helped White people see how policing has been and remains deeply racialized. Unarmed Black and brown Black Lives Matter protesters were quelled with force and support from the National Guard compared to armed White antilockdown protesters who entered state capitals without any police response.[32] We now find ourselves in a moment where protests against police violence are more racially diverse than before.[33] People are learning more about the origins of policing and calling for the defunding and dismantling of the police in favor of a new form of supporting the public good that works for people of color as well as Whites.[34]

The cycle of liberation provides a way to understand how change can occur while providing hope for a more socially just reality. Whiteness is a powerful force we are all socialized to adopt and replicate; however, it is not a condition we are fated to endure forever. To stop Whiteness and remove it from our society, it is critical to acknowledge that the necessary structural changes needed require us to deprogram ourselves and one another from Whiteness as a worldview we assume to be the only way of the world.

If we consider the cycle of socialization and the cycle of liberation together, we could imagine placing people on a horizontal continuum where individuals are deeply entrenched in Whiteness on the one side and actively working in opposition to Whiteness on the other side. However, as both of these cycles illustrate, these processes are never-ending and assume individuals never reach a conclusion of being socialized or unlearning their original socialization. Therefore, when considering how to support White college students in their journey to understand privilege, it is useful to imagine that all of our White students can fall anywhere on this continuum between embracing and rejecting Whiteness at any given point in time. This book seeks to provide insights that can help social justice educators create and leverage "waking up" moments among our White college students to shift them in this continuum, begin their liberation from Whiteness, and embrace a socially just worldview.

Antiracism: An Alternative to Whiteness

In order for social justice educators to help White college students reject Whiteness, we must also understand what we are teaching them to embrace as an alternative worldview. Whiteness is a collective racialized way of knowing and understanding our reality that is grounded in the experience of being White that operates to reinforce racial inequalities and racism. Therefore, the alternative must be a collective way of knowing and understanding our reality that is grounded in decentering the experience of being White while working against racial inequality and racism. A worldview that rejects Whiteness and actively works in opposition to racism as a product of Whiteness is antiracism.

Antiracism is grounded in scholarship that explores and works in opposition to the systemic, structural, interpersonal, and intrapersonal manifestations of privilege and social injustice more broadly and White privilege and racism in particular.[35] Central to antiracism are ideas that understand social inequality as structural and systemic, a belief that all people are and ought to be equal, and emotions that fuel action against racism.[36] If Whiteness entails White racial knowledge, White supremacy, and White emotionality as three anchors that sustain its worldview, it is equally important to consider the corollaries to these three elements within antiracism that I propose to be race critical knowledge, a race critical ideology, and racial emotional resiliency.

Race critical knowledge refers to truths and histories that are centered around multiculturalism and structural social power. Both race critical knowledge and

White racial knowledge shape our understanding of reality; however, race critical knowledge has a more expansive scope in terms of both whose experience is centered and how we think about social power and its relationship to truth and experience. Race critical knowledge challenges ideas that make race peripheral or invisible to our understanding of reality. To make this distinction clear, let us consider the common notion within White racial knowledge that Black oppression is no longer present in the United States. Race critical knowledge would center the experience of being Black in the United States and draw upon Black history and experiences to counter this notion. Further, race critical knowledge would focus on the existence of racial power and its impact on the broader Black community to highlight that Black oppression not only still exists today but also that modern Black oppression is a continuation of long-standing racial oppression woven into the fabric of our social institutions.

Race critical ideology refers to the beliefs and explanatory frameworks related to race and racial inequalities. Critical race theory provides an intentional approach to examine race, racism, and racial power in order to bring about social transformation that provides a basis for race critical ideology. Central to critical race theory are assertions that (1) race is a social construction with a material reality, (2) the phenomenon of racism has become normalized and ordinary, (3) racism and racialized power are manifested and sustained through Whiteness and their perpetual normalization, (4) racism is real and knowable from the lens of racially oppressed groups, and (5) examining points of interest convergence can reveal how race and racism operate to support their continuation through mitigated change.[37] These assertions are grounded in structural and systemic understandings of race and racial inequalities. Whereas White supremacy works to dismiss race and center social inequality around individuals, a race critical ideology centers race and positions social inequality as structural.

Finally, racial emotional resiliency refers to the emotional capacity for individuals to engage in racial experiences that contribute to antiracist action. Racial emotional resiliency allows for individuals to fully experience a range of emotions without having those emotions serve to center Whiteness or diminish their capacity for action. For example, it is common for White people to learn about White privilege and feel shame and guilt for being White and having benefits denied to other racial groups.[38] However, White individuals with racial emotional resiliency would use their feelings to fuel their resolve to act. Additionally, they would not intentionally or unintentionally leverage their feelings to frame themselves as victims seeking comfort from others. Racial emotional resiliency entails an understanding that antiracism work is necessarily uncomfortable to identify and reject Whiteness in ourselves and our interactions with others.

The worldview of antiracism entails an understanding that all people have been originally socialized to adopt Whiteness and thus must commit to a lifelong process of actively working against social inequality and White racism in particular.[39] As such, individuals committed to antiracism understand that everyone must commit to this work and no one is an exception to this rule. Kendi (2019) goes further to remind us that working toward antiracism is more than simply being "not-racist." If one is not actively engaged in antiracism, or ways of thinking and being that reject Whiteness and racism, then that same lack of action works to support Whiteness and racism.[40] Because we are all socialized into Whiteness, doing nothing, or not actively contributing to social inequality and racism, is tantamount to tacit support of hegemonic Whiteness, which is sustained through passivity. As such, Kendi rightfully points out that there is no such thing as being not-racist and that attempts to assert oneself as not-racist actually work in tandem with White emotionality that provides distance from Whiteness as a defensive posture. Instead, a commitment to antiracism requires recognition that we are all on a continuum of supporting Whiteness versus antiracism with every decision we make.

The relationship between Whiteness and antiracism could be conceptualized through the analogy of fencing. In the sport of fencing, two players stand facing each other along a long line. Players move along this line by either advancing or retreating, all the while making strategic decisions about striking the other player or deflecting incoming attacks. If we personified Whiteness and antiracism as the two players in a fencing match, it would capture the relationship between these two worldviews and how they operate relative to each other. Just as the two players share the same field of play on a long ling, Whiteness and antiracism share the same "social field" where they compete to be an active paradigm. However, in this fencing analogy, the player who represents Whiteness would start the match with points to reflect the hegemonic nature of Whiteness and how embedded it is in our social institutions. Meanwhile, the player who represents antiracism would not only start with zero points but also start at the end of their side of the long line and thus need to actively advance *and* score points in order to win. The point behind this analogy is to make explicit that Whiteness is the de facto winner due to how social structures and socialization forces exist to survive without doing anything and therefore explain why being not-racist is not enough and instead requires an active commitment to antiracism.

Studying College Students' Views on Privilege

Examining how college students understand social justice concepts is tricky. The concept of privilege is a value-loaded term that elicits strong thoughts and feelings about society, others, and oneself. Privilege does not have a "neutral" definition because the concept necessarily connects our experiences to others in ways that highlight purposeful structural advantage and disadvantage based on who we are. We simply cannot think about privilege and oppression without considering who we are as social beings, how we perceive ourselves in the world, and what our relationship is to the physical manifestations of privilege and oppression. Social justice concepts are different from those in other disciplines such as math or science. Consider the physics concept of force, the energy that exists as a result of the interaction between two objects. The concept of force does not elicit feelings about ourselves or others. Learning about force as a physical phenomenon does not have any bearing on how we understand ourselves as human beings in society. Force is simply a concept that helps us understand our physical world without impacting our sense of self or our relationships with others. Therefore, studying social justice concepts requires attention to the ways people relate to these concepts.

Further complicating our thoughts and feelings about privilege is the fact that we already have particular ideas, beliefs, and feelings about privilege. According to a 2019 Pew Research Center survey, only 59% of Whites believe that their race is advantageous to them. At the same time, 28% believe their race does not impact them and the remaining 12% of Whites believe that their race hurts them either "a little" or "a lot."[41] How people come to adopt their stances on privilege overall, and racial privilege in particular, is sensible because we are constantly bombarded with explicit and implicit messaging about privilege that shapes our ideas and feelings about this concept. At family gatherings, especially around the Thanksgiving holiday, some relatives may adopt a nuanced understanding of racial privilege as a social fact while others may dismiss the notion of racial privilege because they worked hard for what they have.[42] In social media, White privilege is a well-used hashtag (#whiteprivilege) to identify the unearned benefits White people receive that society denies to people of color. However, a competing hashtag, #blackprivilege, also exists among mostly White people to challenge the notion that White people solely benefit from their racial group membership. In mainstream media, we see television shows that reflect a range of popular attitudes. On the one end of the continuum, there are shows like Netflix's *Dear White People* that portray a sophisticated view of privilege as structural and systemic. On the other end of the continuum are shows like Comedy Central's "South Park" that critique contemporary events around privilege and social identity as politically correct. The varied understanding of privilege reflects the tension between the competing worldviews of Whiteness and antiracism. Because the concept of privilege embodies this broader tension, special considerations are required to explore how people truly understand it.

How people wish others to perceive them will influence how candid they are about their thoughts and beliefs. This statement holds true when people discuss their personal lives or what they consider to be a "sensitive topic." Conventional hegemonic wisdom in the United States stands that race is not something people ought to discuss openly, promoting a "color-blind" stance among people across many races. However, research demonstrates that race actively influences people regardless of if they choose to name it for themselves. White people may act differently in an all-White backstage versus when they are in a front stage that is racially diverse or where there are moral authority figures (e.g., teachers).[43] White people also convey different attitudes about race on surveys versus when participating in interviews.[44] For these collective reasons, studying how college students understand privilege is not simple or easy.

The main ideas and arguments I present in this book emerged from my dissertation research[45] conducted at Great Lakes College[46] during the 2016–2017 academic year. My research used a phenomenological case study designed to explore how eight White first-year college students viewed privilege conceptually, ideologically, and emotionally after participating in a standardized diversity and privilege workshop during the Fall 2016 term. Three forms of data were generated for this research project. First, students participated in 2-hour, semi-structured interviews during the Winter 2017 term. I asked students questions about how they viewed privilege in the abstract and specifically related to race (i.e., White privilege). During these interviews, students discussed (a) how they defined and explained privilege (both in general and specifically to race), (b) their thoughts and feelings when shown a political cartoon depicting racial privilege,[47] and (c) how they felt when participating in their fall diversity and privilege workshop. Second, I generated field notes during each student interview to document students' tone, body language, and other observations about their affect or behavior while responding to interview questions. These observations were particularly useful to reveal emotional reactions to the interview questions and the political cartoon. Third, I asked each student to provide me with a copy of a reflection paper they wrote upon completing the diversity and privilege workshop during the Fall 2016 term. These reflection papers asked students to reflect on the concepts of privilege and oppression and apply them to their own social identities.

I analyzed these data using Gee's (2011, 2014) tools for discourse analysis. I specifically used Gee's seven building tools that consider how language (a) reinforces specific ways of knowing and communicating about our reality (sign systems tool); (b) reflects current social practices (activity tool); (c) creates social significance (significance tool); (d) creates, distributes, or destroys social goods (politics tool); (e) establishes relationships between ideas (connections tool); (f) creates or sustains relationships with people (relationship tool); and (g) helps individuals adopt an identity (identity tool). Collectively, these building tools exposed how these White students viewed privilege related to what it is, how it operates, and how it influences their view of themselves and others. I read all of these White students' reflection papers and interview transcripts multiple times to familiarize myself with the data. I systematically reviewed these data in three waves to identify common and contrasting findings that emerged from these students. In the first wave, I examined data from each individual student and coded stanzas of text that revealed ideas, explanations, and feelings about privilege. I also created in vivo codes within each coded stanza of text using Gee's (2011, 2014) building tools (e.g., "what social goods are being distributed, and to whom, in the text?"). These findings became the specific ideas, explanations, and feelings I present in Chapters 3 through 5. In the second wave, I examined the data across all of these students for differences and similarities which formed the basis of the themes and student groupings around which I discuss the findings (see Tharp, 2018 for a more detailed explanation of the methodology).

Overview for This Book

Every book is a product of its time. The core ideas of this book were developed during my doctoral research around 2016. However, these ideas remained relevant while I wrote this book amidst the racial inequities that were magnified during the start of the COVID-19 pandemic and the murders of Ahmaud Arbery, Breonna Taylor, and George Floyd that sparked national protests to defund the police and promote racial equity. As such, this book offers important insights into how White college students view privilege, based in research and grounded in a sociological understanding of cultural and social structures that are unfortunately timeless.

Who Is This Book for?

This book is written primarily for university faculty and staff who teach content related to privilege, oppression, and social inequality in broad terms and specifically related to race. This audience includes faculty who teach courses in cultural studies, sociology, social work, and education programs. This audience also includes staff who (a) provide diversity workshops across campus, (b) incorporate diversity topics into student leader training, and (c) work in student affairs units that engage students in their sociocultural development. My goal is to provide these educators with empirically based insights to identify and educationally engage their White students' views of privilege. My background entails both workshop- and course-based education experiences, so I pose these insights and recommendations relative to these education environments.

Additionally, this book is useful for high school teachers who also teach content related to privilege, oppression, and social inequality, as well as those engaging their students about social difference more broadly where their White students may challenge the relevance of these discussions generally or specifically for themselves. This audience may include teachers of social studies, human geography, English/literature, and other topics where they intentionally have incorporated a racially diverse curriculum to promote awareness of sociocultural differences. Finally, this book is written to be useful for scholars in the fields of education, the learning sciences, sociology, and cultural studies who share an interest in how students view privilege and social justice concepts broadly. These scholars may find value in the methodology used to collect and analyze the data that ground the discussion of this book.

Book Structure and Format

This book is divided into two parts that collectively illuminate the "how" and "what" related to White college students' views of privilege. Part 1 consists of Chapters 1 and 2, which explore key educational and societal elements that influence student learning. Chapter 1 reviews the literature on student learning and illuminates key principles and processes that influence what students think, believe, and feel. This chapter pays close attention to the presence of prior knowledge and how it is used by students to help or hinder learning. Chapter 2 examines the role that society and social communities play in shaping student learning. This chapter specifically situates students' prior knowledge in the social context of Discourse communities to explain how White college students' ideas, beliefs, and feelings are developed and maintained as part of their White racial group membership. Collectively, these two chapters provide a critical foundation for the rationality of White college students' views about privilege.

Part 2 consists of Chapters 3 through 6, which discuss specific insights related to two distinct ways that White college students view privilege based on empirical research. Chapter 3 reveals core ideas at the center of understanding privilege. Each of these ideas is described and the relationship between these ideas is explained. The result is a glimpse into the web of ideas that collectively reinforce and anchor what is "known" about privilege. Chapter 4 describes differing ideological frameworks used to make sense of privilege. Each framework is presented relative to its operational goal and central beliefs related to privilege. The chapter concludes by illustrating how the central ideas presented in Chapter 3 relate to the central beliefs of each framework. Chapter 5 explores the feelings that emerge from White college students during conversations about privilege. In addition to reviewing these feelings, the ways these feelings influence action and inaction are reviewed as a central focus to understand the relationship between feelings and our own actions that support or hinder learning. Chapter 6 synthesizes the insights shared in Chapters 3 through 5 and explains how ideas, beliefs, and feelings related to privilege work together to reinforce one another and maintain a particular worldview about privilege. This chapter highlights constellations of ideas, beliefs, and feelings that are both particularly entrenched and malleable through education. The arguments presented in all four chapters will be accompanied by empirical evidence from interviews with White college students, excerpts from their written work, and public examples of these ideas, beliefs, and feelings and how they operate together to sustain a way of understanding privilege. The conclusion reflects on synthesis from Chapter 6 to offer key takeaways and suggest specific curricular and pedagogical strategies educators can use in their work.

Notes

1 See Association of American Colleges and Universities (2013); National Leadership Council for Liberal Education and America's Promise (2008).
2 See U.S. Census Bureau (2016) regarding racial demographics in the United States and Espinosa et al. (2019) regarding racial demographic shifts among college campuses.
3 See Brown (2016) for trends regarding academic curriculum, Kolowich (2015) regarding cocurricular trainings, and Schmidt (2008) regarding intergroup dialogue efforts on campuses.

Introduction **17**

4 See Nakashima (2019) for a review of growing White supremacy overall, and CBS News (2019); Coates (2019); Feagin (2013); and Shear (2020) for discussions about White supremacy in the Republican party overall and the Trump presidency in particular.
5 See Bauer-Wolf (2019a, 2019b).
6 See Cohn and Quely (2020).
7 See Somashekhar (2015).
8 See Azziz (2015), Rotenberg (2015), and Mangan (2020).
9 See Case (2013), Hardiman and Jackson (2007), Jensen (2005), Johnson (2006), McIntosh (1989), Rothenberg (2004), and Winant (1997).
10 See Jones, A. (2018).
11 See Omi and Winant (2015).
12 See Hardiman and Jackson (2007).
13 I purposefully use the term "people of color" to refer to all racial social identity groups that are subjugated to highlight the commonality of systemic oppression perpetuated by Whiteness. While the term BIPOC (Black, indigenous, and people of color) has become increasingly common, I hesitate to use this label that highlights the oppression of Black and indigenous communities over others, namely against the Asian community (and more specifically the Chinese community), who have been explicit and intentional targets of racialized violence (Yam, 2021) resulting from racist references to COVID-19 (Fung, 2021). I do not use this term to homogenize all racial groups or make invisible their unique experiences and therefore refer to specific groups when highlighting these specific racialized realities. See Meraji and Demby (2020) for a thoughtful discussion about the benefits and challenges of using either people of color or BIPOC.
14 See Leonardo (2009).
15 See Bonilla-Silva (2014).
16 See Feagin (2013).
17 See Dawson and Bobo (2009).
18 See Hanks et al. (2018) regarding the racial wealth gap, Jones, J. (2018) regarding unemployment disparities, and Stevenson and Mayson (2018) about racially disproportionate arrest data.
19 This use of White supremacy is different from the ways Leonardo (2009) and Bonilla-Silva (2014) use White supremacy to describe systematic White racial domination.
20 See Feagin (2013) regarding racial narratives, Bonilla-Silva (2014) regarding justifications in favor of the racial status quo, Feagin et al. (2001) exploration of sincere fictions, and Matias (2016) regarding Whiteness as an ideology.
21 See Bonilla-Silva (2014), Feagin (2013), Feagin et al. (2001), and Winfield (2007).
22 See Bonilla-Silva (2014).
23 See Leonhardt and Philbrick (2018).
24 See Boler (1999).
25 See Goodman (2011) and Wise and Case (2013).
26 See Matias (2016).
27 See Ibid for more on emotions and how they reinforce Whiteness.
28 See Feagin et al. (2001).
29 See Bonilla-Silva (2014).
30 See Matias (2016).
31 See Horowitz et al. (2019).
32 See Zhou and Amaria (2020).
33 See Cheung (2020).
34 See Potter (2013) regarding the origins of policing and Stockman and Eligon (2020) regarding police alternatives.
35 For scholarship on privilege and oppression broadly, see Adams et al. (2016); Goodman (2011); Watt (2015). For scholarship on White privilege and racism specifically,

see DiAngelo (2018), Kendi (2019), Leonardo (2009), Matias (2016), Omi and Winant (2015), Saad (2020), and Watt (2015).
36 See DiAngelo (2018), Kendi (2019), and Saad (2020).
37 See Delgado and Stefancic (2012) and McCoy and Rodricks (2015) for more on critical race theory.
38 See Goodman (2011) and Wise and Case (2013).
39 See DiAngelo (2018) and Saad (2020).
40 See Kendi (2019).
41 See Pew Research Center (2019).
42 See Cargle (2019).
43 See Picca and Feagin (2007).
44 See Bonilla-Silva and Forman (2000).
45 See Tharp (2018).
46 Great Lakes College is a pseudonym for the institution where the study occurred.
47 See Horsey (2014).

References

Adams, M., Bell, L. A., Goodman, D. J., & Joshi, K. Y. (Eds.). (2016). *Teaching for diversity and social justice* (3rd ed.). Routledge.

Association of American Colleges and Universities. (2013, June 27). *Board statement on diversity, equity, and inclusive excellence.* www.aacu.org/about/statements/2013/diversity.

Azziz, R. (2015, December 4). What can campus leaders do to make protests unnecessary? *The Chronicle of Higher Education.* http://chronicle.com/article/What-Can-Campus-Leaders-Do-to/234463.

Bauer-Wolf, J. (2019a, February 25). Hate incidents on campus still rising. *Inside Higher Ed.* www.insidehighered.com/news/2019/06/27/white-nationalist-propaganda-rise-college-campuses.

Bauer-Wolf, J. (2019b, June 27). White supremacy activity spreads on campuses. *Inside Higher Ed.* www.insidehighered.com/news/2019/02/25/hate-incidents-still-rise-college-campuses.

Boler, M. (1999). *Feeling power: Emotions and education.* Psychology Press.

Bonilla-Silva, E. (2014). *Racism without racists: Color-blind racism and the persistence of racial inequality in America* (4th ed.). Rowman & Littlefield Publishers.

Bonilla-Silva, E., & Forman, T. A. (2000). "I am not a racist but. . . ": Mapping White college students' racial ideology in the U.S.A. *Discourse and Society, 11,* 51–86.

Brown, A. (2016, January 7). Diversity courses are in high demand. Can they make a difference? *The Chronicle of Higher Education.* http://chronicle.com/article/Diversity-Courses-Are-in-High/234828.

Cargle, R. E. (2019, November 21). How to talk to your family about racism on thanksgiving. *Harper's Bazaar.* www.harpersbazaar.com/culture/politics/a25221603/thanksgiving-dinner-conversation-how-to-talk-to-family-about-politics/.

Case, K. (Ed.). (2013). *Deconstructing privilege: Teaching and learning as allies in the classroom.* Routledge.

CBS News. (2019, July 19). *From birtherism to racist tweets: Trump's history of inflaming racial tensions.* www.cbsnews.com/news/from-birtherism-to-racist-tweets-trumps-history-of-inflaming-racial-tensions/.

Cheung, H. (2020, June 8). George Floyd death: Why US protests are so powerful this time. *BBC.* www.bbc.com/news/world-us-canada-52969905.

Coates, T. (2019). *We were eight years in power: An American tragedy.* One World.

Cohn, N., & Quely, K. (2020, June 10). How public opinion has moved on Black lives matter. *The New York Times*. www.nytimes.com/interactive/2020/06/10/upshot/black-lives-matter-attitudes.html.

Dawson, M. C., & Bobo, L. D. (2009). One year later and the myth of a post-racial society. *DuBois Review: Social Science Research on Race, 6*(2), 247–249.

Delgado, R., & Stefancic, J. (2012). *Critical race theory: An introduction* (2nd ed.). New York University Press.

DiAngelo, R. (2018). *White fragility: Why it's so hard for White people to talk about racism*. Beacon Press.

Espinosa, L. L., Turk, J. M., Taylor, M., & Chessman, H. M. (2019). *Race and ethnicity in higher education: A status report*. www.equityinhighered.org/resources/report-downloads/.

Feagin, J. R. (2013). *The White racial frame: Centuries of racial framing and counter-framing*. Routledge.

Feagin, J. R., Vera, H., & Batur, P. (2001). *White racism* (2nd ed.). Routledge.

Fung, K. (2021, March 18). 30% of anti-Asian incidents in 2020 used rhetoric like 'China virus', 'kung flu', report says. *Newsweek*. www.newsweek.com/30-anti-asian-incidents-2020-used-rhetoric-like-china-virus-kung-flu-report-says-1577189.

Gee, J. P. (2011). Discourse analysis: What makes it critical? In R. Rogers (Ed.), *An introduction to critical discourse analysis in education* (2nd ed., pp. 23–45). Routledge.

Gee, J. P. (2014). *How to do discourse analysis: A toolkit* (2nd ed.). Routledge.

Goodman, D. J. (2011). *Promoting diversity and social justice: Educating people from privileged groups* (2nd ed.). Routledge.

Hanks, A., Solomon, D., & Weller, C. E. (2018, February 21). Systemic inequality: How America's structural racism helped create the Black-White wealth gap. *Center for American Progress*. www.americanprogress.org/issues/race/reports/2018/02/21/447051/systematic-inequality/.

Hardiman, R., & Jackson, B. (2007). Conceptual foundations for social justice courses. In M. Adams, L. A. Bell, & P. Griffin (Eds.), *Teaching for diversity and social justice: A sourcebook* (pp. 35–66). Routledge.

Harro, B. (2013a). The cycle of liberation. In M. Adams, W. J. Blumenfeld, C. R. Castaneda, H. W. Hackman, M. L. Peters, & X. Zúñiga (Eds.), *Readings for diversity and social justice* (3rd ed., pp. 618–625). Routledge.

Harro, B. (2013b). The cycle of socialization. In M. Adams, W. J. Blumenfeld, C. R. Castaneda, H. W. Hackman, M. L. Peters, & X. Zúñiga (Eds.), *Readings for diversity and social justice* (3rd ed., pp. 45–52). Routledge.

Horowitz, J. M., Brown, A., & Cox, K. (2019, April 9). *Race in America 2019*. www.pewsocialtrends.org/2019/04/09/race-in-america-2019/.

Horsey, D. (2014). The American dream [Political Cartoon #142]. *The Los Angeles Times*. www.latimes.com/nation/la-tot-cartoons-pg-photogallery.html.

Jensen, R. (2005). *The heart of Whiteness: Confronting race, racism, and White privilege*. City Lights Books.

Johnson, A. G. (2006). *Privilege, power, and difference* (2nd ed.). McGraw-Hill.

Jones, A. (2018, October 12). Police stops are still marred by racial discrimination, new data shows. www.prisonpolicy.org/blog/2018/10/12/policing/.

Jones, J. (2018, October 30). Black unemployment is at least twice as high as White unemployment at the national level and in 12 states and D.C. *Economic Policy Institute*. www.epi.org/publication/2018q3_unemployment_state_race_ethnicity/.

Kendall, F. E. (2013). *Understanding White privilege: Creating pathways to authentic relationships across race* (2nd ed.). Routledge.

Kendi, I. X. (2019). *How to be an antiracist*. One World.
Kolowich, S. (2015, November 20). Diversity training is in demand. Does it work? *The Chronicle of Higher Education*. http://chronicle.com/article/Diversity-Training-Is-in/234280.
Leonardo, Z. (2004). The color of supremacy: Beyond the discourse of 'white privilege'. *Educational Philosophy and Theory*, *36*(2), 137–152.
Leonardo, Z. (2009). *Race, Whiteness, and education*. Routledge.
Leonhardt, D., & Philbrick, I. P. (2018, January 15). Donald Trump's racism: The definitive list, updated. *The New York Times*. www.nytimes.com/interactive/2018/01/15/opinion/leonhardt-trump-racist.html.
Mangan, K. (2020, June 8). After years of delays, college are quickly acting on protesters' demands. *The Chronicle of Higher Education*. www.chronicle.com/article/After-Years-of-Delays/248949.
Matias, C. E. (2016). *Feeling White: Whiteness, emotionality, and education*. Sense Publishers.
McCoy, D. L., & Rodricks, D. J. (2015). Critical race theory in higher education: 20 years of theoretical and research innovations. *ASHE Higher Education Report*, *41*(3), 1–117.
McIntosh, P. (1989, July–August) White privilege: Unpacking the invisible knapsack. *Peace and Freedom Magazine*, 10–12.
Meraji, S. M., & Demby, G. (Hosts) (2020, September 30). Is it time to say R.I.P. to 'POC'? [Audio podcast episode]. In *Code Switch*. National Public Radio. www.npr.org/2020/09/29/918418825/is-it-time-to-say-r-i-p-to-p-o-c.
Nakashima, E. (2019, September 20). DHS: Domestic terrorism, particularly white-supremacist violence, as big a threat as ISIS, al-Qaeda. *The Washington Post*. www.washingtonpost.com/national-security/domestic-terror – particularly-white-supremacist-violence – as-big-a-threat-as-isis-al-qaeda-dhs-says/2019/09/20/dff8aa4e-dbad-11e9-bfb1–849887369476_story.html.
National Leadership Council for Liberal Education and America's Promise. (2008). *College learning for the new global century*. Association of American Colleges and Universities. secure.aacu.org/AACU/PDF/GlobalCentury_ExecSum_3.pdf.
Omi, M., & Winant, H. (2015). *Racial formation in the United States* (3rd ed.). Routledge.
Pew Research Center. (2019, April). *Race in America 2019*. Pew Research Center.
Picca, L. H., & Feagin, J. R. (2007). *Two-faced racism: Whites in the backstage and frontstage*. Routledge.
Potter, G. (2013). *The history of policing in the United States*. https://plsonline.eku.edu/insidelook/history-policing-united-states-part-1.
Roediger, D. (1994). *Toward the abolition of Whiteness*. Verso.
Rotenberg, M. B. (2015, December 3). 4 ways to ease strife on campuses. *The Chronicle of Higher Education*. http://chronicle.com/article/4-Ways-to-Ease-Strife-on/234439.
Rothenberg, P. (2004). *White privilege: Essential readings on the other side of racism*. Worth.
Saad, L. F. (2020). *Me and White supremacy: Combat racism, change the world, and become a good ancestor*. Sourcebooks.
Schmidt, P. (2008, July 16). 'Intergroup dialogue' promoted as using racial tension to teach. *The Chronicle of Higher Education*. https://www.chronicle.com/article/intergroup-dialogue-promoted-as-using-racial-tension-to-teach-985/.
Shear, M. D. (2020, June 28). Trump retweets racist video showing supporter yelling 'White power'. *The New York Times*. www.nytimes.com/2020/06/28/us/politics/trump-white-power-video-racism.html.
Somashekhar, S. (2015, November 17). How Black lives matter, born on the streets, is rising to power on campus. *The Washington Post*. www.washingtonpost.com/national/how-black-lives-matter-born-on-the-streets-is-rising-to-power-on-campus/2015/11/17/3c113e96–8959–11e5-be8b-1ae2e4f50f76_story.html.

Stevenson, M. T., & Mayson, S. G. (2018). The scale of misdemeanor justice. *Boston University Law Review, 98*(3), 731–779.

Stockman, F., & Eligon, J. (2020, June 8). Cities ask if it's time to defund police and 'reimagine' public safety. *The New York Times.* www.nytimes.com/2020/06/05/us/defund-police-floyd-protests.html.

Tharp, D. S. (2018). *Variations among White first-year college students' understanding of privilege.* University of Illinois at Chicago. Dissertation. https://hdl.handle.net/10027/22614.

U.S. Census Bureau. (2016). *Map and graph illustration of the U.S. Redistricting data and changes of the national population by race from 2000–2010* [Graph]. 2010 Census results. http://census.gov/2010census/data.

Vygotsky, L. S. (1978). *Mind in society: The development of higher psychological processes.* Harvard University Press.

Watt, S. K. (2015). *Designing transformative multicultural initiatives: Theoretical foundations, practical applications, and facilitator considerations.* Stylus.

Winant, H. (1997). Behind blue eyes: Contemporary White racial politics. In M. Fine, L. Weis, L. C. Powell, & L. M. Wong (Eds.), *Off White: Readings on race, power, and society* (pp. 40–53). Routledge.

Winfield, A. G. (2007). *Eugenics and education in America: Institutionalized racism and the implications of history, ideology, and memory.* Peter Lang.

Wise, T., & Case, K. A. (2013). Pedagogy for the privileged: Addressing inequality and injustice without shame or blame. In K. A. Case (Ed.), *Deconstructing privilege: Teaching and learning as allies in the classroom* (pp. 17–33). Routledge.

Yam, K. (2021, March 16). There were 3,800 anti-Asian racist incidents, mostly against women, in past year. *NBC News.* www.nbcnews.com/news/asian-america/there-were-3-800-anti-asian-racist-incidents-mostly-against-n1261257.

Zhou, L., & Amaria, K. (2020, May 27). *These photos capture the stark contract in police response to the George Floyd protests and the anti-lockdown protests.* www.vox.com/2020/5/27/21271811/george-floyd-protests-minneapolis-lockdown-protests.

1
EXPLORING HOW STUDENT LEARNING WORKS

As a father of a toddler, I am reminded of and humbled by how much my son is learning every day. He is attentive to absolutely *everything*: His books, favorite television shows including *Dora the Explorer* and *Daniel Tiger's Neighborhood*, the things that anybody says or does – the list goes on and on. Not a day goes by that he doesn't stop, point, and ask, "What's this?" with his little voice, followed by him repeating the answer ad nauseam as he attempts to master the new association he has just learned.

He is in a wonderful stage of soaking up the world around him and mastering both what things are and how they are categorized. For example, he currently loves trucks (a fascination he did not acquire from myself or his mother). We drive down the road and he squeals with delight when we pass by construction zones saying, "Look daddy – a digger!" However, he uses the term "digger" both as a descriptive category for all construction trucks (e.g., bulldozers, dump trucks, excavator trucks) and as a label for actual excavator trucks themselves. As a result of his love of trucks, he has acquired a few different types of toy trucks we play with at home. However, as a toddler still mastering language, sometimes what he says does not reflect my understanding of the world when he asks for his "digger." Sometimes he means an excavator truck. Other times, he means his dump truck or bulldozer truck. When I misinterpret what he means, he will emphatically say "No, a digger!" and eventually get emotionally upset after repeated attempts that result in failure.

While he is attentive to everything I say and do, he is equally attentive to everything that I do *not* say and do. One time I referred to his Little People toys as "guys," and he began to use "guys" to refer to all of his people toys. "Guys" referred to Little People toys that were boys and girls. "Guys" referred to his Dora the Explorer figure. To correct this gendering misclassification, I started

DOI: 10.4324/9781003082378-2

substituting the word "people" in place of "guys" and began to describe the people in terms of perceived gender and race. Even though my wife and I have been steadfast in using this new term and describing his toys more intentionally, he still uses the term "guys" more often than not.

Watching my son learn, unlearn, and relearn concepts is similar to how people learn overall. The benefit of watching my son learn is that it is far easier to help him unlearn and relearn concepts that he has only been learning for the first 2 years of his life. College students face greater challenges and missteps when unlearning and relearning concepts that they have internalized for 18 years or more. These challenges become more significant when the concepts they are unlearning and relearning are mirrors for what they think, believe, and feel about themselves.

How Students Learn

It is critical to begin by stating what may seem obvious to some: Learning is not the same as teaching. Learning is a process a student undergoes that is based upon how they make sense of their experiences and also contributes to a change.[1] Given this definition of learning, it is critical to note that learning is a process that is directly linked to one's own experience that a student can choose to engage in or not. This definition is key because it highlights that students have agency in what they learn and that their experiences influence not only what they learn but also the extent to which they will decide to engage in a learning process at all.

Teaching refers to the activities or experiences that help facilitate learning. Teaching can be formal, including when educators design curriculum and structured activities around learning outcomes. Teaching can also be informal and occur through our social environment, including conversations we have with other people, reading the news, or watching movies. Taken together, learning can happen anytime and anywhere because teaching is occurring all the time and everywhere.[2] There are multiple formats and media that facilitate teaching in our society; however, students can decide how they will engage these experiences and what they will choose to learn from them. Because we should not assume that all teaching leads to learning, it is even more important to explore the learning process and understand how educators can create teaching experiences students will engage with to facilitate their own learning.

It is equally critical to clarify what we mean when we talk about *what* is being learned. Learning entails more than the acquisition of facts and other forms of static knowledge based on memorization and knowledge retrieval. Learning entails both the development of knowledge, beliefs, behaviors, and feelings as well as how these bits of information are organized in relationship to one another within a broader social context.[3] Said differently, learning involves integrating various types of contextualized information to understand our material reality, including ourselves as physical beings in society.

The Role of Prior Knowledge and Experience

Student learning results in a change related to how they (a) organize information and (b) use their organized information to make sense of the world. They may need to make room for new information or reclassify old information based on the things to which they have been exposed. What is clear is that the process of learning happens in relation to students' prior knowledge and experience. No college student is a blank slate waiting to be filled; therefore, it is important to clarify the role prior knowledge and experience play in the learning process.

Prior knowledge and experience refer to the existing information students have and how that information is organized.[4] Students have prior knowledge and experience about nearly every topic you can imagine, including complex concepts. Consider the concept of gravity as an example. Imagine a young child tossing a ball up into the air. This child has not received formal schooling to learn about the concept of gravity; however, they realize that when they throw the ball up in the air, it will come back to the ground. By the time this same child attends elementary school and is taught the concept of gravity, they have the opportunity to reorganize their prior experience with tossing a ball (and other objects) into the air and watching it return to the ground in relationship to the new concept of gravity they were taught.

The same is true about the concept of privilege. By the time students attend a workshop or course focused on privilege, they already have a lot of information about privilege, learned from a combination of formal and informal teaching experiences. They have prior information about what privilege means, who does and does not have privilege, why some people have privilege while others do not, and how the existence of privilege makes them feel. Therefore, when teaching students about privilege, the very first thing educators will encounter is the prior knowledge and experiences of their students that can either help advance or create challenges when they learn new information about this concept.

One factor that influences student learning is the extent to which students' prior knowledge and experience is activated. Their prior knowledge and experience can be activated through intentional prompts from an educator to help students recall information and bring it to the surface for consideration. For example, an educator could ask students to think about a time they experienced privilege in order to bring their ideas, beliefs, and feelings to the surface for exploration and to help them add and organize new information into their understanding. However, prior knowledge and experience can be activated from interactions that seem similar or familiar to past experiences. Consider a situation where a White student is surfing social media and views a friend's post about Black Lives Matter protests which says, "this is essential reading for all White people." Even though the word "privilege" is never uttered, the White student's prior knowledge and experience may be activated if the post seems familiar to past experiences interacting with others about racial differences and how privilege skewed their perception of reality. In both examples, prior knowledge and experience are activated and therefore are actively operating to interpret and potentially integrate new information about privilege.

A second related factor that influences student learning is the quality and relevance of students' prior knowledge and experience. When students' prior knowledge and experience about a topic are accurate and relevant, the ability to receive and integrate new information can be seamless. The challenge emerges when students' prior knowledge and experience fall short of either or both accuracy and relevancy. If students' prior knowledge is accurate but not completely relevant, it can be misapplied to a new experience and skew how the new information is viewed, integrated, and organized with existing information. Consider the way the word privilege is used colloquially when someone says, "It is an honor and a privilege to be here today." The connotation of privilege reveals an accurate understanding of privilege as a generic benefit. However, this understanding of privilege allows *everyone* to have privilege regardless of identity and is not connected to social structures. While this person's understanding of privilege is not wrong, it is an irrelevant application of a colloquial definition of privilege when a sociological definition of privilege is required.

On the other hand, if a student's prior knowledge and experience is relevant but only partially accurate or incomplete, their insufficient information reveals a potential gap where new information is needed. Consider a different example of a White, working-class student who claims that they do not have privilege because they lack economic advantages that other people have in life. This student can reasonably claim that they do not have privilege by citing examples around social class. However, the error in their understanding arises from the notion that privilege resides in *individuals*, whereas privilege is a *structural* phenomenon that is tied to multiple social group memberships. This means a single person can experience privilege and oppression at the same time associated with different identities.

However, if students' prior knowledge and experience are simply inaccurate and therefore necessarily irrelevant, it creates a new challenge in that the information they have is organized in ways that takes space from new information that would provide a more accurate understanding of the concept. For example, consider a person who argues that the concept of privilege does not exist at all – *no one* has privilege. They may hold this understanding because of existing information they use to view all advantages a person may appear to have as solely a matter of hard work. As such, it makes sense to them that there is no such thing as privilege because no one has any benefits and therefore everyone is "simply" living their own lives. Students will be most successful in their learning when their prior knowledge and experience are both accurate and activated. However, if educators intentionally activate students' inaccurate information for the purpose of examination, that can be used to purposefully create dissonance between new and existing information.

Prior knowledge and experience most often may refer to conceptual knowledge about any given topic. However, students' prior knowledge and experience are broad enough to include ideas, beliefs, and feelings. Even though beliefs and feelings are not types of knowledge per se, they do influence what someone understands to be true in different ways. For example, some (primarily Christian) children believe in the existence of Santa Claus as a magical overweight man who lives at the North Pole, constantly monitors children's actions, and rewards good behavior by bringing all children across the world toys and candy in a single night once a year. To believe in Santa Claus supports specific ideas about him, such as needing flying reindeer in order to deliver toys and candy to every child within a 24-hour time period or having the magical ability to transform his body in order to fit down chimneys or otherwise enter locked homes. Without a belief in the magical nature of Santa Claus, the ideas children have might need to be different. Feelings have a slightly different influence on ideas than beliefs. While beliefs help provide a rationale for various bits of information, feelings reveal an emotional embodiment of information. Using the same example of Santa Claus, consider how the story of Santa Claus can make children feel. When children receive toys and candy, they might feel good about themselves as well-behaved children. As such, they may feel that they deserved such a reward, which could only have been known because of Santa's ability to monitor their behavior and judge them to be worthy and therefore special. Those same feelings may then inspire future good behavior because they reinforced their knowledge about and belief in Santa and his magical surveillance capabilities. Just as the ideas, beliefs, and feelings held by children about Santa Claus are distinct yet interconnected forms of prior knowledge that influence how Santa Claus is understood, so too are the ideas, beliefs, and feelings held by White people about privilege. Therefore, each of these types of information warrants a brief exploration regarding what they are, how they are learned, and how they influence one another overall and in the context of the concept of privilege.

Learning and Ideas

The development of conceptual knowledge involves both receiving information and organizing that information in purposeful ways. Research exploring differences between novices and experts revealed that expertise was not necessarily reflective of having more information, but how that information is organized on the basis of an advanced understanding of key ideas and how they relate to one another.[5] For example, imagine how a young child might understand information about animals versus a zoologist. A young child might know multiple types of animals such as cows, dogs, chickens, frogs, and spiders. A young child would likely lump all of these animals together under the broad category of "animals" and possibly into subcategories of animals found in a home (dogs, frogs, and spiders) and animals found on a farm (cows and chickens). However, a zoologist would know additional information about each animal regarding the presence of a backbone, how they give birth to offspring, and if they are cold- or warm-blooded. A zoologist could use their additional insight to develop a more sophisticated way of categorizing this same list of animals based on animal taxonomies. They could group these same animals based on their phylum category as vertebrates (cows, dogs, chickens, and frogs) versus invertebrates (spiders), or even their class category as mammals (cows and dogs), birds (chickens), amphibians (frogs), and arachnids (spiders). In this example, zoologists would not necessarily be considered experts because they know more than a child, but because they have organized their vast amount of information in ways that allow them to understand and think about animals in more complex ways. A young child could answer basic questions about these animals' names, the sounds they make, and where they typically live. However, a zoologist could answer more complex questions about these animals' lifestyles, reproductive processes, and how they are similar to and different from one another based on their additional information that is organized in advanced ways that support higher level analysis and understanding.

The process of learning and organizing information may seem to be a straightforward psychological process of creating and expanding one's cognitive schemas for concepts as they are learned. However, scholarship by diSessa (1993, 1988) and diSessa and Sherin (1998) illustrates that it is not that simple because complex concepts require mastery of how multiple ideas relate to one another. The concept of privilege is a complex social concept that requires learners to have specific information about it, such as (a) the existence of various advantages (i.e., rights, benefits, and access to resources), (b) the knowledge that one receives these advantages based on one's social identities, (c) the influences of these advantages on one's individual experience, and (d) the distribution of these advantages through social institutions. However, simply putting these pieces of information together would suggest that privilege applies to the distribution of advantages linked to social identities through social institutions that benefit *any and all* social identity groups. What is missing in this schematic categorization of these bits of information is how they are related through an understanding of institutionalized social power that varies based on social identity categories such as race. When relating these same ideas to one another with this understanding as a sort of conceptual glue, it changes how we think about privilege. Relating the components of privilege through institutionalized social power prevents privilege from being misapplied to topics such as affirmative action that appear to benefit people of color only because it works to level out institutionalized social power that benefits White people.

diSessa and Sherin (1998) proposed a new way of thinking about conceptual knowledge as coordinating classes or systematic ways of engaging information about our reality. Coordinating classes consist of bits of information that are purposefully organized based on their relationship to one another. The way these bits of information are organized and related to one another supports an endless cycle of engaging information in the world and integrating new ideas and experiences into their existing organization of information. Stated simply, all concepts have key characteristics that are purposefully organized in someone's mind to inform how they interpret new ideas and experiences for integration into their evolving understanding. However, when a student has internalized inaccurate information or organizes their information based on a limited, localized set of personal experiences, that complicates how they engage new information. As a result, the student may reject new information or how it is presented if it conflicts with their existing set of ideas and how they relate to one another.

Thinking about conceptual knowledge as a coordinating class is particularly useful for considering how White college students conceptually understand privilege. To have a robust understanding of privilege requires students to organize multiple bits of information that are purposefully organized around the idea of institutionalized social power (see Figure 1.1). With this understanding of privilege, students would know what to look for in order to identify privilege in their lived experiences. As a result, these same students would then integrate new examples of privilege and grow their understanding of privilege in the real world that would help them identify it in the future.

However, consider what this looks like if students do not have these same bits of information or have other ways of organizing variations of this information. Imagine that a student views privilege to be a natural result of hard work without any regard to social identity (see Figure 1.2), a common view among White working-class students. This alternative understanding of privilege would dramatically alter what they view as privilege in their lived experiences. Anytime someone works hard *and* experiences an advantage would be viewed as having privilege that is earned. Therefore, this student would integrate multiple examples of privilege that are not based on social identity or institutionalized social power.

Imagine for a moment that these two students are having a conversation about privilege with one another. They would likely not understand how the other person could think about privilege as they do because when they look for

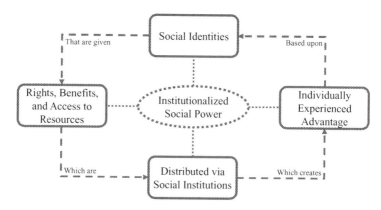

FIGURE 1.1 Visualizing Information About Privilege Organized Around Social Power

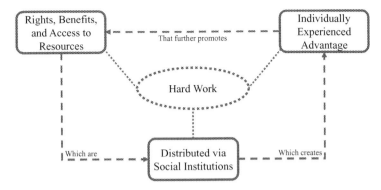

FIGURE 1.2 Visualizing Information About Privilege Organized Around Hard Work

privilege in the world, it does not register to them. Therefore, regardless of how many examples they provide to one another to prove their point, those examples, which were integrated into their respective understanding of privilege based on the bits of information they have and how they are organized, would also not be convincing. The reason for this disconnect would be that they literally are not viewing privilege in the same way. It is a difference of how they define privilege and use that definition of privilege to further make sense of their world. In this way, the coordinating class framework provides a critical framework for how and why students have different ideas about privilege.

Learning and Beliefs

In addition to the cognitive processes associated with receiving and organizing new information about concepts, individuals also develop beliefs – ideological stances used to explain how and why bits of information relate to one another. There is a difference between the ideas an individual has about a concept and how they choose to explain the reason or rationale associated with those ideas. If we consider an earlier example of a child tossing a ball up into the air and learning that it will always return to the ground, the child must also come up with an explanation for *why* the ball always returns to the ground. Does the ball return to the ground because of the gravitational pull of the Earth? Does the ball return to the ground because it is heavy? Does the ball return to the ground because it is God's will? All these explanations reveal certain beliefs about the world – a belief in science or the existence and nature of a deity. Therefore, it is equally essential to consider the beliefs individuals have and how they influence their understanding of concepts.

The literature on ideology is useful to ground this exploration into the role that belief plays in learning. Ideology refers to mental frameworks used by individuals in social groups to understand their social world.[6] While *individuals* draw upon an ideology to make sense of their world, ideologies are situated within *social groups* and expressed through social discourse.[7] Using the same example in the previous paragraph, the different beliefs a child may use to explain why a ball always returns to the ground comes from the social groups to which they belong. A belief in science stems from a shared understanding within a scientific *community*. A belief in the existence and power of a deity stems from a shared understanding within a religious *community*. Therefore, individuals draw upon the beliefs expressed through the social groups to which they belong to make sense of their individual experiences.

Because ideologies are situated within social groups, ideologies transcend time and space. Individuals live and die; however, social groups are constantly being maintained as new individuals enter social groups, thus making ideology ahistorical.[8] Halbwachs (1992) used the notion of collective memory to capture this important aspect of ideology. Collective memory refers to stories, ideas, and beliefs that are socially constructed and shared among members of social groups. When members of a social group have a shared social experience, the act of recollection within a social group serves to both maintain and refine what is remembered.

To clarify how collective memory operates and its significance, consider how sport fans talk about championship games from the past. Fans of a specific team are members of a social group who maintain memories about these fantastic experiences by retelling these stories and passing them on to future generations of fans. As a result, these fans are connected to a love of a specific team and also a set of stories, ideas, and beliefs about that team that connect fans over time. For example, when the Chicago Cubs baseball team made it to the World Series championship in 2016, news stories featured young and old Cubs fans talking about their love of the team, sometimes referring to significant events or past games they did not directly experience but learned from their parents and grandparents as part of becoming a fan.[9]

Taken together, ideologies are mental frameworks that are situated within social groups and maintained over time. When individuals use ideology to make sense of their reality, their beliefs influence how they behave in the world. As a result, ideologies are situated within social groups, used by individuals, and manifested in our material existence.[10] In the case of sports fans, being a fan often entails adopting negative feelings and behaviors toward rivals. Therefore, the shared stories about a team that fuel beliefs about a team's superiority over other teams can manifest in behaviors ranging from insults to physical brawls with fans from a rival team.

The material impact of our ideologies has far more serious repercussions when they relate to social differences and social inequality. As discussed previously, everyone in the United States is socialized to learn and adopt Whiteness as a racialized way of understanding reality. Part of being socialized into Whiteness involves learning and adopting a set of beliefs about various racial groups and how these racial groups relate to one another. However, these beliefs have contributed to the creation and maintenance of structural and systemic racial privilege and oppression.

Even though ideologies are used by individuals to make sense of their world, these beliefs can be false.[11] Given that ideologies exist within social groups and influence our material reality, it is important to consider how social groups use ideologies to create and sustain social power. For example, a commonly held false belief within the White racial community is that White people are superior to other racial groups. The origins of this belief can be traced back to a need to justify the enslavement of Black people in order to economically benefit White people in the United States.[12] Because ideologies persist over time, this belief in White superiority evolved over time to maintain social and economic advantages through tangible racial violence and structural inequities. During the time of Ancient Greece, Aristotle posited a climate theory based on the belief that extremely hot or cold climate produces morally, intellectually, and physically superior people. His theory was used to rationalize Greek superiority over non-Greeks and justify early systems of slavery. During the colonial and early days of the United States, White Puritans adopted similar notions of superiority justified by the great chain of being that lighter skinned people were literally closer to God than dark-skinned people and applied these beliefs to indigenous and Black peoples to justify colonization, missionary conversion, and modern systems of slavery. During the early 1900s, White scientists adopted similar notions of White superiority and applied the pseudoscientific reasoning of eugenics based on genetically based racial differences evident in both phenotypical appearance and moral character to support postslavery social control policies such as forced sterilization. During the post–civil rights movement, beliefs in White superiority were grounded in notions that Blacks were more violent and dangerous as a matter of genetics and cultural practices, supporting the origins and rapid growth of mass incarceration.[13] The basic belief that White people are superior to other racial groups persisted and evolved over time within the White racial community to justify the creation and maintenance of racial violence and inequality over Black people in particular, and communities of color more broadly, that has been documented as existing throughout our history and into the present day.

For a concept indelibly tethered to social groups such as privilege, the literature on ideology is useful for clarifying from where these beliefs emerge and how these beliefs shape our conceptual understanding. Beliefs about privilege are learned from others who share our social identity group memberships and further reinforced or refined through our individual experiences. In this way, we learn a set of beliefs about privilege from our social groups and integrate them into our way of understanding the world as we experience reality ourselves. In this way, our beliefs reflect an intuitive understanding of our reality based upon our localized social experiences.[14] Over time as we experience more of the world and expand our social groups, our beliefs may evolve and replace our intuitive understanding of the world with an understanding that is more sophisticated and critically thought-out.

Racialized ideologies influence both what individuals might believe about society and how they chose to engage others in the world, whether or not race is explicit. Bonilla-Silva (2014) explored how long-standing false racial beliefs about White superiority have evolved into color-blind notions in the post–civil rights world. This evolution of racialized beliefs allows individuals to distance themselves from explicitly racist beliefs in favor of using what appears to be supposedly race-neutral explanations to talk about the existence of racial inequalities. Four common ideological frames have evolved under this set of color-blind beliefs that include abstract liberalism, naturalization, cultural racism, and minimization of racism. Each frame relies on distinct explanations about racial privilege that can overlap with one another. The most common and interconnected frame, abstract liberalism, uses ideas associated with economic or political liberalism (e.g., individualism, individual choice) to explain away the role of race in social inequality. The naturalization frame relies on arguments that racial differences are innately hardwired into our physical self biologically or psychologically. Cultural racism relies on arguments that racial differences stem from social group habits that are based upon stereotypes (e.g., Blacks are lazy). However, minimization is a frame that generically dismisses the existence of structural or institutional forms of inequality in favor of any other explanation.[15] While these false racial beliefs can be adopted by individuals of any racial social group, they are commonly found among Whites and are passed along through this social group.

Based on this wealth of scholarship, the relationship between conceptual understanding and ideological explanation is quite salient when considering social concepts including privilege. Let us reconsider Figures 1.1 and 1.2 to show how central ideas about privilege are understood in relationship to beliefs about privilege. Imagine that there are two college students who hold different beliefs. One student, Katy, believes that all social groups are equal in worth, and therefore, no social group is superior to another. The other student, Jessica, believes that some groups are superior to others. As Katy and Jessica interact with social inequality in the world, these beliefs will influence how they explain the existence of privilege and core ideas for this concept.

Katy's belief that social groups are equal in their worth will influence the ideas she chooses to adopt about privilege. When faced with evidence of inequality between social groups such as the racial wealth gap, Katy's beliefs will influence her to look for reasons to explain this phenomenon outside of these individuals and their racial groups. If social groups are equal in worth, the racial wealth gap might be the result of structural forces imposed upon different racial groups. This belief would influence Katy to hold ideas about privilege that involve institutionalized social power as a vehicle to distribute benefits through social institutions to select social identity groups. As a result, Katy's ideas about privilege would reinforce her belief that social groups are equal in their worth (Figure 1.3).

Jessica would approach the existence of the racial wealth gap a bit differently. Jessica's belief that some social groups are superior to others would influence her to look for reasons to explain the racial wealth gap that are associated with qualities or characteristics associated with race. As a result, she might argue that these differences are linked to how hard people within different racial groups work, encouraging her to adopt ideas about privilege that any benefits awarded through social institutions are earned through individual hard work, and therefore, individuals have the same ability to choose how hard they wish to work in order to gain these benefits (Figure 1.4). Taken together, Jessica might employ her understanding explicitly by saying that Black people are lazier than White people (an example of the cultural racism frame) or that White people are naturally smarter and end up in higher paying jobs (an example of the naturalization frame). However, Jessica could also express her beliefs implicitly by denying the

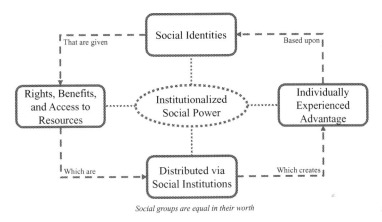

FIGURE 1.3 Visualizing the Relationship Between Information About Privilege and a Belief in Equality

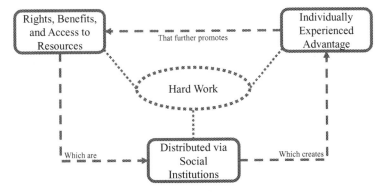

FIGURE 1.4 Visualizing the Relationship Between Information About Privilege and a Belief in Superiority

role of race at all and suggesting that the wealth gap simply reflects those who work harder than others (an example of the abstract liberalism frame).

If Katy and Jessica were having a conversation about privilege, their diametrically opposed beliefs would cause them to be baffled by the other's explanation. Katy would reject Jessica's explanation that social group differences or individual hard work is the reason why certain social groups have advantages over others. Jessica would balk at Katy's insistence that social structures distribute benefits unequally and would likely accuse Katy of making excuses for the choices people make themselves. As a result, each student would reject the other student's understanding of privilege because it would be challenging for them to consider each other's ideas about privilege because they do not square with their beliefs about the nature of social groups in society. For both Katy and Jessica, their ideas are purposefully organized in order to support their respective beliefs about privilege. Their different beliefs about privilege also helped them to include and organize a curated set of ideas that reinforce their respective beliefs. Therefore, their different sets of ideas and beliefs collectively support how they reject the other's understanding of privilege.

Learning and Feelings

Emotions also influence how we understand and explain the world. Emotions refer to an individual's feelings that are informed by what that individual perceives and believes within their social context.[16] Feelings mediate the extent to which someone experiences pleasure versus displeasure and remains in a state of calm versus alertness. They also influence our actions and behaviors related to these states of being.[17] In this way, emotions are similar to both ideas and beliefs because they too are influenced by our social experiences while also informing how we interact with our social world. As such, emotions influence the learning process through what we notice, what we pay attention, how we understand and remember information and experiences, and our approach to problem-solving and reasoning.[18]

I know this is true for myself and have noticed the difference in my thoughts and behaviors when I feel happy or upset. On days when I feel joyful and happy, I have a bounce in my step, and it is hard to bring me down. I tend to notice things around me that make me smile, like flowers in my neighborhood, the way my son smiles when he does an authentic belly laugh, or the extra satisfying way food tastes. On these happy days, what I notice in my environment helps reinforce my happy mood. However, on days when I feel angry and upset, I am a bit like Eeyore from Winnie the Pooh. I tend to notice things that irritate me, like my creaking floor, the weeds in my front yard, or the shrill scream my son makes when he wants attention. On these gloomy days, what I notice in my environment are reflections of my mood – all the things that bother me and reinforce my feeling upset.

While there is a physiological component to how emotion operates, emotions are neither hardwired within us nor universal for all people. The belief that emotion is universal and innate reflects a classical view of emotion as a brute reflex, a view that is widespread and deeply embedded in our society. Instead, emotions are constructed as individuals experience the world and make sense of those experiences over time. Furthermore, our social interactions also influence how we make sense of our experiences and thus how we construct our emotions and emotional responses.[19] Therefore, the way we express our feelings varies widely between people and cultures.

However, our feelings and the distinctive ways they influence us reflect the social rules and norms in society[20] and cannot be separated from existing social relations of power.[21] As individuals experience emotion and exhibit emotional reactions through their behavior, it is critical to attend to how emotions and emotional responses are learned in association with social group membership in the broader context of social power. For example, cisgender men and women are socialized in different ways when they feel sad. Cisgender men are discouraged from expressing their sadness through tears, which are viewed as a sign of weakness that contradicts what men ought to be. However, cisgender women are encouraged to express sadness through tears because they are viewed as more emotional and sensitive, thus reinforcing the perception of what women ought to be. Harro's (2013) cycle of socialization explicitly connects our emotions to how we are socialized related to social identity groups and the power dynamics between these groups in a few important ways.

During the socialization process, individuals learn views about social identity groups and how they relate to each other from their social interactions with those they know and love (e.g., family, friends) and institutions they trust (e.g., education, medical, legal). While learning *views* about ourselves and others, they also learn how we ought to *feel* about ourselves and others. Members of privileged groups are taught to view themselves as good, superior, and admirable, whereas members of oppressed groups are taught to view themselves as bad, inferior, and contemptible. Positive views of ourselves can cultivate emotions of happiness and pride, whereas negative views of ourselves can cultivate emotions of sadness and shame. A few examples may make this connection explicit.

As a White person, I learned to view myself as better than others without anyone ever saying this to me explicitly. For example, during high school, I was in advanced placement classes. Being in these advanced classes made me feel good. It nurtured and reinforced a view of myself as smart, hardworking, and that I deserved to be in these high-level courses. Without ever consciously thinking about it, I assumed that the other students in these courses were also smart, hardworking, and deserving: Nearly all of them were also White. After all, schools would never place students in advanced classes if they were not good enough to be there, right? On the contrary, in the few general education courses I took that were more racially diverse, it seemed like those peers were not as smart or hard working as I was. I never had a reason to question me or my peers' being in those classes, nor would I have wanted to jeopardize how being in those classes made me feel about myself. What would it have done to my sense of self had I questioned if I truly deserved to be in these courses? It would have threatened the view of myself as smart, hardworking, and deserving. Therefore, I did not question the "what" or the "why" behind my placement in advanced courses and simply accepted it as truth. In other words, the way I felt related to my personal experience grounded by my privilege as a White person, which was enough to help me sustain beliefs that contributed to this view of myself.

At the same time, as someone who grew up in a working-class family, I also internalized beliefs about myself as inferior to others. My senior year of high school, I qualified to compete in the Illinois High School Association State speech tournament. (For the unfamiliar, speech teams consist of students performing in a range of events focused on public speaking and performance.) I will never forget how nervous and excited I felt about the chance to perform. My parents even took me to buy new dress clothes to compete, including a new blazer. After a few rounds of competition, I failed to advance, and my time in the tournament was over. When I received feedback from the judge whose score knocked me out of the competition, I saw that I was given the lowest overall score possible solely because I did not unbutton the bottom button of my blazer. While my coach was kind enough to explain what that meant (in the world of male fashion, the bottom button ought to remain unbuttoned at all times) and told me to ignore that feedback, it was forever burned into my consciousness. I had never owned a blazer before, and I never saw my father or any men in my family wearing suits or blazers, so such cultural knowledge was foreign to me. Even though it was unreasonable for me to know this cultural fashion rule, I could not shake feeling ashamed and inferior for my not knowing, linking my not knowing to being working class, and feeling like I didn't belong at the tournament in the first place. Many years after that, I still feel nervous when dressing up for a job interview or social occasion and cannot shake the thought of being revealed as an impostor who does not belong.

As we are socialized to adopt certain views about ourselves and others, we also learn how to behave within our respective social identity groups and how to interact with others different from ourselves. Both social affirmations and rewards along with social admonishments and punishments are distributed through our social interactions to support and reinforce hegemonic views of ourselves, others, and how we ought to interact with one another. These rewards and punishments influence both how we feel about ourselves and others.

Returning to the example related to gendered expressions of sadness, cisgender boys and girls commonly receive different reactions to when they express sadness by crying. If a cisgender boy cries to express feelings of sadness, he may be given negative attention by men in his life for expressing himself in this way. Such admonishments might sound like "Boys are not supposed to cry" or "Are you a girl? You need to toughen up!" as ways to check the boy's behavior relative to his social group membership. As a result, the boy may feel bad about himself and grateful to other men in his life for helping him to be strong. On the contrary, if a cisgender girl cries to express feelings of sadness, she may be given positive attention from women in her life who seek to provide care, compassion, and comfort. Such attention would serve as a positive reward that provides social permission for her to express herself in this way that does not conflict with what is acceptable behavior from a girl. As a result, the girl may feel affirmed in who she is and grateful for how men and women provided her support.

At the center of this entire socialization process are emotions that drive our continued participation in this cycle as we maintain and reproduce these learned views and behaviors for others to learn. By going along, both privileged and oppressed groups retain a certain degree of certainty because our views and behaviors are congruent with what our social world is designed to expect from us. However, privileged groups also have affective interests in maintaining systems of dominance because their privileged status produces material and emotional well-being.[22] Therefore, the socialization process shapes how we learn emotions that cannot be divorced from the context of social power. The embodiment of our emotions is thus another area where social power is internalized within us. Cheryl Matias' (2016) exploration of White emotionality explores how White people are socialized to use emotions to protect their belief in their racial superiority and defend themselves in interracial experiences when these beliefs feel threatened. Let us consider a few different examples to illustrate this point.

When White people express pity and sadness for those less fortunate than themselves, it reinforces the social hierarchy while further emphasizing the goodness of the White person for seeming so caring. Such pity acts as a socially acceptable expression of racialized disgust. For example, in 2019, Donald Trump described the city of Baltimore as "disgusting," "dirty," and "dangerous" in a series of tweets intended to highlight how some cities needed more help and attention.[23] These comments by a White person about a predominantly Black city never explicitly talked about race. However, these comments effectively played on racialized beliefs about Black people as inferior to Whites that manifested themselves in emotional disgust that served to reinforce a positive view of White spaces (and therefore the White people in them) relative to Black spaces and Black people. As a result, these comments help the White speaker appear benevolent and compassionate even though their comments actually operate to reinforce a view of White superiority over people of color.

When White people believe they ought to be color-blind and politically correct, they may be inclined to feel nervous or fearful when interacting with people of color. These feelings stem from not wanting to do or say the wrong thing to offend people of color. If a White person said or did something offensive, it could tarnish their image as "a good White person." However, these feelings are seldom present when White people interact with other White people, revealing how such feelings operate to protect themselves from negative attention, not a desire to avoid hurting others from their actions or comments.

When White people are called out for racist comments or behaviors by others, particularly people of color, they might express sadness or guilt to turn the tables and deflect the focus of the conversation away from their comments and behaviors and toward themselves as a well-meaning person. The "White women's tears" meme perfectly captures this dynamic and highlights how frequently (and effectively) crying is used to deflect accountability for a White person's racism. Furthermore, White people observing this situation may view the person of color as causing trouble because they called attention to a White person's racism. As a result, expressing sadness and guilt becomes an effective emotional tool to shut down conversations about race while simultaneously painting people of color as being too aggressive or angry for simply bringing attention to racism.

One example of this came shortly after public attention and protests over the police murder of Breonna Taylor and George Floyd. In June 2020, Stacy Talbert, a White female police officer in Georgia, recorded a video where she provided an emotional recount of a delayed fast-food order experience. While describing her experience she is on the verge of tears, stating how nervous and anxious she felt because she feared that her food was tampered with given the broader context of mistrust toward police. However, the entire video shifts attention away from police accountability and is encapsulated when the officer says, "Please, just give [police officers] a break . . . and if you see an officer, say thank you because we don't hear that enough anymore."[24]

Sometimes White people are more intentional about how to weaponize their emotions to maintain power in racial interactions. Armed with prior knowledge and experience that a White person's emotional distress will always receive attention, especially when juxtaposed with people of color, White people may use emotions to leverage situational outcomes. Another viral example of this from May 2020 involved Amy Cooper, a White woman who was walking her dog without a leash in Central Park. When a Black man asked that she leash her dog and started to record the encounter, the White woman threatened to call the cops and said that "an African-American is threatening her life" and then proceeded to follow through on her threat in an increasingly emotional phone call with the police.[25]

These examples of White emotionality highlight that White people, as members of a White racial community, are all socialized to embody racialized emotionality in particular ways. However, emotions are also a powerful entry point to promote student learning, including about the concept of privilege. When a student has an emotional response, it provides an opportunity to explore what they are feeling and why they are feeling a certain way and to examine the ideas or beliefs that are connected to their feelings. A student's feelings may reveal particular ideas and beliefs about themselves, others, and how they relate to other people, including people from different social identity groups than themselves. Research has examined that students' understanding of privilege is linked to how they feel about themselves and who is to blame.[26] Feelings of guilt and shame are most common among White students examining privilege[27] as students experience cognitive dissonance between their prior knowledge that anchored their positive self-image as people who were deservingly advantaged in a just world juxtaposed to new truths that identify White people as undeserving beneficiaries of systemic social inequality. However, educators can leverage students' emotional reactions to bypass resistance and promote learning,[28] particularly in order to move students' past emotions that deflect responsibility or prevent action.[29]

To summarize this discussion thus far, emotions shape learning by influencing both what we notice and how we feel about what we notice. However, both our emotions and the ways in which we express them are learned over time through our social group memberships, including our social identity groups. These learned emotions also serve to reinforce social group boundaries and existing social power dynamics between privileged and oppressed groups. Therefore, there will always be an emotional component to learning that is magnified when engaging concepts and experiences related to social inequality. These emotions constitute another form of prior knowledge that exists among students that can be used by educators to support learning.

Based on this wealth of scholarship, the relationship between conceptual understanding and ideological explanation is quite salient when considering social concepts including privilege. Let us reconsider Figures 1.1 and 1.2 to show how central ideas about privilege are understood in relationship to beliefs about privilege. Imagine two college students who hold different beliefs. One student, Katy, believes that all social groups are equal in worth, and therefore, no social group is superior to another. The other student, Jessica, believes that some groups are superior to others. As Katy and Jessica interact with social inequality in the world, these beliefs will influence how they explain the existence of privilege and core ideas for this concept.

How we understand the nature of privilege, including who does and does not have privilege and why, is inextricably linked to perceptions and feelings about ourselves and our social group memberships. The relationship between ideas, beliefs, and feelings becomes clear when reconsidering our earlier example of Katy and Jessica's ideas and beliefs about privilege depicted in Figures 1.3 and 1.4. Katy's ideas about privilege are supported by a belief that social groups are equal in their worth. When Katy is faced with examples of systemic and structural racism that provides advantages to White people, she is likely to feel frustrated with systemic inequality and hopeful that these systems can be dismantled. Therefore, conversations about privilege are not personalized because Katy understands privilege as structural, not individualized. However, Jessica's ideas about privilege are supported by a belief that some social groups are superior to others. When Jessica is faced with the same examples of systemic and structural racism that advantages White people, she is likely to feel frustration toward the person who initiated the conversation about privilege because it threatens her sense of self and deservingly superior that is supported by her beliefs. It is also likely that she might feel guilty about being the beneficiary of privilege but might subsequently use emotion to pivot the conversation away from her as a White person by emphasizing how hard she has worked and the challenges she has overcome in life. Such emotional positioning is linked to feeling that privilege is individualized, not structural. In these fictitious examples, it is clear how our emotions and emotional reactions are influenced by our ideas and beliefs while simultaneously operating to maintain our existing ideas and beliefs.

Conclusion

In order for educators to provide effective teaching that leads to student learning, educators must understand the influence of prior knowledge and how it is cultivated among their students. While this is true for any education experience, it is critically important when cultivating learning relegated to social inequality and privilege. Students' prior knowledge about privilege is cultivated both through their experiences with privilege and the way they are socialized to understand privilege relative to their social identities. Socialization is a pervasive and systemic process that creates and reinforces social power through the adoption of ideas, beliefs, and feelings related to privilege. These internalized understandings both replicate social power in society as a whole and operate to maintain social identity group memberships and intergroup boundaries. While these ideas, beliefs, and feelings related to privilege are distinct in what they are and how they operate, they exist together and are interconnected. When educators understand the role of prior knowledge, three different types of prior knowledge, and how such prior knowledge is cultivated in society relative to social inequality concepts including privilege, they will have the necessary humility for the daunting educational task before them.

Notes

1 See Ambrose et al. (2010).
2 See Vygotsky (1978) for more about his sociocultural view of education.
3 See Bransford et al. (2000) and Sawyer (2006).
4 See Ambrose et al. (2010) and Bransford et al. (2000).
5 See Bransford et al. (2000).
6 See Hall (1986).
7 See Gee (1996).
8 See Althusser (1971, 2003).
9 See Frye (2016).
10 See Althusser (1971, 2003).
11 Ibid.
12 See Kendi (2016).
13 See Alexander (2012), Kendi (2016), Kivel (2013), and Winfield (2007).
14 See Philip (2011).
15 See Bonilla-Silva (2014).
16 See Boler (1999).

17 See Kleinginna and Kleinginna (1981).
18 See Ting et al. (2017).
19 See Barrett (2017).
20 See Averill (2017).
21 See Gordon (1981, 1989) and Boler (1999).
22 See Bonilla-Silva (2019).
23 See Chapman (2019).
24 See Griffith (2020).
25 See Ransom (2020).
26 See Chizhik and Chizhik (2002).
27 See Wise and Case (2013).
28 See Adams (2016).
29 See Hardiman et al. (2013) and Matias (2016).

References

Adams, M. (2016). Pedagogical foundations for social justice education. In M. Adams, L. A. Bell, D. J. Goodman, & K. Y. Joshi (Eds.), *Teaching for diversity and social justice* (3rd ed., pp. 27–54). Routledge.

Alexander, M. (2012). *The new Jim Crow: Mass incarceration in the age of colorblindness*. The New Press.

Althusser, L. (1971). *Lenin and philosophy* (B. Brewster, Trans.). Monthly Review Press.

Althusser, L. (2003). *The humanist controversy and other writings* (F. Matheron, Ed. and Trans., and G. M. Goshgarian, Trans.). Verso.

Ambrose, S. A., Bridges, M. W., DiPietro, M., Lovett, M. C., & Norman, M. K. (2010). *How learning works: Seven research-based principles for smart teaching*. Jossey-Bass.

Averill, J. R. (2017, July). The social construction of emotion: Myths and realities. *Emotion Researcher*. Retrieved July 22, 2020, from https://emotionresearcher.com/the-social-construction-of-emotion-myths-and-realities/#.

Barrett, L. F. (2017). *How emotions are made: The secret life of the brain*. Houghton Mifflin Harcourt.

Boler, M. (1999). *Feeling power: Emotions and education*. East Sussex, UK: Psychology Press.

Bonilla-Silva, E. (2014). *Racism without racists: Color-blind racism and the persistence of racial inequality in America* (4th ed.). Rowman & Littlefield Publishers.

Bonilla-Silva, E. (2019). Feeling race: Theorizing the racial economy of emotions. *American Sociological Review*, 84(1), 1–25.

Bransford, J. D., Brown, A. L., & Cocking, R. (2000). *How people learn: Brain, mind, experience, and school*. National Research Council.

Chapman, W. (2019, July 31). Fact-checking Trump on Baltimore. *U.S. News and World Report*. www.usnews.com/news/cities/articles/2019-07-31/fact-checking-president-trump-on-his-baltimore-tweets.

Chizhik, E. W., & Chizhik, A. W. (2002). A path to social change: Examining students' responsibility, opportunity, and emotion towards social justice. *Education and Urban Society*, 34(3), 283–297.

diSessa, A. A. (1988). Knowledge in pieces. In G. Forman & P. Pufall (Eds.), *Constructivism in the computer age* (pp. 49–70). Lawrence Erlbaum.

diSessa, A. A. (1993). Toward an epistemology of physics. *Cognition and Instruction*, 10(2&3), 105–225.

diSessa, A. A., & Sherin, B. (1998). What changes in conceptual change? *International Journal of Science Education*, 20(1), 1155–1191.

Frye, A. (2016, October 13). 'Lovable losers'? That's not how young fans see the cubs. *Chicago Tribune.* www.chicagotribune.com/redeye/redeye-how-young-fans-approach-rooting-for-the-cubs-20160922-story.html.

Gee, J. P. (1996). *Social linguistics and literacies: Ideology in discourses* (2nd ed.). Taylor & Francis.

Gordon, S. L. (1981). The sociology of sentiments and emotions. In M. Rosenberg & R. Turner (Eds.), *Social psychology: Sociological perspectives* (pp. 551–575). Basic.

Gordon, S. L. (1989). Institutional and impulsive orientations in the selective appropriation of emotions to self. In D. D. Franks & E. D. McCarthy (Eds.), *The sociology of emotions* (pp. 115–135). JAI Press.

Griffith, J. (2020, June 17). Officer in video complaining about fast-food order says people missed the point. *NBC News.* www.nbcnews.com/news/us-news/officer-viral-video-complaining-about-fast-food-order-draws-ire-n1231353.

Halbwachs, M. (1992). *On collective memory* (L. A. Coser, Ed. and Trans.). University of Chicago Press.

Hall, S. (1986). The problem of ideology: Marxism without guarantees. In D. Morley & K. Chen (Eds.), *Stuart Hall: Critical dialogues in cultural studies* (pp. 25–46). Routledge.

Hardiman, R., Bailey, B. W., & Griffin, P. (2013). Conceptual foundations. In M. Adams, W. J. Blumenfeld, C. R. Castaneda, H. W. Hackman, M. L. Peters, & X. Zúñiga (Eds.), *Readings for diversity and social justice* (3rd ed., pp. 26–35). Routledge.

Harro, B. (2013). The cycle of socialization. In M. Adams, W. J. Blumenfeld, C. R. Castaneda, H. W. Hackman, M. L. Peters, & X. Zúñiga (Eds.), *Readings for diversity and social justice* (3rd ed., pp. 45–52). Routledge.

Kendi, I. X. (2016). *Stamped from the beginning: The definitive history of racist ideas in America.* Bold Type Books.

Kivel, P. (2013). *Living in the shadow of the cross: Understanding and resisting the power and privilege of Christian hegemony.* New Society Publishers.

Kleinginna, P. R., & Kleinginna, A. M. (1981). A categorized list of emotion definitions, with suggestions for a consensual definition. *Motivation and Emotion, 5,* 345–379.

Matias, C. E. (2016). *Feeling White: Whiteness, emotionality, and education.* Sense Publishers.

Philip, T. M. (2011). An "ideology in pieces" approach to studying change in teachers' sense-making about race, racism, and racial justice. *Cognition and Instruction, 29*(3), 297–329.

Ransom, J. (2020, July 6). Amy Cooper faces charges after calling police on Black birdwatcher. *The New York Times.* www.nytimes.com/2020/07/06/nyregion/amy-cooper-false-report-charge.html.

Sawyer, R. K. (2006). *The Cambridge handbook of the learning sciences.* Cambridge University Press.

Ting, C. M., Amin, H. U., Saad, M. N. M., & Malik, A. S. (2017). The influences of emotion on learning and memory. *Frontiers in Psychology, 8,* article 1454. www.frontiersin.org/articles/10.3389/fpsyg.2017.01454/full#h2.

Vygotsky, L. S. (1978). *Mind in society: The development of higher psychological processes.* Harvard University Press.

Winfield, A. G. (2007). *Eugenics and education in America: Institutionalized racism and the implications of history, ideology, and memory.* Peter Lang.

Wise, T., & Case, K. A. (2013). Pedagogy for the privileged: Addressing inequality and injustice without shame or blame. In K. A. Case (Ed.), *Deconstructing privilege: Teaching and learning as allies in the classroom* (pp. 17–33). Routledge.

2
HOW SOCIAL GROUPS CONTEXTUALIZE LEARNING ABOUT AND OUR UNDERSTANDING OF PRIVILEGE

Growing up, I was not the world's biggest sports fan. As a child, I was surrounded by sports culture even though I did not care for sports other than a mild interest in baseball. Most of the other boys I knew were big sports fans who knew the names and stats for multiple players. The men in my family loved watching games and talking about sports at nearly every family party. At school, there were "fan days" where students were encouraged to wear clothing in support of their favorite sport teams. In total, my peers, family, and school life were saturated with other males who loved sports. Therefore, it became useful to learn about sports so that I could fit in. Relatedly, as a White male in White male social spaces, it was common and acceptable to be a fan of sports teams with Native mascots.

Fast forward to college where I first became aware of racial privilege and joined student organizations committed to social justice. One notable memory at college involved attending an event about Native American appropriation. I learned how widespread Native American appropriation was in society, including sports mascots. After I attended this event, I decided to be more conscientious about this issue and would vocally object to native appropriation. Conversations with family members during and after college would include my critique of appropriated sport mascots often while I wore an activist T-shirt that said, "people are not mascots."

Fast forward once again to my early professional career. I was working in a cultural center on a college campus at a time when our local hockey team, the Chicago Blackhawks, was in its prime, winning consecutive championship games. Everyone was instantly a fan of the team and had matching attire. Likewise, I knew the secret to fitting in and had a professional looking polo shirt with their team logo embroidered on the chest – an image of an indigenous man's face with colored feathers in his hair. One day, I came to work wearing this polo

DOI: 10.4324/9781003082378-3

shirt when I had a meeting planned with a group of male administrators who I wanted to fit in with and who I believed were also big sports fans. However, a staff member in my department was gracious and brave enough to point out that what I was wearing was offensive and problematic given the work we did in our cultural center. In that moment, I did not find that staff member to be gracious at all, and instead of thanking this colleague, taking ownership for my mistake, and changing my outfit, I was defensive and offered multiple rationalizations that protected my self-image and also reinforced Whiteness.

The first two acts of my story highlight how social spaces and communities influence what we think, believe, feel, and do in our lives that allow us to fit in with others and retain a certain sense of self. In the first act of my story, I wanted to fit into male spaces and learned enough about sports to act and sound like a part of these social groups. Furthermore, as a White person in the world, being a fan of a team with a Native mascot was never a problem. In the second act of my story, I spent time in a different social group where a different set of ideas and beliefs was shared among us and normalized around racial justice. However, the final act of my story reveals the fluidity of our involvement in social communities and how we draw upon the various social communities we have been a part of over time, including the multitude of learned ways of thinking and being. Even though wearing a polo shirt with a Native mascot violated what I knew and believed as a social justice educator, my defensiveness was grounded in rationalizations that centered Whiteness and my desire to fit in that were reminiscent of a different set of ideas and feelings that I retained from my childhood experiences.

The takeaway of this story is that people can align with multiple social communities over time. When we align with different and contradictory social communities, we do not jettison our existing ideas, beliefs, and feelings. Instead, we acquire multiple sets of ideas, beliefs, and feelings that allow us to behave in ways to fit into these social groups and social spaces. Therefore, when it comes to understanding how students learn about privilege, it is critical to explore how these distinct social communities shape what we learn and how we decide to use what we have learned depending on the social context in which we find ourselves. This chapter examines how we learn to belong and how we demonstrate our belonging in ways that connect back to privilege.

Learning to Belong: Socialization

Human beings are social animals who are unique in our capacity to seek and maintain community in social groups. We are strongly influenced by a desire for social relationships. We develop the capacity to read other people in order to anticipate and meet someone else's needs. We make decisions about our behaviors in order to live in harmony with those around us.[1] Our capacity and desire for community are evident through the multitude of social communities that exist in our lives. These include social groups based on our social identities (e.g., race, gender) and personal identities. The types of social groups to which we belong might be based on the country where we live, the city or town where we live, the language(s) we speak, our racial identity, our field of work, our hobbies, the sports teams we cheer for, the music we listen to, the types of art we enjoy, the college we graduated from . . . this list could go on and on.

Every social group to which we belong has its own distinct way of being or culture. While the concept of culture is used to describe any number of features within a society, here I refer to the subjective nature of culture defined by Bennet (1998) as "the learned and shared patterns of beliefs, behaviors, and values of groups of interacting people" (p. 3).[2] Sharing a set of beliefs and values with others allows us to work together, support one another, and create social harmony that allows social group memberships to be particularly fulfilling. At the same time, we cannot enjoy these benefits of social groups until we learn how to belong in the first place.

Broadly speaking, socialization refers to the process of learning the norms and culture of a social group through our social interactions. Socialization is a vital process to prepare individuals to become members of social groups. Through socialization, we learn particular ways of thinking, feeling, and acting that connect us to other individuals in our social group while also aligning us with these social groups. In this way, socialization provides a useful function to maintain social groups over time by passing on the culture shared by individuals aligned with social groups to future generations.

However, the socialization process is tethered to existing social power relations within social groups. Consider the example of a family social group. Parents not only teach their children ways to think, feel, and act but also teach social power dynamics between the roles of a parent and child within their social group. Parents have social power over their children and exercise that power to create and maintain rules and boundaries such as bedtimes or healthy eating habits. In the context of large social groups, such as our nationalities linked to the countries in which we live, we are socialized to learn the culture of our country along with the social power dynamics that exist within the country. Such power dynamics include the relationship between people and authority figures (e.g., students and teachers, patients and doctors, civilians and police officers) as well as those linked to our social identities based on privilege and oppression. In addition to learning ways to think, feel, and act that allow us to participate in society, we also learn ways to think, feel, and act about ourselves and others based on these social power relations.

Bobbie Harro's (2013) cycle of socialization framework provides a detailed overview of how individuals are socialized to adopt thoughts, feelings, and behaviors that maintain social power dynamics between privileged and oppressed social groups. The cycle begins with people being born into the world without knowledge or awareness of social identity groups or the existing power relations between groups. However, through interactions with individuals they love (e.g., family and friends) and institutions they trust (e.g., schools), they acquire ideas, beliefs, and feelings about themselves and others, even when they are not explicitly said, modeled, or taught. Individuals learn just as much from what others do *not* say or do around certain social groups. Therefore, existing social inequalities are observed and assumed to be normal, especially if they are noticed without any acknowledgment or question. Over time, individuals acquire a sense of self-related to one's own social identities and ideas, beliefs, and feelings about people who are associated with different social groups than themselves which are further reinforced through a mixture of implicit and explicit punishments and rewards related to maintaining prevailing social group boundaries. Because human beings are social and seek a sense of belonging with other people, emotional desires for security and certainty fuel our choices to replicate ideas, beliefs, and feelings that maintain social power dynamics in order to preserve our "membership" within our social groups.[3] While the cycle of socialization explains how we learn power dynamics among privileged and oppressed groups alike, it is particularly useful to explain how and why individuals from privileged social identity groups are more likely to participate in reproducing existing social power dynamics.

Social Groups and Discourses

Everyone is socialized into their respective social groups. However, over time, individuals may identify with social groups that are different from the original social groups into which they were socialized. Consider the example of a first-generation college student who may come from a working-class family and goes on to become a medical doctor. While this college student may have been originally socialized into a working-class social group, over time, they likely also become socialized into multiple additional social groups different from their original social group, such as a medical professional social group and an upper-class social group. When individuals are socialized into multiple social groups with different (and at times conflicting) ideas, beliefs, and feelings, they retain both ways of seeing and interacting in the world.

Instead of thinking about how individuals belong to social groups in binary terms in which we either do or do not belong, it is useful to consider how individuals make choices regarding which social groups they actively participate in at any given moment through their communicative practices. Gee's (1999) theory of discourse provides a useful way to consider how our communication practices reflect the social group(s) we are actively and intentionally participating in at any given moment through the concept of "big D" Discourse. While "little d" discourse refers to the ways we communicate with others on a daily basis, including our verbal and nonverbal communications, "big D" Discourse refers to how we communicate and express ourselves that align with the social groups to which we belong.[4] Therefore, the concept of Discourses describes social groups while emphasizing that individuals have agency to decide how and to what extent they communicate and express themselves in order to participate in various social groups given their particular context.

Individuals who have been socialized into multiple and sometimes conflicting Discourses understand how to communicate and express themselves to actively and intentionally participate as a member of any particular Discourse. Consider a person who is both a medical doctor and a parent. In a static understanding of social group membership, this person is both a parent and a medical doctor all the time. However, they may not always be communicating and expressing themselves in ways that actively and intentionally participate as a parent or a medical doctor in every social context. Such a person might wake up and participate in a Parenting Discourse by helping get their children ready for the day, making them breakfast, and talking with them using special nicknames (e.g., Mommy/Daddy). However, once this same person arrives at work, they participate in a Medical Doctor Discourse by wearing a stethoscope around their neck, speaking with patients using a particular script to guide their conversation, performing a medical exam on their patients' bodies, providing instructions for self-care, and using formal titles to introduce themselves (e.g., Doctor). Even though this person is behaving differently in different contexts, they are still the same person who makes discursive choices to align with a particular social group at a given moment given their social context.

What and how we communicate is inherently social and influenced by the Discourses in which we actively participate. Our ability to alter how we communicate and express ourselves to actively and intentionally participate in multiple Discourses is supported by socialization processes that teach us how to do so through what we think, believe, and feel that are expressed through our discourse with others. This socialization process teaches us how to participate in various Discourses while simultaneously reinforcing how we communicate a particular set of ideas, beliefs, and feelings in order to establish and maintain an active sense of belonging within these Discourses.

What and how we communicate serve as "building tools" that allow individuals to construct meaning that strengthens our relationship to a particular Discourse through our active participation. These "building tools" allow individuals to (a) create social significance, (b) reflect social practices, (c) adopt an identity, (d) build or maintain relationships with others, (e) manufacture and distribute social goods, (f) create relationships between ideas, and (g) reinforce epistemologies.[5] Therefore, our "little d" discourse can reveal which "big D" Discourse we are participating in and the ways in which we have been socialized into that same "big D" Discourse.

Using the same example of a person who is a parent and a medical doctor, this person uses multiple communicative practices to actively construct their participation in a Medical Doctor Discourse. When this person goes to work, they wear a doctor's coat and a stethoscope. During their workday, they use a particular script when talking to patients (e.g., "What brings you in today?"; "Does that hurt?";

"Say 'ahhh'") and may prescribe medicine as needed. Based on these bits of information about how this person communicates both nonverbally through their attire and verbally through what they say to patients, we can see how their communicative practices construct and maintain their participation in a Medical Doctor Discourse. Doctor office visits reflect a distinct social practice where they adopt their identity as a doctor. In this interaction, they have a doctor–patient relationship, where the doctor conducts an examination which reflects a particular epistemology and distributes wellness (or knowledge that will contribute to wellness) as a social good. Based on the conversation between the doctor and patient, certain things may become more significant than others through connections between various ideas shared when talking about symptoms. Collectively, these communicative practices construct this person's participation in the Medical Doctor Discourse. If this person decided to participate only partially in the Medical Doctor Discourse (e.g., not wearing their lab coat or wearing a mechanic's jumpsuit, wearing a toolbelt versus a stethoscope, using a different script in the office visit), it is possible that patients would question whether or not they were a *real* doctor, thus revealing how our participation in a Discourse operates in social contexts.

Our relationship to any Discourse is influenced by how much we actively and intentionally participate in ways that connect us to others who also actively and intentionally participate in the same Discourse. This is especially true when considering social identities as Discourses. Consider traditionally hegemonic Cisgender Discourses of "Masculine" and "Feminine." Participation in either a Cisgender Masculine or Feminine Discourse entails multiple communicative practices that distinguish the Discourse to which you belong. Consider the question "What does it mean to act like a boy/man or girl/woman?" The answer to this question would reveal a list of these communicative practices that we learn, which allow us to participate in these Discourses.

Our socialization into these Cisgender Discourses is readily apparent when someone asks an expecting mother if she is having a "boy or girl." What the mother says indicates not only which set of communicative practices the baby will learn but also the communicative practices others will use when interacting with the baby. A short stroll through the children's clothing section in a department store will reveal some of these communicative practices. Children participating in a Cisgender Masculine Discourse have clothing with cool colors (e.g., blue, green) that feature "strong" things such as dinosaurs, trucks, and superheroes. Children participating in a Cisgender Feminine Discourse have clothing with warm colors (e.g., pink, yellow) that feature "cute" things such as flowers and princesses. When friends and family members bring gifts for this baby that are associated with a particular Discourse, they help create relationships between the baby, themselves, and others who also participate in that given Discourse (e.g., fathers, sons, grandpas, and uncles sharing a Cisgender Masculine Discourse; mothers, daughters, grandmas, and aunts sharing a Cisgender Feminine Discourse).

Participation in a Discourse is not necessarily "all or nothing." It is possible for people to participate to varying degrees in a Discourse. Using the same example with Cisgender Discourses, we can imagine individuals who we would say are cisgender women who might not seem to fully participate in a traditional Cisgender Feminine Discourse. Consider the popular movie series *The Hunger Games*. The protagonist of the movies, Katniss Everdeen, is physically strong, assertive, and strong-willed and uses these characteristics to fight oppression and help lead a rebellion. However, she wears her hair long and at times will wear dresses and make up and acts more subdued in her interactions with others. Contrast her to another supporting character, Effie Trinket, who consistently wears dresses and make up in her role to help civilize youth around proper etiquette. Most people would characterize both of these characters as cisgender women even though they do not participate in a Cisgender Feminine Discourse in the same way or to the same degree.

Another movie, *Dear White People*, is full of examples of Black and White characters participating in Racial Discourses to varying degrees as they navigate social situations and spaces to feel a sense of belonging to others on a college campus. The protagonist, Samantha White, is a biracial Black woman who leads the Black Student Union to advance racial justice issues while simultaneously balancing romantic relationships with two different men, Reggie (a Black man) and Gabe (a White man). A constant theme throughout the film is how Sam participates in a Black Discourse to varying degrees that influences the extent to which her Black and White peers view her as "Black enough." The film also displays characters who attempt to participate in different Racial Discourses than those into which they were originally socialized. Another Black female character, Colandrea Conners, actively and intentionally tries to minimize her interactions with Black spaces and students on campus. Further, she works to minimize her participation in a Black Discourse while simultaneously attempting to participate in a White and Upper-Class Discourse through her attire (wearing designer clothing), her speech (never using slang), her expressed ideas and beliefs (finding upper-class White men desirable over Black men), and even her name (being called "Coco") while interacting with White, upper-class students on campus. The way that her character alternates her language and behavior throughout the film and interacts with both Black and White characters alike demonstrates how individuals have agency over which Discourses they participate in and how much they choose to participate in a given Discourse depending on the social context.

While individuals can choose to participate in various Discourses, that does not guarantee their acceptance by other members of that Discourse. It is for this reason that individuals cannot readily claim to belong to any social group of their choosing. In order for someone to be accepted by other members of a Discourse, they need to communicate in similar ways (e.g., appearance, speech, and language) while having a shared understanding (e.g., ideas, beliefs, feelings) that communicates oneself as consistently aligned with a Discourse. How many times have you been in a room where a racially diverse group of people are talking when a White person will turn to a person of color and say something like, "for a moment I forgot you weren't White." Or perhaps a person of color will turn to the White person and say "you can't say that/talk that way." Such situations, whether in a workplace or social setting, reflect the extent to which sufficient participation can facilitate belonging in a Discourse; however, the ability to maintain one's belonging is dependent on consistent and active participation that facilitates acceptance of others, especially when attempting to participate in a Discourse different from those a person was originally socialized into.

In addition to helping us understand the nature of social groups, Discourses can be understood as social groups that embody different positions related to broader social issues and realities. Racial Discourses reflect various embodiments of a racialized experience. Professional Discourses (e.g., teachers, medical doctors, construction workers) reflect various embodiments of occupationally oriented experiences. Just as we are socialized into various social groups related to social identities and professional occupations, we are also socialized into various topical Discourses. However, some Discourses can reflect different sides of a contentious topic. The broader topic of abortion in the United States has two clear sides (e.g., Pro-Choice, Pro-Life) with distinct ways of understanding the topic and providing expression as being on a particular side. The same is true for the broader topic of racial privilege and social inequality. For the topic of racial privilege and social inequality, we can envision two sides: A side that supports the status quo and maintains social inequality and a side that challenges the status quo and advocates for social equity. When considering the specific topic of privilege and race, these Discourses can be labeled a Whiteness Discourse and an Antiracism Discourse.

Whiteness Discourse

The Whiteness Discourse is an extension of Whiteness. While Whiteness refers to a collective racialized way of knowing and understanding our reality that is grounded in the experience of being White, a Whiteness Discourse refers to the communicative practices which simultaneously align with and reinforce Whiteness. These communicative practices include a specific set of ideas, beliefs, and feelings related to privilege in general and specifically related to race. When individuals participate in a Whiteness Discourse, they express distinctive yet commonplace ideas about the notion of privilege, beliefs which underpin explanations of privilege, and feelings that arise when faced with the concept of privilege. These ideas, beliefs, and feelings are considered normative within society because individuals are socialized into a Whiteness Discourse as a default way of participating in society. Therefore, the collective social experiences we have, including our interactions with most social institutions, are predicated on participating in a Whiteness Discourse to be successful. As a result, participating in a Whiteness Discourse is not only normative and pervasive but also rewarded through our interpersonal relationships (e.g., sharing similar ideas and beliefs as a way to maintain friendships) and institutional environments (e.g., expressing similar beliefs and emotional expressions to advance in the workplace).

Participating in the Whiteness Discourse entails adopting specific ideas about the notion of privilege and racial privilege that are congruent with White racial knowledge. In general, individuals who participate in the Whiteness Discourse are quick to dismiss the concept of privilege by arguing that situations of privilege are situational or highly individualized versus being viewed as connected to social identity groups or existing as a structural or institutional phenomenon in society. On the contrary, what others might claim to be privilege is viewed by participants of the Whiteness Discourse as the result of individual merit, luck, or chance or the result of someone else's personal bias. Therefore, privilege is not seen as a real social phenomenon but is instead a reference to individualized experiences that are either earned or beyond an individual's control. As such, privilege as defined in this book simply does not and cannot exist.

Individuals who participate in the Whiteness Discourse espouse beliefs about and related explanations of the existence of privilege that are related to and build upon these existing ideas. Broadly speaking, participating in the Whiteness Discourse entails believing in White supremacy in ways that either appear to be blind to social identities or simultaneously emphasizing individuality among Whites yet social patterns among people of color. This belief commonly involves a view that all *individuals* are inherently equal and the existence of benefits and advantages are tied to individual circumstances. When White people have benefits, they were earned or derived by luck or chance. However, people of color have benefits from an unfair acknowledgment of social identities that undoes the innate equality among all individuals. Within this belief system, White people are either never responsible for unearned benefits or assumed to have worked hard for earned benefits. Meanwhile, people of color are always responsible for any disadvantages they experience, yet if they have what appears to be an advantage, it must have been unfairly gained from bias against White people. Overall, the prevailing belief among participants in the Whiteness Discourse prevents acknowledgment of White privilege while allowing for racial privilege to be experienced among people of color, all of which reinforces the belief that White people are superior.

A particular set of emotions and emotional displays accompanies these ideas and beliefs among individuals who participate in the Whiteness Discourse that overlap with White emotionality. Overall, individuals express a range of feelings than range from internally directed discomfort, sadness, and shame to externally directed frustration and contempt. What these feelings have in common is that they arise when individuals who participate in the Whiteness Discourse are faced with claims or evidence regarding the existence of social inequality. In certain circumstances, these individuals feel internally directed feelings as they experience tension between evidence or claims of social inequality relative to how they view and feel about themselves and society. Often, these emotions are manifested through comments such as "social inequality is a shame" or "I just feel so bad about social differences" that imply a sense of "but what can we do?" In other circumstances, these individuals feel externally directed feelings when they feel accused of contributing to social inequality because they have a social identity that receives privilege. These emotions are expressed through comments such as "It's not my fault" or "I never owned slaves." Additionally, internally directed feelings may also lead to counterclaims about people of color who are *really* responsible because they talk about privilege or perhaps benefited from social equality initiatives, which are viewed as evidence of reverse discrimination. What these feelings and emotionally driven reactions have in common is that they avert attention away from the topic of privilege and responsibility away from these individuals or White people as a group. The specific emotions themselves are less distinctive than their primary purpose, which is to maintain the status quo and protect Whiteness as a way of seeing and moving through the world. In other words, the way these feelings function to protect Whiteness by centering the White experience and othering people of color is central to participating in the Whiteness Discourse.

There are endless examples of high-profile people who actively participate in the Whiteness Discourse. Tucker Carlson, a television personality on Fox News, hosted a segment on his cable television show critiquing diversity trainings happening in the federal government,[6] including trainings on "White privilege" that the White House decided to halt because they are viewed as "divisive, anti-American propaganda."[7] In Carlson's 11-minute segment, he critiques the lunacy and "crackpot race theories"[8] presented in these trainings related to privilege, and in doing so, expresses central ideas, beliefs, and emotional responses consistent with the Whiteness Discourse. Consider the following comments shared throughout his television segment:

- "Critical race theory is racism. . . . It is vicious, it is cruel, it divides the country. . . . It makes Americans hate each other . . . and you cannot say this enough because it is true, it is also the very definition of the racism they are claiming to fight."[9]
- "Hey, working class guy driving the truck . . . it's your fault, you did it. You are the real enemy here, and there is nothing you can do to change that. Systemic racism, sorry."[10]
- "Jeff Zucker, the head of CNN . . . is the embodiment of privilege if there ever was one. According to critical race theory, [he] got his job precisely because of systemic racism. SO why does he still have it? Why can he still bear to hold [his] job?"[11]
- "[In one training] the trainers demanded that the men make a list of associations about White male culture, this is so sick. . . . Is anyone actually okay with this? Does anyone want to be subjected to this? Want your sons subjected to this? They didn't do anything wrong, they were just born a certain way. This is evil, and it's also the most corrosive thing we can do."[12]

These comments reveal his understanding that privilege is individualized versus structural when he suggests that privilege places blame on individuals, such as the "working-class guy driving the truck." He further emphasizes an individualized understanding of privilege when he points to Zucker as a *real* example of privilege while simultaneously suggesting that if he had privilege, it would be resolved with a personal decision to leave his job. Carlson reveals his belief that privilege does not exist in the first place when he ends his commentary about Zucker's privilege by saying he was the embodiment of privilege *if there ever was one*. Additionally, Carlson turns the tables to suggest that critical race theory is actually racism because it focuses on race, suggesting that there is no legitimate reason to talk about race, let alone racial structural inequalities, unless the person themself is actually promoting racism or attempting to "make Americans hate each other." Justified by his beliefs in the nonexistence of privilege, he exhibits multiple emotions of frustration, anger, and contempt through his words, tone, and facial expressions. He expresses frustration with the existence of these trainings that no one wants to be subjected to claims that individuals, specifically White and working-class people, are wrongly blamed and describes these trainings as "sick" and "evil." These emotional reactions are notable in how they operate to shift the focus away from privilege as a structural and systemic phenomenon by focusing instead on individuals and accusing diversity trainers for wrongly blaming people for being White.[13]

As mentioned previously, people of color also can and do participate in the Whiteness Discourse. Candace Owens, a Black female conservative commentator and spokesperson for Turning Point USA, is known for critiquing the existence of White privilege. In an interview with Glenn Beck hosted on Facebook,[14] she argues that White privilege does not exist by stating, "You want to know why White people do better than Black people? Because White people as a whole make better decisions than Black people do."[15] In this statement, she expresses a similar focus on privilege as individualized through individual decision-making while simultaneously relying on racial stereotypes that reinforce White superiority over people of color, explicitly making the link between ideas and beliefs connected to Whiteness. These ideas and beliefs are further reinforced in a moment where Beck highlights Booker T. Washington's focus on individual betterment, and Owens offers agreement by stating that White privilege is an "excuse for Black Americans not to apply themselves."[16] Owens then holds up examples of Black people who rose up through their individual decision-making. While Owens does not exhibit frustration or anger in her commentary, she finds the notion of White privilege comical, often laughing or chuckling with a slight distain during the conversation, which serves to trivialize the notion of privilege and reinforce the notion that individuals are to blame for any supposed inequalities that are observed in society.

In addition to these examples of high-profile people, there is ample evidence of how people participate in the Whiteness Discourse. Consider how many times you have heard a family member, friend, student, colleague, stranger, or even yourself, express any of the following sentiments in the context of race or racial inequality through your life:

- "I don't see color/race/differences . . . just that we are all human."
- "Racism is a relic of the past" or "Slavery ended a long time ago."
- "Some people are just luckier than others."

- "I don't have White privilege, I'm poor/working class."
- "It's not *their* fault they were born White."
- "It's not what you have, it's how you choose to use it."
- "I earned everything I have and would never accept a handout."
- "If *those people* would try harder/apply themselves they might be better off."
- "Some people are just naturally lazier/more hardworking than others."
- "If people would spend less time focusing on race and more time bettering themselves, they would be as successful as anyone else."

All these sentiments have a few things in common. First, they share two central ideas that (a) social identities are not significant and (b) advantage is based on the individual instead of structures or systems. Second, they share a central belief that some people are better than others . . . and those people *happen to be* White people. Third, there is an emotional desire to deflect attention away from Whiteness in order to eliminate any tension between their experience of reality and the way they view that reality, including how they feel about themselves and others.

To summarize, the Whiteness Discourse is one of many Discourses that people in the United States are socialized to participate in from the earliest of ages. Participating in the Whiteness Discourse related to the topic of privilege revolves around ideas that privilege does not exist in any structural sense, the belief the White people are superior to others as an explanation for racial inequality, and manifestations of emotions that protect the normalcy of Whiteness as a worldview and the innocence of those who profess it. However, even though we are all socialized to learn how to participate in the Whiteness Discourse, including its understanding of privilege, there is an alternative Discourse that many people can and do learn – the Antiracism Discourse.

Antiracism Discourse

Just as the Whiteness Discourse is an extension of Whiteness, the Antiracism Discourse is an extension of antiracism. The Antiracism Discourse refers to the communicative practices that align with a collective way of knowing and understanding reality that is not centered around the White experience and actively works against racial inequality and racism. Generally speaking, participants in the Antiracism Discourse affirm the existence of privilege in general, and racial privilege in particular, as a structural and systemic phenomenon. Contrary to participants in the Whiteness Discourse who seek to minimize privilege as a phenomenon and discredit those who focus on privilege, participants in the Antiracism Discourse seek to raise attention to the pervasiveness of privilege and give voice to alternative perspectives and experiences as evidence of its existence and impact on others, including those who experience oppression and privilege alike. Because participating in the Antiracism Discourse exists in direct opposition to the Whiteness Discourse, both the communicative practices related to the Antiracism Discourse, as well as those who participate in the Antiracism Discourse itself, are a threat to Whiteness and its hegemonic ability to operate as socially normative, acceptable, and desirable. Therefore, it is not uncommon for the Antiracism Discourse or those who participate in this Discourse to be framed as extreme or out of touch with reality. Indeed, these comments are partially true in the sense that participating in the Antiracism Discourse *is* out of touch with the normative practices of Whiteness and *is* extreme in its goal of dismantling oppressive systems and structures that have operated in the United States since its colonial founding over 400 years ago.[17]

Participating in the Antiracism Discourse entails adopting specific ideas about privilege and racial privilege that draw upon race critical knowledge. Central to their ideas is an understanding of privilege in general, and racial privilege in particular, as a structural and systemic phenomenon. A core idea involves privilege being associated with social power that is distributed through structures and systems based on social group memberships. Related to their view of privilege as structural and systemic, they understand privilege as pervasive across time and space. Therefore, they are able to connect what participants in the Whiteness Discourse would claim are isolated events and situations as interconnected. For example, the idea that privilege is pervasive across time and space supports an understanding of racial privilege as a common thread that supported Black chattel slavery, Jim Crow policies and practices, and the modern-day prison industrial complex across the United States.[18] A more specific idea about privilege being pervasive across time and space also involves an understanding of privilege as rooted in colonization and imperialism as a pervasive institution that enables privileged social groups to steal land and natural resources from other social groups. Overall, participants in the Antiracism Discourse understand privilege as a very real phenomenon that can be witnessed through individuals' stories and experiences yet are grounded in structures and systems that have persisted from the past into the present.

Individuals who participate in the Antiracism Discourse are grounded in a race critical ideology that is reminiscent of critical race theory. A central belief among participants in the Antiracism Discourse is that race is a social construction that has been used to create structural racial inequalities. Therefore, it follows that privilege not only exists but also was purposefully and intentionally manifested, cultivated, and perpetuated in order to create and sustain social power for White people at the expense of people of color. However, while individuals have contributed to the creation and maintenance of privilege, participants in the Antiracism Discourse believe that the existence of privilege is embedded in our social systems and institutions. Generally speaking, participants in the Antiracism Discourse are more concerned about *how and where* privilege operates within and across our society as a systemic phenomenon instead of focusing on privilege on an individual level. This belief in the structurally embedded nature of privilege enables participants in the Antiracism Discourse to examine their own role in perpetuating privilege without being easily distracted by what privilege say about them personally. To say this more colloquially, "it's not about *me*, it's about *our us and our society*."

Participants in the Antiracism Discourse exhibit racial emotional resiliency that supports their ability to identify and interrogate privilege without taking it personal or becoming deterred when uncovering their own involvement in perpetuating and benefiting from privilege. Overall, these individuals express feeling upset by the existence of privilege and frustration at its persistent presence in society. When faced with evidence of how they themselves are culpable for perpetuating privilege or benefiting from it, they express regret that is coupled with a commitment to act differently in the future. Their emotional reaction is linked to an understanding that their original socialization into Whiteness guarantees they will say or do something that may hurt others and therefore focus on how to prevent repeating their mistakes in the future. Instead of attempting to explain why they were well-intended to prove their commitment to antiracism, they simply take responsibility for their actions and expect their future behavior to speak for itself regarding how committed they are to antiracism. Relatedly, participants in the Antiracism Discourse may express feelings of hopefulness and resolve because they believe that just as Whiteness was purposefully and intentionally created to unfairly distribute social power, through personal commitments and dedication to structural change, these structures and systems can be changed. What is most notable among participants in the Antiracism Discourse is that their feelings and the ways these feelings are operationalized are directed toward structures of privilege versus individual people with privileged social identities. Even though participants in the Antiracism Discourse may critique individual people with privilege, these critiques are centered around systemic privilege that is manifested in these individuals. Said differently, these critiques are not directed toward an individual person in and of themselves but toward an individual person as evidence and an extension of systemic and structural privilege.

While it is far more common to find academics who participate in the Antiracism Discourse, there are multiple media and entertainment personalities who participate in the Antiracism Discourse, with many more who began participating after the murder of George Floyd.[19] Francesca Ramsey, a Black female entertainer and video blogger, hosts an MTV web series where she frequently talks about privilege and social inequality. On one of her webisodes, she tackles the misguided assumption that her show hates White people and employs multiple ideas, beliefs, and emotional expressions in her response.[20] She employs a structural and systemic understanding of privilege by explicitly stating that her critiques are of "systems and institutions"[21] and not about individual White people. She leverages ideas about privilege as being guided by social power and highlights how social inequality is pervasive across time and space by stating that she is against "the historical roots of oppression that have led to today's societal conditions which allow institutions with White leadership to systematically discriminate against people of color."[22] This comment also showcases Ramsey's underlying belief that social inequality was purposefully and intentionally implemented through social institutions. Finally, she demonstrates racial emotional resiliency by expressing frustration with social inequality, not individual White people, as well as through her hopefulness that having challenging conversations about race and privilege can lead to greater awareness that can change our social institutions.

Jon Stewart, a White male television and film personality who was the former host of *The Daily Show* also provides a clear example of participation in the Antiracism Discourse. In a short video clip where he speaks about defunding the police, Stewart leverages multiple ideas and beliefs central to the Antiracism Discourse.[23] He emphasizes the importance of looking at structures and systems by stating the need to look at the "context" while explicitly naming the existence of structures and systems that maintain racial segregation.[24] He draws upon the intentional design of social inequality and its pervasive nature by stating, "*we built a segregated system and we built it up for over 400 years* [emphasis added]."[25] While he seems upset with the existence of structural discrimination in his comments, he concludes with a sense of resolve when stating that we must commit to doing the work to dismantle these structures because "they don't just dismantle themselves. . . . I feel like our efforts should be in dismantling them as best we can."[26] In total, he understands racial inequality as being intentionally implemented in structures and systems to benefit certain racial groups over others; however, he expresses emotional resolve that fuel his motivation to change these systems that are beyond any single individual.

While these examples illustrate individuals actively participating in the Antiracism Discourse, individuals must constantly make the choice to intentionally participate in this Discourse. Since everyone is socialized to participate in the Whiteness Discourse by default, most people may not constantly and consistently participate in the Antiracism Discourse. Consider Elizabeth Warren, a White female Democratic senator from Massachusetts. During her bid to become the 2020 Democratic presidential nominee and vice-presidential nominee, she consistently made statements about racism that is structural and systemic coupled with specific policy proposals to address racism at a structural level.[27] However, when Warren took and published the results of a DNA test in order to prove her Native American ancestry,[28] doing so was congruent with participating in the Whiteness Discourse. Taking a DNA test in order to provide evidence of one's ancestry aligns with the belief that elements of our social identity, including race and ethnicity, have a genetic component. Such claims stem from scientific racism and the eugenics movement that has been used to support claims that social differences are the result of genetic differences.[29] This understanding directly contradicts a central idea within the Antiracism Discourse – that race is socially constructed (not a genetic fact). While Warren has communicated a structural analysis of racism and works to dismantle institutionalized social inequality, it is also true that she has communicated an understanding of race that is guided by

White racial knowledge. The intention of this example is to highlight that participation in both the Whiteness and Antiracism Discourses are choices we make that are evidenced through our communicative practices. Once again, individuals are not singularly and solely members of a Whiteness or Antiracism Discourse, but instead make choices about which Discourses they participate in at any given moment. Therefore, it is important to look for the extent to which individuals choose to participate in the Antiracism Discourse and what ideas, beliefs, and feelings are present when doing so.

To summarize, the Antiracism Discourse is a Discourse that individuals may choose to participate in at some point during their life. Participating in the Antiracism Discourse related to the topic of privilege revolves around ideas that privilege exists as a structural and systemic phenomenon that was purposefully and intentionally implemented to maintain social power for select racial identity groups linked to how these groups have been socially constructed relative to one another. Further, participation in the Antiracism Discourse is marked by feelings that are directed toward social inequality as a structural force coupled with hopefulness that structural inequalities can be dismantled. Like all other Discourses, participation in the Antiracism Discourse is not a group to which someone is a static member, but instead requires consistent commitment to participation. Therefore, even individuals who actively participate in the Antiracism Discourse may not always participate or participate consistently in this Discourse. Therefore, it is important to consider the extent to which any person is participating in the Antiracism Discourse along with the social context that informs their level of participation at any given time.

One more example may prove useful to illustrate what participation in either the Whiteness or Antiracism Discourse looks like when participants in each Discourse are engaging with each other. In an extended interview in 2014 between Bill O'Reilly, a former Fox News television show host, and Jon Stewart, then host of *The Daily Show*, O'Reilly and Stewart discuss the topic of White privilege in a way that illustrates how they participate in ways consistent with the Whiteness and Antiracism Discourses, respectively.[30] During their conversation, they both employ most of the ideas, beliefs, and emotions discussed thus far in this chapter. Below are a few segments of their exchange in chronological order:

Segment One – What is Privilege[31]

O'Reilly: There is not [White Privilege]. . . . If there is White privilege, then there has to be Asian privilege because Asians make more money than Whites. . . . They make more money, [have more] higher education, [are] more affluent, so it's Asian privilege, not White privilege.

Stewart: White people . . . set the system, so that's what privilege is, is, that White people set the system . . . but there has been a systemic, systematized subjugation of the Black community.

Segment Two – Does Privilege Exist Today[32]

O'Reilly: Look, that was *then*, this is *now* . . . maybe you haven't figured out that there is no more slavery, no more Jim Crow, and the most powerful man in the world is a Black American.

Stewart: Slavery and Jim Crow are dead, but the residual effects of that systemic subjugation exist today.

Segment Three – Is Privilege Individualistic or Structural[33]

O'Reilly: But you don't put forth, alright, this 'Oh, White privilege, and if you fail, then that's why you fail,' alright? America is a place where if you work hard and get educated and [are] an honest person, then you can succeed. That's what should be put out there, not all this other stuff.

Stewart: White people do more drugs in this country than Black people, but Black people make up a far higher majority of drug arrests

O'Reilly: Do you know why that is?

Stewart: Yes! . . . because Black people, it's about real estate to some extent. There has been a systemic subjugation through real estate. Black people are ghettoized in this country.

O'Reilly: They're forced to live there. They have to live there. Is that what you are telling me?

Segment Four – Privilege and Guilt[34]

O'Reilly: This is the usual White guilt liberal stuff.
Stewart: This isn't guilt, this is fact. I don't feel guilty.

Segment Five – Emotional Intensity About Privilege[35]

O'Reilly: If you wanna say it's White privilege because Whites didn't have it as bad as Blacks, fine. But that's not what's happening here in contemporary society.

Stewart: Yes, it is!

O'Reilly: No, it's not! Let me repeat this, and I'll do it slowly so even you can understand. If you work hard, if you get educated, if you are an honest person, you can make it in America.

Stewart: If you live in a neighborhood where poverty is endemic it's harder to work hard, it's harder to get an education.

O'Reilly: It's all relative. Yes, it's harder if you are a ghetto kid. But can you do it, yes!

Segment Six – Privilege and Social Identity[36]

O'Reilly: [White privilege] doesn't exist to any extent where individuals are kept back because of their color or promoted because of their color. Look, you and I are lucky guys. We made it, we worked hard. It's not because we're White! . . . what you're doing is promoting victimhood.

During their exchange, O'Reilly explicitly and repeatedly states his belief that people are equal and that what others would call privilege is actually a reflection of individual choices to work hard, stating that "America is a place where if you work hard and get educated and an honest person, then you can succeed . . . not [White privilege]."[37] His belief is supported by ideas that success is linked to individual choices or luck but is not tethered to one's racial identity. He further reiterates an individualistic notion of privilege by stating that, *if* privilege exists, Asians have privilege over White people because they are relatively better off. He also explicitly states that privilege is situational and occurred in the past but does not exist today by citing the individual accomplishments of a single Black man who became President of the United States. During the interview, O'Reilly visibly expresses frustration, anger, and contempt in the form of exacerbated signs and eye rolls, primarily toward Stewart as the person who was seen as instigating the conversation. At one point, he even states that the topic of White privilege is an attempt to make White people feel guilty. All of his emotional reactions operate to deflect attention away from structural analyses of privilege and tend to become more visibly manifested when attempting to divert the conversation toward his understanding of privilege as individualistic.

On the other side of the conversation, Stewart makes clear his belief that privilege was intentionally developed to benefit White people at the expense of Black people. This belief fueled specific ideas about privilege as "systemic" and evidenced through empirical racial disparities (i.e., housing discrimination, drug arrests). When challenged to divorce racial injustices from the past in the present, he insists that the impact of slavery and Jim Crow persists into the present day because of the core idea that privilege is structural and systemic and thus can persist across time and space. Stewart also exhibits emotional frustration and feeling upset during the exchange. However, his emotional reaction is centered in the desire for O'Reilly to acknowledge the systemic and structural nature of privilege. At one point, he even states that he does not feel guilty about privilege, suggesting his emotional resolve to work toward undoing privilege systemically versus being stuck in how he personally feels about the existence of privilege.

Highlighting this exchange serves four key purposes. First, it provides a holistic glimpse into what participation in the Whiteness and Antiracism Discourses might look like in reality. Second, it demonstrates how the ideas, beliefs, and emotions central to participating in the Whiteness and Antiracism Discourses can converge together toward their respective goals of protecting or dismantling

Whiteness. Third, the video clip itself provides evidence of how emotional responses arise both on their own and when exposed to ideas and beliefs from the opposite Discourse that are often emotional triggers. Finally, throughout the conversation, there are moments where both O'Reilly and Stewart "back off" each other and joke around, showing how people make choices about when and how to participate in Discourses as they navigate social settings.

Exploring College Students' Understanding of Privilege Relative to Discourses

Exploring how college students understand privilege in relation to participation in either the Whiteness or Antiracism Discourse should be important and useful to educators for a few reasons. First, college students, particularly undergraduate students, are coming to college from a multitude of spaces and places that reflect various normalized ways of understanding privilege. Considering how college students participate in these Discourses helps educators remember that the ideas, beliefs, and feelings expressed by these students exist in relationship to the various social groups that have socialized them to see and understand reality in a particular way. Second, contextualizing college students' understanding of privilege relative to these two Discourses regarding privilege and social inequality highlights the ways in which their distinct ideas, beliefs, and feelings are interconnected to one another. For example, participants in both the Whiteness and Antiracism Discourse believe in the notion of equality; however, they employ this concept in very different ways. Also, participants in both Discourses commonly express similar feelings of frustration or feeling upset; however, they direct those feelings to different places. The ability to see the connections between these different understandings of privilege leads to a third reason Discourses are important – they remind us that students can be viewed on a continuum based on the extent to which they choose to participate in these ideas, beliefs, and feelings, offering hope for educating students who actively participate in the Whiteness Discourse and reminding us of the importance of continuing to develop students who participate in the Antiracism Discourse to varying degrees.

Chapters 3 through 5 will provide a more in-depth exploration and analysis of the respective ideas, beliefs, and feelings related to privilege that were observed among eight White college students during a qualitative, phenomenological research study.[38] All eight of these students were first-year students at Great Lakes College (GLC) who self-identified as White. Beyond these commonalities, these students had different constellations of social identities and experiences. The following brief summaries of each student provide a glimpse into their positionalities, how they showed up during their interviews, and an overall synopsis of their understanding of privilege. These descriptions help to contextualize these students' understanding of privilege as purposeful within the context of their prior knowledge and experience.

Anna

Anna identified as a "chronically ill," bisexual woman who was upper-middle class and agnostic. She stated that she was from the Mid-Atlantic region of the country. Anna was feeling ill during her interview, which possibly contributed to her less precise language and challenges to find the right language to express her thoughts and feelings. While she was somewhat subdued, she seemed quite eager to participate in the interview. Anna described privilege as the advantages given to people that place them ahead of others. She demonstrated the most thorough understanding of privilege, often referring to social group "superiority complexes" and discussing the relationship between the past and present. She also expressed emotion that was connected to a desire for activism. In addition to discussing race, she also frequently invoked examples of gender and ability status to explain her understanding of privilege.

Carol

Carol identified as a "straight" female who is also upper-middle class and able-bodied. She identified as a Midwesterner, having moved to three different Midwestern states during her childhood. Carol identified as Catholic, having attended both Catholic elementary and high schools. During her interview, she appeared very confident while simultaneously expressing a theatrical flair. She was very friendly, a bit giggly, and quite expressive in her body language during her interview. Carol defined privilege as the benefits a person receives based on their background or race; however, she only viewed herself as "slightly privileged" and did not believe in the existence of White privilege. Throughout her interview, she talked about her job experiences coupled with direct accusations toward people of color as perpetrating reverse discrimination against her. She wondered what life would be like if no one ever knew about the existence of slavery and expressed visible anger and contempt toward people of color.

Jamie

Jamie grew up in the southeastern United States and identified as a "very White passing" White-Hispanic female who was also "gay or queer," lower-middle class, and able-bodied. She did not identify herself with any religious affiliation. She had a happy disposition during her interview. She had mild facial expressions that occasionally grew into a smile and laughter. Jamie was very deliberate in her responses, often taking time to think after each question. Jamie understood privilege as the unearned benefits (including both material and social benefits) an individual receives based on their social identities, not based on their personal skills or achievements. As a White-passing person with a German father and Cuban-American mother, along with her experiences as a queer woman, she described herself as "pretty well informed" about privilege and referred to these social identities often.

How Social Groups Contextualize Learning   63

Jane

Jane identified as a bisexual, cisgender female who was able-bodied, "solidly middle class," and "culturally Catholic." Jane grew up in a suburb of the midwestern city where GLC is located. She viewed herself as "pretty familiar" with privilege thanks to her "good teachers," feminist books, and the experience of a nationally watched legal battle over transgender rights at her high school. Jane began her interview rather reserved, but she relaxed rather quickly, which contributed to long, energized descriptions that were accompanied by many facial expressions. Her facial expressions seemed to match how confident she felt about her responses to the interview questions, smiling when feeling most confident and scrunching her face when she seemed to feel less confident. Jane defined privilege as "the way society is built that benefits a certain group of people" through structural means. While she expressed a strong understanding of privilege as structural, she also repeatedly referred to her belief that human bias was innate to all people. She most often talked about privilege through the lens of gender and was most likely to express self-doubt when talking with her peers about privilege.

Jason

Jason identified as a "straight" male who was middle class, a practicing Roman Catholic, and "able" regarding his ability status. He was extremely reserved and succinct during his interview. He did not disclose much about himself or his views and declined to share more even when explicitly invited. Jason understood privilege as a social construct that was relative based on an individual's "innate" social identities. He was adamantly explicit that we lived in a zero-sum reality where social hierarchies were natural, and therefore, individual people of color were not to blame but instead should be pitied. Overall, he viewed social identities as "nominal" and instead focused on the importance of our actions.

John

John identified as a "straight" male who was nonreligious, upper-middle class, and "very capable of a lot of different things." However, when asked about other identities he had, he adamantly stated that he identified "most importantly as a human being" more than anything else and rejected social identity labels throughout his interview and reflection paper. He was a Midwesterner who was soft-spoken and polite during his interview. However, as the interview progressed, his responses became increasingly emphatic as he spoke louder and with greater intensity. John understood privilege to occur when people receive benefits without earning them or when someone has less than you do yourself, frequently tying this definition to someone's family rather than their social group memberships. He felt strongly that focusing on privilege divides people instead of focusing on our similarities, and he concluded the interview with gratitude for allowing him (and others like him) to have their views heard.

Lucy

Lucy identified as "Caucasian" while also stating her ethnicities as "a bunch of stuff" without being sure about them. She also identified as middle class, "straight," female, and did not believe herself to have any disabilities. Lucy identified as Catholic and had attended Catholic school her entire life. She also stated that she identified as politically conservative, which meant "pro-life, I don't like big government . . . lower taxes for everyone, not socialism at all," and proudly voted for Donald Trump in the 2016 election. Lucy was very polite during her interview, originally a bit reserved, but grew more comfortable over time. Her responses to questions were brief and peppered with fragmented sound bites from conservative discourse, followed by uncertainty. Lucy understood privilege as "something you're born into" that provides "an advantage over someone." However, she struggled to describe privilege, often following statements with "I don't know." She was visibly and verbally uncomfortable discussing race and often focused on social class.

Scott

Scott shared that he was one-sixteenth Cherokee, but because he did not identify with native culture, he viewed himself as White. He also identified as a cisgender male who also was able-bodied, agnostic, and lower-middle class. While Scott identified as "homosexual," he shared that he did not experience much oppression related to his sexual orientation. Scott added that working was also important to his identity, stating, "I work . . . I take a lot of pride in that for sure." Scott was a Midwesterner from a large family with a "strong female influence" that made him "pretty familiar" with privilege. He was mild-mannered during his interview and did not exhibit many visible verbal or nonverbal expressions. Scott defined privilege as when society gives individuals a "one-up over other people for no reason other than just what you are born with." Throughout his interview and his reflection paper, he focused most on race and specifically spoke about the Black Lives Matter movement.

The next three chapters will identify specific ideas, beliefs, and feelings with respect to participation in either a Whiteness or Antiracism Discourse using quotes from these White college students as evidence of how this looks and sounds in reality. Reflections and observations about how these different sets of ideas, beliefs, and feelings are related to one another will be shared at the conclusion of each chapter in order to pave the way for recommendations on how educators might engage these ways of understanding privilege to support learning.

Notes

1 Lieberman (2013).
2 Bennett (1998).
3 Harro (2013).
4 Gee (1999).
5 Gee (2014).
6 See Fox News (2020).
7 See Schwartz (2020).
8 See Fox News (2020, 8:55).
9 See Fox News (2020, 0:43).
10 See Fox News (2020, 0:58).
11 See Fox News (2020, 5:21).
12 See Fox News (2020, 9:42).
13 See Fox News (2020).
14 See Beck (2020).
15 See Beck (2020, 1:55).
16 See Beck (2020, 3:17).
17 See Feagin (2013).
18 See DuVernay (2016).
19 See Carras (2020).
20 See Ramsey (2016).
21 See Ramsey (2016, 0:27).
22 See Ramsey (2016, 2:13).
23 See NowThis News (2020).
24 See NowThis News (2020, 0:33).
25 See NowThis News (2020, 0:37).
26 See NowThis News (2020, 1:32).
27 See Haines (2020), Warren Democrats (2020), Warren Delivers Commencement Address at Morgan State University (2018).
28 See Perrigo (2018).
29 See Meraji (2019); Winfield (2007).
30 Comedy Central (2014).
31 Comedy Central (2014, 2:15).
32 Comedy Central (2014, 3:39).
33 Comedy Central (2014, 4:30).
34 Comedy Central (2014, 5:39).
35 Comedy Central (2014, 7:38).
36 Comedy Central (2014, 9:11 / 10:14).
37 Comedy Central (2014, 4:30).
38 See Tharp (2018).

References

Beck, G. (2020, June 7). *Is there White privilege?* [Video file]. Facebook. www.facebook.com/GlennBeck/videos/286495025812529/.

Bennett, M. J. (1998). Intercultural communication: A current perspective. In M. J. Bennett (Ed.), *Basic concepts of intercultural communication* (pp. 1–34). Intercultural Press.

Carras, C. (2020, June 12). White celebrities partner with NAACP to 'take responsibility' for racism. *Los Angeles Times*. www.latimes.com/entertainment-arts/story/2020-06-11/i-take-responsibility-video-white-celebrities-naacp.

Comedy Central. (2014, October 16). *The daily show: Bill O'Reilly extended interview* [Video file]. YouTube. www.youtube.com/watch?v=8raaT7SRx18.

DuVernay, A. (Director). (2016). *13th* [Documentary Film]. Netflix.

Feagin, J. R. (2013). *The White racial frame: Centuries of racial framing and counter-framing.* Routledge.

Fox News. (2020, September 9). *Tucker: Critical race theory is a lie from start to finish.* [Video clip]. *Fox News.* https://video.foxnews.com/v/6188946152001?playlist_id=5198073478001#sp=show-clips.

Gee, J. P. (1999). *Introduction to discourse analysis: Theory and method.* Routledge.

Gee, J. P. (2014). *How to do discourse analysis: A toolkit* (2nd ed.). Routledge.

Haines, E. (2020, July 2). Warren discusses fight to end systemic racism as some discuss her as potential VP. *The Washington Post.* www.washingtonpost.com/politics/2020/07/02/warren-discusses-fight-end-systemic-racism-some-discuss-her-potential-vp/.

Harro, B. (2013). The cycle of socialization. In M. Adams, W. J. Blumenfeld, C. R. Castaneda, H. W. Hackman, M. L. Peters, & X. Zúñiga (Eds.), *Readings for diversity and social justice* (3rd ed., pp. 45–52). Routledge.

Lieberman, M. D. (2013). *Social: Why our brains are wired to connect.* Crown Publishers.

Meraji, S. M. (Producer) (2019, July 10). Is 'race science' making a comeback? [Audio podcast episode]. In *Code Switch.* National Public Radio. www.npr.org/sections/codeswitch/2019/07/10/416496218/is-race-science-making-a-comeback.

NowThis News. (2020, June 23). Jon Stewart on defunding the police and dismantling racist institutions. [Video]. *YouTube.* www.youtube.com/watch?v=oiyCcBkn1b0&feature=youtu.be.

Perrigo, B. (2018, October 15). Elizabeth Warren just shared a DNA test showing she has Native American ancestry. *Time Magazine.* https://time.com/5424597/elizabeth-warren-dna-test-native-american-ancestry/.

Ramsey, F. (Host) (2016, November 3). Why does MTV decoded hate White people?!? (Episode 410). [Web series episode]. In *Decoded.* MTV. www.mtv.com/episodes/jb01t0/decoded-why-does-mtv-decoded-hate-white-people-season-4-ep-410.

Schwartz, M. A. (2020, September 5). Trump tells agencies to end trainings on 'White privilege' and 'critical race theory.' *National Public Radio.* www.npr.org/2020/09/05/910053496/trump-tells-agencies-to-end-trainings-on-white-privilege-and-critical-race-theor.

Tharp, D. S. (2018). *Variations among White first-year college students' understanding of privilege.* University of Illinois at Chicago. Dissertation. https://hdl.handle.net/10027/22614.

Warren Delivers Commencement Address at Morgan State University. (2018, December 14). Elizabeth Warren, US Senator. www.warren.senate.gov/newsroom/press-releases/warren-delivers-commencement-address-at-morgan-state-university.

Warren Democrats. (2020). *A working agenda for Black America.* https://elizabethwarren.com/plans/agenda-black-america.

Winfield, A. G. (2007). *Eugenics and education in America: Institutionalized racism and the implications of history, ideology, and memory.* Peter Lang.

3
CORE IDEAS ABOUT PRIVILEGE[1]

When I asked White college students participating in my research study to define privilege, every student indicated that it referred to a type of benefit or advantage. However, this is where the similarities ended among students' conceptual understanding of privilege. The other ideas that they explicitly and implicitly invoked centered around either a structural or individual understanding of privilege.

To illustrate the differences between these ideas, imagine what would happen if participants in the Whiteness and Antiracism Discourses were on separate teams playing the word association game *Outburst!*, a game where teams take turns guessing items associated with a category (e.g., the category of animals might have answers such as dog, cat, mouse).[2] During the game, players shout out whatever comes to their mind first, thus revealing their prior knowledge and experience related to any given category. What do you suppose individuals participating in the Whiteness and Antiracism Discourse teams would say if the category was "things associated with privilege"?

Individuals participating in the Whiteness Discourse would likely say the following things: "depends on each person," "earned," "lucky," "individual bias," and "relic of history." All these answers center privilege around the experience of the individual in a particular context. These answers reflect White racial knowledge, a set of ideas regarding privilege that are associated with participation in the Whiteness Discourse.

However, individuals participating in the Antiracism Discourse would likely say the following things instead: "Based on social identity," "form of social power," "intentionally distributed," "institutionalized superiority," and "pervasive over time." All these answers center privilege around structures and systems beyond any single individual. These answers reflect race critical knowledge, a set of ideas regarding privilege that are associated with participation in the Antiracism

DOI: 10.4324/9781003082378-4

Discourse. In this imaginary thought experiment, consider how foreign the answers would sound to individuals participating in the opposite Discourse, likely causing much frustration toward one another for what they said.

On the basis of my research, I observed four core ideas central to race critical knowledge and another four core ideas central to White racial knowledge. These two sets of ideas reflect specific understandings about privilege that are connected to their participation in the Antiracism and Whiteness Discourses, respectively. I present each of these ideas in the context of their respective Discourses with examples from the White college students in my study. I follow this presentation of ideas with an explanation for how these ideas are connected to one another to form a compelling internal logic. Afterward, I provide a discussion of how these opposing sets of ideas are related to one another.

Core Ideas About Privilege Central to the Antiracism Discourse

Anna, Jamie, Jane, and Scott expressed four ideas about privilege that are central to race critical knowledge and consistent among people who participate in the Antiracism Discourse. These ideas included privilege pertaining to social power, privilege as a manifestation of institutionalized superiority, privilege as intentionally implemented, and privilege as pervasive from the past into the present. Collectively, these ideas coalesce around an understanding that the benefits and advantages of privilege exist and are maintained at a structural and systemic level in society.

Social Power

The notion that privilege is a manifestation of power granted to individuals because of their association with certain social groups, or a form of *social power*, reflects the first and most foundational core idea about privilege central to race critical knowledge. Scott expressed this idea about privilege in simple terms early in his interview when he framed privilege as "where society gives you a one-up over other people for no reason other than just what you are born with." In his brief definition, Scott used the phrase "a one-up" to describe social power associated with the social identities a person was born into.

Jane also discussed social power as central to privilege multiple times during her interview. At first, she invoked the notion of social power when describing the opposite of privilege as "discrimination." Because discrimination refers to unfair negative treatment based on a person's social identities, her choice to frame privilege as the opposite of discrimination reveals her understanding of privilege as an unfair positive treatment based on a person's social identities. The idea of social power emerged again when she discussed why White people have racial privilege in the United States:

> Because America was founded by White people, and there was slavery. And so, the remnants of that still persist in [this city], with, you know, segregation. There are remnants of that in a lot of major cities as well. Um, sort of modern times the xenophobia that's happening has, um, and also Hispanic people being viewed as lesser as well . . . because since the founding of this country there have been overwhelmingly White people in power. I mean, the president of the United States, the last one [Barack Obama], was the first one after like 44 presidents. So, he's the first one who was not a White person, so that says something.

Jane explained how White people as a collective racial social group have privilege because members of their racial social group have been and remain in power at the highest levels of government, including the office of the Presidency. Jane also made connections between the privilege White people have today and the system of slavery and persistent racial segregation, further reinforcing how she understood power to be connected to racial social group memberships. Further still, she expressed how perceptions about different racial social groups are connected to the distribution of social power by talking about xenophobia and views of Hispanics as lesser than White people, also reinforcing the idea that power is tied to social group memberships. Later in her interview, Jane made these connections between power and social group memberships explicit:

> I think the root cause of racial privilege is the way this country was founded. . . . [B]ecause it was founded by all White people, with enslaved African Americans, or enslaved Africans, and then African Americans. Then Jim Crow and all of that, you know, the history of America basically has always put, um, people of color lesser.

Once again, Jane explained how racial privilege was connected to power granted to White people and denied to Black people based on their racial social group memberships through particular structural practices in society (i.e., slavery, Jim Crow).

Jamie provided a similar understanding about racial privilege in her explanation of why White people have privilege and people of color do not have privilege. Her explanation leverages the idea that power is distributed based on racial social group status. However, Jamie goes one step further to connect social power to ingrained beliefs about racial superiority and inferiority:

Tharp: When thinking about racial privilege in the United States, who has racial privilege?

Jamie: White people . . . because of a history of oppression of people of all other races that they consider to be less than them, often backed by

	pseudoscience when it got later, but earlier backed by the belief that they were somehow less than human.
Tharp:	And who does not have racial privilege in the United States?
Jamie:	People of color . . . because White people don't let them have privilege really. They try to keep them as confined to a certain level as they can.
Tharp:	When you say White people don't let them, do you mean individual White people?
Jamie:	Not really, kind of I guess as a whole, White culture, I mean White supremacy. I'm not saying any individual White person is like, 'No, I don't want this Asian man to be at the same level as me.' No, they are not saying that, but every White person has in some way benefited from a history of White supremacy, and that history of White supremacy is built around making sure it's not penetrated by people of color.

In this exchange, Jamie clearly explained her understanding that privilege is connected to racial social groups that receive (or are denied) power based on their social group status. When she stated that White people do not allow people of color to have privilege, she clarified that she was referring to White people as a collective racial group as opposed to individual White people, adopting a view that social power is structural and not individualistic. Similar to Jane, Jamie connected our socialized beliefs about racial social groups to the way social institutions distribute power to White people as a collective racial social group.

Overall, the idea of social power is a foundational core idea for two key reasons. First, it establishes that privilege is structural because it is tethered to social group memberships versus individual people. Second, it centralizes power within the context of our social group memberships. Together, the idea of social power supports an understanding that the benefits and advantages associated with privilege are substantive and structural.

Institutionalized Superiority

An idea related to social power is that of privilege reflecting *institutionalized superiority* of select social groups. Not only does privilege get distributed to select social groups, but the distribution of privilege is also linked to a collective belief that those social groups are superior, which is codified into social norms, policies, and practices at a structural level. The notion that privilege is connected to a collective belief in the superiority of a particular social group that is ingrained into society reinforces privilege as a structural phenomenon beyond any single individual, their individual social identities, or their individual actions. Furthermore, the belief in a social group's superiority exists beyond an individual's bias and also positions these beliefs as a collective way of viewing and understanding social groups reflects how people are socialized to think about social group differences in the United States.

Scott, Jamie, Jane, and Anna all explicitly spoke about how widespread perceptions of social group superiority and inferiority were linked to privilege. Scott spoke to this simply and directly when he explained that privilege exists with a "superior and a minority" group that is "very deep-rooted in the whole race structure and the way society works." Jamie discussed how early colonists perceived the indigenous people as inferior to themselves and that these collective "thoughts and ideas are still ingrained in society today." Jane described how the United States was founded on racism, meaning that "the majority race, White people, believ[e] that another race is not as worthy of human dignity." In all these comments, they clearly link a collective belief in social group superiority to social structures.

Anna repeatedly spoke about the ways that collective beliefs related to the superiority of a social group were ingrained into society. In her interview, she explained how social institutions were "pushing [people of color] back" when she stated the following:

> It's just the perceptions that people have of other groups of people or the lack of representation of certain people. . . . I think the things that are pushing them back are just these like societal norms and these ideas and perceptions of them. . . . And there [are] systematic things that oppress people. There are things put in place that that limit people's abilities and options.

Anna's comments elsewhere in her interview contextualized her comments above that White people were viewed positively and had privilege relative to people of color. In these comments, she identified negative perceptions of select social groups and connected these to systemic oppression that limits these social groups. Throughout her interview, Anna returned to the idea of privilege as a form of institutionalized superiority when explaining why people of color do not have privilege:

> Because they've been put in boxes, they have been put in a box both literally and figuratively . . . just this idea of being less than and just this system where things don't favor them and jobs look at them differently. And this belief system that has been so fused with our society and government and the way we work as people.

Anna's commentary described how the collective perception of people of color as inferior among White people (the "boxes" they are put in) are "fused" within our social institutions. She later spoke about these social group perceptions as "superiority complexes" that were ingrained in society. Her commentary provided a critical point that beliefs in the superiority of a social group are located in a broader, collective "belief system," not an individual's bias for or against a social group. Her framing these beliefs in group superiority as collective versus individualized underscores the notion of privilege as a structural phenomenon while rejecting a view of privilege as linked to individual bias (an idea central to the White racial knowledge discussed on p. 14).

Intentionally Implemented (Including Colonization)

If privilege is rooted in social power and based upon an institutionalized belief in the superiority of one's own social group, it necessarily must also be *intentionally implemented* by social groups through social structures in order to create and maintain social power over other social groups. The notion that privilege is intentionally implemented further reinforces a structural understanding of privilege through social group memberships. There are social and structural aspects through which privilege is intentionally implemented. Socially, privilege is intentionally implemented through socialized beliefs among racial social groups about the superiority of White people and inferiority of people of color. Structurally, these beliefs are integrated into our social systems, introducing and reinforcing notions of group superiority and inferiority through policies and practices that obfuscate the intentional inequalities through which social groups are treated.

For example, racist federal housing policies and real estate practices in the 1930s helped White families purchase homes in suburban areas that were purposefully denied to Black families based on beliefs regarding Black inferiority and undesirability.[3] These policies and practices contributed to racial inequalities in wealth because of how property ownerships facilitated the accumulation and transferable of wealth, further privileging White people over people of color. However, the results of these policies and practices further reinforced racialized beliefs, such as the belief that White families worked hard to earn their homes while Black families were less likely to own homes due to being lazy.

Anna, Jamie, Jane, and Scott all used the idea of privilege being intentionally implemented within our social structures and systems. Jane and Scott spoke to this idea directly and succinctly. Jane explained that privilege is a result of "the system [being] set up that way." Scott similarly explained how privilege is "very deep rooted just in the whole race structure" and that "it's just ingrained into the way that things work." In both of their comments, privilege was the result of a decision made to advantage certain social groups that were embedded into social structures.

Anna and Jamie provided detailed commentary about how privilege is intentionally implemented to advantage select social groups. Anna spoke about socially ingrained "superiority complexes" that contributed to the intentional implementation of privilege. She discussed how these "superiority complexes" are infused into social structures through an example related to gender when asked why privilege exists:

> [In] the 1300s men and women in America would stay home and you would work on your own farm, and you would work together, and the

men would have different tasks. But [men and women] were almost at a fair playing field. So, you would have men make all the cooking things so that the woman can cook, and the men would go kill things so that the woman can cook. But it was almost this partnership. And then men started finding work outside their home and women were left to do all the work at home. And that the idea of this like fair partnership sort of like dissolved in the idea that women had to stay at home and do the work which was necessary for like living. So he would go make the money, but she's going to stay home and take care of the kids and be active in the household. . . . And just the idea that because he was going out and doing work and doing this kind of work, that woman's work was less valuable, and just that idea that there is a difference and therefore one person or one large group of people decides that they're better than the other people.

Anna's answer explored how beliefs in superiority linked to gendered social groups evolved from a division of labor into different values on the type of labor performed that were embedded into families and workplaces. She explained how ingrained beliefs in social group superiority were transferred into the type of work performed by different social groups, which helped create and reinforce beliefs about what types of work was valuable and desirable.

Near the end of her interview, Anna returned to this idea once again when asked to discuss the root cause of racial privilege in the United States. In her response, she succinctly connected racial social group superiority to social structures and explicitly discussed colonization:

Superiority complexes. This belief system based on trivial things that were set up by someone who had all the answers already. Just this idea of White people being better because they knew X, Y, and Z, but they freaking created X, Y, and Z. . . . Like the idea that people could come and try and colonize America, to come and move to America, almost starve to death and die, and literally only survive because Native Americans knew how to farm and like help them. . . . And then those White people could still feel superior because of the color of their skin and because they wore different types of clothing and spoke a more proper language. And had formal texts and things like that, and have this system of money and then they felt because Native Americans had different systems already in place and different ways of living that [those were] inferior to them.

Anna's reply explicitly described the dialectical relationships between a belief in one's own social group superiority and its infusion into social structures. In her racial example of White colonists interacting with indigenous people, White people believed they were superior, and so, they created social systems to make them superior, such as determining cultural norms (e.g., proper attire and language) and social structures (e.g., financial institutions). At the same time, the social systems White people created also reinforced their beliefs in their own superiority. Anna became noticeably agitated when describing how English colonists viewed themselves as superior even after needing help from indigenous people in order to survive, serving to further underscore how she viewed the intentional implementation of privilege to be absurdly unfounded.

Like Anna, Jamie also described how beliefs in the superiority of one's own social group were infused into social structures during her interview. When asked the reason privilege exists, along with who or what was to blame for privilege, Jamie also explicitly discussed colonization:

> Do you want me to go all the way back to European colonialism? (chuckles) It kind of exists from back then. People came and mixed and saw people who looked and acted and were different from them and tried to make them more like them, and kind of wiped out entire populations of people, and certain people stayed on top for a very, very long time. Those kinds of things and thoughts and ideas are still ingrained in society today despite the fact that we try our best to be equal, because they [spent] that many years on the top, [it] kind of made them the norm. . . . [T]hey kind of instilled a history of their own dominance and that prevails in many ways today.

Jamie's ability to both identify and describe colonization as the cause of and source of blame for privilege provided a clear example of how privilege was intentionally instituted from the early foundations of the United States. She described how White Europeans viewed themselves as superior and then "ingrained" those beliefs into society and "instilled a history of their own dominance" that prevails into the present. Jamie's description, while less precise, accurately described colonization as a systemic and pervasive process where White Europeans viewed themselves as superior to other social groups which formed the basis for the creation and implementation of policies and practices that rationalized and justified their actions across social institutions (e.g., government, business, finance, education). In her description, it is clear that she views colonization as *the* example of how privilege was and still is intentionally implemented through social structures.

The idea of privilege being intentionally implemented, both in the abstract and through the specific naming of colonization, highlights that the advent of privilege was a choice. It was a choice to view one's own social group as superior to others. It was a choice to create and maintain policies and practices that manufactured a material reality to match a narrative of social group superiority. It was a choice to maintain these policies and practices by doing nothing to change them once they became normative within society. While choices are made by individuals, the concept of privilege is still structural because it lives in the fabric of societal norms, policies, and practices that are maintained by social groups as a collective.

Situated in Both the Past and the Present

A final core idea about privilege is how it exists in, and stretches across, the past and into the present. When individuals understand privilege as a phenomenon that transcends moments in time, it forces us to consider how it exists and persists through social structures. The idea that privilege is *situated in both the past and the present* is connected to the previous three ideas of social power, institutionalized superiority, and intentional implementation. In some ways, this idea about privilege is a natural extension of the previous three ideas. The social power bestowed upon select social groups contributes to a collective belief in their superiority that was purposefully ingrained into our social structures. Social structures are built to outlast individuals; therefore, it makes sense that the codification of privilege into social norms, policies, and practices has been able to persist over time. In other words, a temporally transcendent view of privilege also provides an opportunity to consider the extent to which privilege is a structural concept.

Jamie, Anna, and Jane explicitly discussed the origins of privilege in the past that persisted into the present. Jamie described how "a history of privilege . . . leads up to it still existing in all these forms today." Anna was similarly deliberate when using the idea of privilege as situated in the past and present to describe how she would explain the reason privilege exists to a friend:

> There are these beliefs that people have that started *waaaay* before you were born, like way before we were born, that gave people this certain idea which people still have those ideas from beliefs today. It's not to say that like privilege or oppression is in the past, it's just to say that the origins are in the past.

Anna's explanation positioned the idea of institutionalized superiority ("these beliefs") as starting in the past, by emphasizing and repeating that it began in the past ("way before we were born") and persists to the present. She went further to clarify that privilege was not solely situated in the past, only its origins.

Jane also described how privilege in the past contributes to privilege in the present because "[privilege] was founded by all White people, with enslaved Africans. . . . Then Jim Crow and all of that, you know the history of America basically has always put people of color lesser . . . so the remnants of that still persist." Jane went further when she shared how she would explain privilege to a friend:

> There are remnants and continuations of things that have been established, that have existed in this country since its establishment that we can't just ignore because they are still causing a problem, and because they haven't been fully eradicated from the society, or fixed or addressed properly in some cases. You get the benefit of it. (Softly) I feel like that's not very good. . . . (Regular volume) I feel like it's too overarching. I don't know,

> I feel like it would be really easy for someone to brush that off, and say "well that's not true, like slavery is over. So, it's over" you know what I mean? I mean, like the argument's been made a billion times if you will, annoyingly.

In Jane's comments, she explained how privilege experienced today are extensions from how privilege was ingrained during the establishment of the United States. However, she suddenly expressed doubt about the effectiveness of her explanation when predicting how her friend might use a commonly heard retort that dismisses privilege as solely in the past. In her back and forth with herself, it is clear that the temporal nature of privilege existing in the past and continuing into the present is a central idea to her understanding of privilege that is important for others to understand.

How Accurate Ideas Fit Together

These four key ideas about privilege work together to support a structural understanding of privilege in the United States. Generally speaking, all four ideas position privilege outside of individuals and instead position it within social structures and institutions from where it operates. Furthermore, these four ideas support one another to describe the nature of privilege in a particular way. The idea that privilege pertains to social power situated within social groups versus individuals is pivotal to a structural understanding of privilege. This core idea supports the idea that power was bestowed upon social groups is:

1. Based upon beliefs about select social groups being superior to others that was institutionalized (institutionalized superiority).
2. Reflecting a purposeful decision made to codify social power (intentionally implemented).
3. Something that has necessarily occurred in the past yet persists into the present (situated in the past and the present).

Furthermore, these three ideas operate to maintain one another as well. The social power based upon beliefs about social groups reflects *institutionalized superiority* of select groups over others that was *intentionally implemented* though social norms, policies, and practices *in the past and into the present* that further creates and sustains collective beliefs about social groups leading *institutionalized superiority* and thus closing the loop of these ideas (see Figure 3.1).

These four ideas operate to maintain a particular internal logic about the structural nature of privilege. However, without all four pieces, the logic is not as strong or stable, making it subject to various avenues of critique as an individualistic phenomenon.

Without the core idea of *social power*, it is overall harder to maintain a stance that privilege is structural versus individualistic. Imagine trying to explain

Core Ideas About Privilege 77

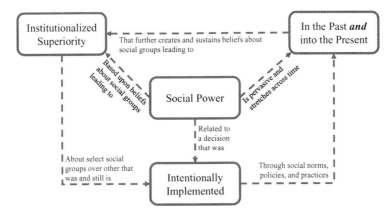

FIGURE 3.1 Visualizing the Relationship Between Race Critical Knowledge Ideas

privilege without the idea of its being based upon power distributed via social group memberships. Without framing privilege around social group memberships, it is much more difficult to rule out the ways in which an individual's actions contribute to the presence or absence of privilege. It is possible to hold the other three core ideas in place and anchor them around a different idea based on individual choices that lead to people deserving privilege.

Without the core idea of *institutionalized superiority*, it is harder to describe why certain groups receive benefits over others. Without the idea that privilege is supported by institutionalized beliefs in group superiority, it is easier for other ideas, such as power hungry or greedy people, to be inserted in its place to describe what helped create and sustain privilege for some over others. However, such alterative ideas are more individualistic than structural and could easily be viewed as the work of a "few bad apples" because most everyone doesn't view White people as better than people of color. Furthermore, trying to explain privilege without this idea almost sounds like a conspiracy theory, which similarly rests upon a view of one or more sinister individuals versus a broader cultural way of knowing and viewing racial groups that implicates how our culture operates.

Without the core idea of *intentional implementation*, it is harder to describe how privilege simultaneously exists and is maintained across multiple social institutions. If you found evidence of privilege being intentionally implemented through policies and practices, it would seem to be the work of a select group of individuals within a particular social institution versus something widespread or pervasive in our society. Alternatively, it is possible for privilege to be viewed as a spontaneous occurrence that simply happened without a particular intention. Such a view of privilege as coincidental would make it hard to view privilege as being sustainable over time.

Without the core idea of *past and present*, any discussion of privilege lacks sufficient evidence to view it as structural. If privilege is only viewable through a single moment in time, there will always be countless other ways to describe the state of inequality because there would not be a constant thread. There would not be reason to hold onto other ideas about privilege as intentionally implemented or based upon institutional superiority because each instance of privilege would be viewed independently from one another.

In sum, if one or more of these four core ideas are not present, it is much more likely that privilege would be viewed as individualistic and not structural or systemic. While it is still possible to maintain a structural understanding of privilege, it would be easily subject to critique without other ideas to sustain such a stance. Given that we live in a society where Whiteness is the norm and status quo, and Whiteness seeks to maintain and replicate itself, conceptualizing privilege without these four ideas would be seemingly hard to sustain in the long term.

A useful example to see how these ideas operate can be readily seen in the debate about affirmative action in college admissions. As Charles Ogletree Jr., a Harvard law school faculty member, put it in an opinion piece in favor of affirmative action:

> We must keep affirmative action – and keep refining it. It is a small but significant way to compensate victims of slavery, Jim Crow laws, discrimination and immigration restrictions. It is also a means to assure that institutions such as Stanford will celebrate and foster that which they simply cannot avoid: diversity in a democratic society. Affirmative action admissions policies seek to realign the balance of power and opportunity by doing what is, at heart, quite simple: affirmatively including the formerly excluded.[4]

Advocates for affirmative action view it as a race-conscious approach to policy and practice with the goal of removing barriers and increasing access to opportunities that can mitigate social inequality. Advocates believe affirmative action helps to address long-standing social inequity that favors White people in society, which may be the result of pervasive attitudes about racial differences that influence existing policies and practices, such as the use of standardized tests in admissions processes which disproportionality favor White people.[5]

All four ideas central to race critical knowledge are used to adopt this stance on the topic:

- There are unequal opportunities afforded to White people as a racial group (social power).
- These unequal opportunities are present today and have existed over time (privilege situated in the past and present).
- Pervasive attitudes that view White people as superior to other racial groups fuel the distribution of unequal opportunities (institutionalized superiority).
- Policies and practices that make it easier or more likely for White people as a racial group to be provided these opportunities need to be revised (intentionally implemented).

These ideas operate together to produce a cohesive view of affirmative action as a policy solution to address long-standing racial inequalities. The core idea of social power frames the social problem around unequal opportunities being afforded to White people as a racial group. This framing is supported by the idea of privilege being situated in the past and present which provides empirical support for this view. The ideas of intentional implementation and institutionalized superiority are conjoined to support the target of affirmative action, policies and practices that remove barriers which are connected to pervasive attributes that favor White people.

Core Ideas About Privilege Central to the Whiteness Discourse

Carol, Jason, John, and Lucy expressed four ideas about privilege that are central to White racial knowledge and consistent among people who participate in the Whiteness Discourse. These ideas included privilege being situational, occurring in the absence of choice and chance, being grounded in individual bias, and being ahistorical. Collectively, these four ideas coalesce around an understanding that the benefits and advantages viewed as so-called privilege exist among unconnected individuals in society.

Situational

The first and most central idea within White racial knowledge is that privilege is individually *situational* and therefore not linked to anything or anyone else. The notion that privilege is situational requires any instance of privilege to be viewed as an isolated occurrence and thus requires any explanations about privilege to be based upon the current and present circumstances. Therefore, this first idea is a powerful one that necessarily ensures that privilege is viewed at the level of the individual and influenced by things that are immediately connected to that individual.

Carol, Jason, John, and Lucy all expressed the notion of privilege as situational. John succinctly stated this idea when saying "privilege is a relative thing based on how you feel compared to the others around you." Carol, Jason, and Lucy shared this notion and notably all discussed a job interview as a situational context where privilege might be evident. In many instances, this idea was explicitly stated. For example, when Carol was asked to describe indicators of privilege during her interview, she stated the following:

> I'm only thinking like, in situational like, situations, maybe like again, like my personal experience of an interview. Like I would immediately think of privilege if you know people were giving me more respect or paying more attention to me, and when the other people in the room were of a different race or a different background. Um, so then I would, that something would like click off in my mind. If either I'm being treated better or I am being

treated worse than the other people surrounding me. I think that would be like a light bulb in my head.

In her statement, Carol explicitly described privilege as situational and proceeded to use an example of a job interview as a specific circumstance where privilege was apparent. She understood the benefit of increased attention due to racial differences in the context of an interview to be a situation where privilege would be present. However, in this context, privilege is situational based on who receives better treatment relative to others regardless of the race of the individuals present. While Carol identified race as a factor in privilege, she did not view privilege as tethered to a particular racial social group.

Jason also openly expressed a situational view of privilege during his interview. When asked if racial privilege existed today, he replied, "I think it'd depend on the situation" because "some situations might have it." He also spoke about a job interview as a situation in which privilege may manifest itself:

> Um, it would depend if race is considered. For example, like if the job application, if they didn't ask your race, then I'd say there's no privilege involved with regards to race. Because they wouldn't know and they obviously don't care, but if you do mark down your race, then I would say, there probably is some privilege involved. I mean you couldn't tell which privilege or, you know, what they're looking for or, you know, who's actually privileged from your point of view, but the job interviewer does have a point of view. . . . [I]f you write down your race, you are either selected for or against so, whoever they decide to select for or against, you know, will have privilege or not.

In his comments, Jason described how privilege is present in a situation only if it is actively invoked in order to gain an advantage. In his view, privilege is situational when someone decides to provide or solicit information for their advantage. Therefore, privilege could be linked to anyone based on their particular intention and actions. In the case of racial privilege, he asserted that privilege is not present as long as no one asks or talks about race because doing so would suggest that someone's race may be advantageous in that particular situation.

Lucy discussed privilege as situational implicitly during her interview. When describing how she understood privilege, she offered a job interview as a useful example stating that privilege would occur if "[the interviewer is] looking for a certain like, type of person like, they're looking for a female, but then like a male goes in for an interview, then like he wouldn't have a privilege." She continued by stating that women have privilege in job interviews because "[businesses are] trying to look for more females, so maybe like I could have an advantage like, so they could diversify their company." In her comments, she selected an example where women are situationally privileged because of the intentional attention toward gender on the part of a business. Her idea of privilege as situational is similar to that of both Carol and Jason where privilege exists when someone intentionally calls attention to social identity.

It is worth noting that Carol, Jason, John, and Lucy used the idea of privilege as situational in two particular ways. First, privilege was not inherently linked to social group memberships. Therefore, this idea suggests that anyone can experience privilege – people of color and White people, women and men. Second, the example of a job interview highlighted that privilege might be more likely to appear in competitive contexts. In competitive contexts, there are finite resources over which multiple people are competing. In the context of a job interview, there may be multiple people competing for a single position. In competitive contexts, someone wins at the immediate expense of others. As such, if anyone can experience privilege (or feel privilege, as John put it), a situational notion of privilege suggests that privilege is present when someone is believed to have unfairly altered the competition.

Choice and Chance

If privilege is situational, it raises an important question: What manifests privilege in one instance yet not in another? The answer to this question can be found in the second core idea that *choice and chance* negate the existence of privilege. At first glance, choice and chance are opposites. Choice entails intentional action on the part of someone while chance refers to forces outside of one's control offered thought of as "luck." However, in the context of refuting the existence of privilege, they both provide a useful way to rule out privilege because the advantages an individual have are either the result of personal choices that "earned" such advantages or the result of luck beyond their control. In both cases, this idea operates to absolve individuals with advantages or benefits from being viewed as having privilege while simultaneously reinforcing a individualistic understanding of privilege. If privilege is explained away due to a matter of personal choice or unexplainable chance beyond personal control, privilege can never be understood as a structural phenomenon.

Carol, Jason, and John all explicitly discussed personal choice as a vehicle for being deserving of success and thus central to dismissing privilege. Carol stated that "everyone makes choices . . . so, I feel like choice is a big aspect of privilege." Jason implied this idea of choice through the notion of merit by asserting that "when you've earned something" it is not linked to privilege and later claimed that "most people, maybe even all people, have at some point earned what they have." John offered a similar view that "anything achieved is almost never a privilege."

The link between personal choice resulting in merit that leads to deserved advantages was clear in Carol's commentary describing the opposite of privilege:

> I did theatre in high school and [when] my director would do auditions for roles, she would have paper, like she would have your paper that you filled out with your information, and then she would put a sticky note on paper

and then give you a number. And then she would have just a bunch of sticky notes on the stage while we were auditioning, and she would write based off of the sticky notes and then she would take notes. That's how she would assign roles. I mean there were males that got female roles. Like one guy got Queen of Hearts just because of the notes . . . there was no determination of looks just pure acting talent.

In Carol's explanation, she provides an example of a theater auditioning process to highlight how someone's merit negates privilege. She describes how the auditioning process was not conscious of students' social identities and purely based on "pure acting talent." However, given her previous comment that choice is a big part of privilege, it stands to reason that merit is the result of good personal choices. Therefore, she infers that students who made good choices that resulted in the development of their skills are what earned them theater roles as opposed to their social identities. This point is further underscored when she highlights how a male student was cast in a traditionally female role (the Queen of Hearts) based on his talent.

The second notion of chance emerged when benefits and advantages were not seen as the result of hard work based upon individual choices. Jason, Carol, and Lucy all used the notion of chance through words such as "chance," "fate," or "luck" to describe ways that privilege exists without any empirical explanation. Jason repeatedly used this idea about privilege during his interview and described a core characteristic of privilege as being "fated, there's no control." Furthermore, he explained that "luck would determine [privilege], random chance" when asked who or what was to blame for the existence of privilege. Carol also summarized her view as who do and do not have privilege as a matter of chance stating that "some of us are lucky, and some of us aren't."

Lucy provided deeper insight into this idea of privilege as a matter of chance when describing the circumstances that contribute to privilege:

I guess what type of job you get in life, like so my major's actuarial science. When I graduate, obviously I want to be an actuary, but if I can't find a job, like that's what happens a lot. People are over-qualified for their jobs at the end, like I may have to work, you know at McDonald's or something [giggles]. Like it's just for like a minimum wage job when like my education, I could do a lot more with it. But that's just kind of bad luck, I guess.

Lucy's comment explains how her job search after graduating from college could end either with a job using her college degree or with work in an unrelated minimum wage job. Even though she views her future college degree as valuable enough to make her "over qualified" for a minimum wage job, she believes that not securing a job in her field would be "bad luck." In her interpretation of this situation, she does not use the idea of choice to highlight how her own choices contribute to how successful she would or would not be.

Collectively, the idea of choice and chance collectively work to shield a person from being associated with privilege. When someone makes good choices that lead to success, the resulting benefits were earned and not a matter of privilege. However, if someone's choices do not lead to success, they do not blame themselves for not making better choices and instead lean on the notion of chance beyond one's control. Overall, this idea about privilege operates to dismiss any structural view of privilege because benefits are individually earned and the lack of benefits is simply "bad luck."

Individual Bias

A closely related idea to privilege being situational as a result of personal choices is that it is the product of *individual bias*. In the situations that Carol, Jason, and Lucy discussed, they all described an intentional choice to notice, solicit, or use information about someone's social identities. When privilege is viewed as a product of individual bias, the focus of privilege remains at the level of the individual. Individual bias suggests that select individuals have bias against others, and therefore, bias resides in a handful of "bad apples" versus being seen as pervasive. Therefore, because any individual could have bias, any individual might find themselves in a situation where privilege is operating.

Carol, Jason, John, and Lucy all expressed this idea about privilege in multiple ways. Carol described how privilege is receiving something based off of "how someone chooses to see you and how they react based off of how they see you." John stated that privilege exists when "people focus on how other people's lives are different from theirs." Lucy declared that the root cause of privilege is found in "everyone's thoughts . . . you're just kind of born into thinking a certain way" and that it would stop "if everyone could just stop being so biased." In these short excerpts, privilege is linked to how individuals *choose* to perceive others. In their extended commentary, these students understood individual bias as associated with both direct and indirect experiences with different social identity groups.

Carol offered an indirect experience as the cause for privilege through the following comments:

> There might be stories. I feel like traumatic stories . . . like maybe there's this one story about a Black guy that did something horrible. And then in that person's mind, just for the rest of their life, they have that in the back of their mind, in the back of their head. . . . I mean there could be a Black girl that's my age that, you know . . . she heard about some White guy that went around and raped a bunch of girls. Now she has that image of rich White men raping women.

Carol explained how an indirect personal experience (i.e., "stories") form impressions about different social identity groups in the "back of their mind" that individuals carry "for the rest of their life." Her explanation was an implicit description of bias as a perspective about a social group that is internalized within an individual. Further, her commentary provides examples of bias toward Black men as well as White men to underscore how bias is something anyone is capable of. By offering examples of bias against both Blacks and Whites, it reinforces her view that privilege could be experienced by any individual.

Both Carol and Lucy also discussed direct experiences and how they contribute to individual bias. Lucy described how someone's community where they grew up informs how they were "born into thinking":

> I've always just grown up around, you know, like Caucasians, that's just my town. Like there's nothing bad about it I don't think. Then there's other towns that are more, you know, more African American or more Latino, like, so then everyone's just kind of growing up in that specific like society. There's just like, you're just growing up with those thoughts.

For Lucy, the community where you grow up shapes the thoughts you have about your own and different social identity groups, especially when they are relatively racially heterogeneous. She explicitly offered a personal example growing up in a predominantly White community as evidence that she then used to extrapolate the same conclusion for Black or Latinx people growing up in predominately Black or Latinx communities. In her commentary, she implies that it is rational for people to hold bias against racially different people based on their level of exposure to racial difference. Much like Carol did in her comments, Lucy also demonstrates how bias is something anyone is capable of, including both people of color and White people alike.

Carol offered a similar example of direct experience that contributed to bias based on who surrounds you in your environment. She offered the following extended commentary when asked to describe what contributes to the existence of privilege:

> I think I grew up in a bubble. . . . I grew up in schools where the Black people were the minority and most of us were White . . . so you don't really hear, you hear stories on the news, and on things like that. But let's face it, most of the stories on the news are bad stories. So, maybe yes, we are hearing bad stories about White people, but since you are surrounded by other White people that aren't like that, then maybe, you know, you don't think about White people like that. But for most people, if they are to grow up in entirely White neighborhood then, you know, then they see all these stories of some horrible things happening about Black people. They might have that stigma because they don't know any other people of that race that aren't like that. So, in their experiences in their mind, that's how it is. So, like bubbles.

In her comments, Carol described her experience growing up in a predominantly White community and attending a predominantly White school. While she did not have much direct experience with Black people, she described how she and other White people would view news media that commonly portrays Black people negatively, a perception they would internalize. However, she further reasoned that her direct experience with other White people as counter examples rebuffed negative portrayals of White people in news media. Overall, she rationalizes that the demographic makeup of our communities and the access it provides to interact with other social identity groups influences the perceptions about others that we internalize (i.e., "stigma").

It is notable that both Carol and Lucy discuss how experiences in predominantly White spaces influence more favorable perceptions of White people and more negative perceptions of Black and Latinx people. Their views of individual bias resulting from the racial makeup of their social environment positions people generically but implicitly refers to White people, as blameless for the environment in which they live. It actively dismisses the ways in which people, including White people, can make choices about where they live and attend school. While Carol and Lucy offered comments that *could* have been the beginning of a discussion of institutionalized beliefs in social group superiority, they opted not to engage a structural analysis of why or how social spaces became and remain racially segregated. The result is a discussion about bias that has a cause due to unnamed intentional choices made by White people that pivots to equalize how anyone, including people of color, can be and are biased toward White people.

This aspect of choice present in the broader idea of individual bias as a means in which privilege is situational was more explicit in John's and Jason's comments. John shared that privilege is evident when people choose to "contrast ourselves with other people in our social setting . . . then that prejudice or stereotype can extend" to others. Jason's previous comments about a job interview as a context where privilege is situational highlights how these ideas are present and interconnected. The same quote of his is repeated here, but this time with select words italicized by the author to highlight the idea of individual bias:

> Um, it would depend if race is considered. For example, like if the job application, if they didn't ask your race, then I'd say there's no privilege involved with regards to race. Because they wouldn't know, and they obviously don't care but *if you do mark down your race, then I would say, there probably is some privilege involved.* I mean you couldn't tell which privilege or, you know, what they're looking for or, you know, who's actually privileged from your point of view but *the job interviewer does have a point of view.* . . . [I] *f you write down your race, you are either selected for or against so, whoever they decide to select for or against, you know, will have privilege or not.*

The italicized portions of Jason's quote illustrate how individual bias is based upon our choice in how we perceive others and on what information. For Jason, the choice to disclose your race is an attempt to seek bias in your favor. Furthermore, the interviewer's perspective of you that includes social identity is subject to their bias as well. Therefore, it follows that the recognition of social identity in any form is a gateway to individualized bias. However, it is notable that if a job applicant does not disclose their race, but the interviewer was aware of their race when they hired them, the applicant is blameless even though they experience this benefit.

Overall, the notion of individual bias operates in a peculiar way that focuses on the person who actively acknowledges social identities. However, individual bias does not implicate the actual people who receive benefits as biased themselves. Therefore, the idea of individual bias can be framed as a problem of people who choose to see difference without ever implicating people who benefit based upon perceptions of difference.

Ahistorical

A final core idea about privilege within White racial knowledge is that privilege exists situationally within and across moments in time. While privilege may have existed in situations over time, such instances are viewed as *ahistorical* and independent from one another. The understanding of privilege as ahistorical reinforces a situational view of privilege that is based upon either individual choices or unexplainable chances. When contemporary instances of privilege are viewed independently from other instances of privilege over time, it is difficult to see how White people are consistently benefiting at the expense of people of color through long-standing institutionalized policies and practices.

Carol, Jason, John, and Lucy used the idea of privilege being ahistorical throughout their interviews. They typically expressed this idea when separating the past from the present. When asked about the existence of privilege, John explained how privilege "comes from some place other than the here and now, it comes from past achievements. And it also comes from the here and now focusing on the difference in achievements." In his explanation, he simultaneously offered dual arguments that intertwine the idea of privilege as ahistorical with choice and chance. First, he described how past achievements, likely through good individual choices, contribute to what is misunderstood regarding privilege. Second, he dismissed the past when stating that focusing on differences in the "here and now" is causing privilege. In total, John connects the past to the present only to explain individual achievement but separates past from present when considering privilege in the present.

Carol offered a similar ahistorical view of privilege that explicitly severed past situations of privilege and inequality to present-day situations when explaining why privilege exists today:

[Sigh] All right, the reason privilege exists. Probably, you could take it the historical way in terms of, yes, slavery and, yes, you know, Englishmen tended to be White . . . and even after slavery there were still, you know, there are always people that still look like that. Then, for some reason, I don't know why, but it tended to be, you know, those that were Black went more towards the city, they weren't getting jobs. Then, for some reason, over time, it just built up this overall stereotype that White people are the ones that get the good education, they get the jobs, they get the money, and Black people don't. I don't know why necessarily, I don't know if it's because that historical aspect, or if it's because there are times where, like the White people are just getting jobs, getting jobs and so it just became a thing. I don't know.

Carol's explanation of privilege began by identifying slavery and the overwhelming proportion of White colonists as forms of racial inequality in the past and separately identified racial inequities between White people and Black people related to jobs and education. While she implied that some people might connect privilege to the past, she does not adopt that for herself and instead repeatedly expressed uncertainty for the cause of present-day racial inequities saying "I don't know" and "for some reason." It is striking that Carol named two instances of privilege and social inequities over time and opted for a chance rationale instead of connecting these two situations together. Furthermore, her choice to frame slavery as historical operated to create distance between the present-day and the past as if something from history did not have relevance to the present day.

The desire to view the past as irrelevant was explicitly connected to the idea of privilege as ahistorical when reacting to a political cartoon titled *The American Dream*. In this cartoon, a White man and a Black man were depicted as gameboard pieces on separate paths that do not come together. Each path had spaces that were captioned with examples of racial privilege and oppression in the United States that straddled a 400-year period.[6]

Lucy invoked the idea of privilege as ahistorical when she reacted to the cartoon stating how "we need to start looking toward the future and stop looking at the past." Jason invoked the idea of privilege as ahistorical when he problematized the cartoon stating "now Blacks aren't slaves, or they've never been slaves" as a rationale to "cut off this area and keep it toward the, uh, modern things." While Jason made these comments, he described how he would modify the cartoon while pointing at spaces that included slavery, Jim Crow laws, lynching, denial of voting rights, KKK, sharecropping, segregation, and the Civil Rights era. However, the parts of the cartoon that he was fine keeping involved spaces that referred to contemporary inequities such as the wealth gap, poor schools, and affirmative action. Jason's reaction to the cartoon was not only ahistorical but also used an ahistorical view of privilege to solely focus on items that can be viewed as problematic for individuals beyond race and therefore for any *individual*.

88 Core Ideas About Privilege

John's ahistorical view of privilege seemed to fuel an even stronger reaction to the cartoon. John described how he wanted to modify it:

> [Pause] I'd want to cross the whole thing out. I wouldn't want people to believe in the concept of racial privilege. I would point out that it starts at the beginning of America, that was established by White people. But I'd also point out that there's no end in sight, and the end is what matters, presumably the end can be everyone hand in hand being on the same space. Yeah, the ending is the same space. So presumably, we're just trying to get to the end space when we're together, and I'd make sure that people know that yes, we were held back before, but we're closer together now, and as long as we keep trying to become closer together, and we don't focus so much on [how] it's so hard for us to be together.

John's desire to eliminate the entire cartoon reflects his ahistorical view of privilege where the past does not matter because only the present and the future are relevant. John stated that he did not want anyone to believe that racial privilege exists or existed because, as he stated earlier, privilege comes from the "here and now" based on how we view difference. Therefore, his view of privilege supported his desire to modify the cartoon by emphasizing an ending where everyone is together holding hands with minimal, if any, attention to the past.

Carol shared John's view of the past as irrelevant and the notion that focusing on the past contributes to social inequality in the present. Her idea about privilege as ahistorical emerged when she described the cartoon in her own terms and proceeded to wonder about the implications of not teaching about the past at all:

> I'm noticing is it's a lot of history. Slavery and Jim Crow Laws and KKK, and a lot of things that don't exist anymore, necessarily . . . it makes me wonder how different our world would be if we didn't teach our kids today about slavery or the KKK or anything like that. What if they didn't know about any of it. They would have to make their own opinions. . . . If no one knew that slavery existed, if no one knew that White people came to America first, if no one knew about any of that stuff. . . . I would hope that people would see, White people and Black people [as] the same.

During the first half of Carol's commentary about the cartoon, she noticed that much of the content was historical and "doesn't exist anymore" implying that the past was no longer relevant. That view of the past as irrelevant became clearer when she imagined what the world would be like if children were never taught about past social inequalities. For her, talking about the past contributes to inequality in the present day because a focus on the past seemingly prevents White people and Black people from viewing themselves and one another as equals. She continued by stating the following:

I feel like a lot of stereotypes exist because of the past and because, I don't mean to, I don't know if this is going to come off right, but because the Black race feels they have the right to suffer because of all of the horrible things that happened to them in the past. . . . I feel like [history] has put that into our minds, [and] sometimes it does bother me a little bit. If I'm being perfectly honest, you see [messages that] you put us through slavery, but I didn't put you through slavery. Like, you know, this was soooo long ago. It's almost like let the past be the past. Don't make me out to be a bad guy just because, you know, ancestors from hundreds of years ago possibly put your ancestors through slavery.

During the last half of Carol's commentary, it became clear that her ahistorical views are grounded in the belief that Black people invoke past situations of social inequality to legitimize their suffering today. Carol implied that Black people invoke the past as a way to blame White people, even though White people today did not directly participate in past social inequalities (i.e., "I didn't put you through slavery.").

Overall, the idea of privilege as ahistorical impedes a structural view and analysis of privilege. It does so by segmenting moments in time where privilege exists as discrete situations where they ought to be individually viewed through the lens of individual choices or chance occurrences: Two other key ideas about privilege central to White racial knowledge. However, as the examples referring to the political cartoon highlight, maintaining an ahistorical view of privilege also serves to erase the past. When a belief that present-day social equality is predicated upon the erasure of past social inequalities, it functionally removes evidence of White privilege that simultaneously maintains White innocence while purporting to focus on more relevant present-day situations that can be easily explained away through choice and chance. Ahistoricism, therefore, is itself an extension of privilege because White people benefit at the direct expense of people of color when the present is decontextualized from the past.

How Inaccurate Ideas Fit Together

These four ideas about privilege central to White racial knowledge and used within the Whiteness Discourse support a decontextualized and individualistic view of what participants of the Antiracism Discourse would view as privilege. Overall, all four ideas compartmentalize privilege into discrete and unconnected instances that are either explainable by considering what individuals do and do not do or inexplicable for reasons that are unknowable. Consistent with the broader purpose of the Whiteness Discourse, these ideas that are central to White racial knowledge collectively operate to maintain the status quo by supplanting complex ideas about privilege with relatively simplistic ones that require no

90 Core Ideas About Privilege

further consideration. The idea that privilege is best understood as situational is the bedrock upon which the other three ideas emerge:

1. When privilege is viewed as situational, each situation can be viewed independently as the result of individual choices that lead to earned benefits or an unconnected coincidence as a matter of chance (choice and chance).
2. A situational view of privilege allows for any evidence of privilege that results in subsequent inequality to be blamed upon individuals who choose to view their social identity group positively and those different from themselves negatively (individual bias).
3. When privilege is viewed as discrete situations, this logic can extent temporally to separate the past form the present where the present day is the only relevant context which considers past instances to be irrelevant and problematic (ahistorical).

Unlike the core ideas used by participants in the Antiracism Discourse, which operate like a web of ideas, the core ideas used by participants in the Whiteness Discourse operate like planets orbiting a sun. Instead of these ideas collectively reinforcing one another in a shared logic, they are loosely tethered together by the way of reinforcing a common central idea: That privilege is situational. A situational view of privilege is more easily adopted when individual *choices* or seemingly random *chances* are viewed as an explanation, when evidence of privilege can be attributed to bad individuals who held *individual bias* toward others, or when an *ahistorical* view of the work suggests that the past is irrelevant and therefore never connected to the present (see Figure 3.2).

Furthermore, these ideas are not directly dependent on one another to maintain a situational view of privilege. While the presence of all four ideas makes it

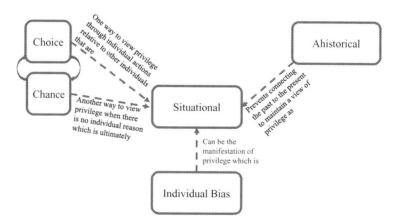

FIGURE 3.2 Visualizing the Relationship Between White Racial Knowledge Ideas

harder to challenge the idea of privilege at situational, they operate in a manner similar to the game of "whack-a-mole." These ideas are offered to defend the core idea of privilege as a situational phenomenon and can be cycled through in order to offer new and different rationales in support of a situational view.

It is important to remember that these ideas operate with a distinct advantage; they can exist without much effort or critical thought. These ideas are useful in their simplicity and require less effort to be maintained. Because these ideas exist in a societal context where people are socialized into the Whiteness Discourse, they do not require constant cultivation because the status quo view of the world is that privilege does not exist. That is why these ideas are not, and do not need to be, interwoven to maintain their own logic.

Using the same example of affirmative action in college admissions can again help illuminate how these ideas operate. Opponents against affirmative action view it as overreach that at the very least ignores the merits of each person and at its worst is tantamount to reverse discrimination against White people. Opponents favor policies and practices that view each person on their own and divorced from their social identities and what may have happened beyond the scope of that individual. These agreements are present in the multiple court cases that have and continue to challenge affirmative action. All four ideas central to White racial knowledge are used to adopt this counter position on the topic:

- Each person should be viewed on their own divorced from their racial identity (situational).
- Each person deserves to be considered regardless of what happened in the past since it is not relevant to their being considered for an opportunity (ahistorical).
- Acknowledging racial identity makes it easier for people to discriminate against Whites (individual bias).
- Each person deserves to be considered based on their own merit based upon the choices they have made that make them worthy (choice and chance).

These ideas operate together to produce multiple arguments in service of an individualistic view. The core idea that privilege is situational dismisses the idea of affirmative action because every*one* should be viewed in the context of themselves as separate from others regardless of race. A common argument is based on the idea of choice and chance, specifically that every person's merits, which are the result of the choices they made, ought to be the determining factor in admission decisions. A closely related argument is based on the idea of individual bias that any approach that is conscious of race introduces bias into the process that serves to discriminate against those with merit because of their race. A third argument based upon the ahistorical idea of privilege goes further to suggest that affirmative action policies go too far because they penalize hardworking students who earned the right to admission because of past inequalities that have no relationship to their qualifications in the present.

Different Ideas, Common Categories

While the specific ideas used by participants in each Discourse are very different from one another, each one can be paired with a relatively similar idea found among participants in the opposite Discourse based on common idea categories. These idea categories include the basis for the *manifestation* of privilege, the level of *accountability* people have for the benefits they receive, the role of *perception* toward people similar and different, and the way privilege is understood relative to *time* (see Table 3.1). By noticing the different ideas within the context of idea categories, this illuminates areas where our conceptual understanding of privilege may be impressionable.

The oppositional ideas of privilege being rooted in social power versus being situational are different ways of thinking about the basis upon which privilege is manifested. The idea of social power positions the advantages and benefits of privilege as a result of power that is unequally distributed based upon social identity group memberships within society. However, a situational view of privilege shifts the focus away from society as a whole in favor of considering privilege as a manifestation of individual and localized contexts. An example of what these ideas look like can be observed when people talk about being race conscious or "color-blind." Race consciousness is based upon the idea that privilege is a manifestation of social power, and therefore, being conscious of race is a part of challenging racial inequalities. However, a "color-blind" approach, most often heard in comments such as "I don't see race, I only see a person," focuses solely on the context of someone as an individual and therefore brackets out any aspects of the individual that connects them to other people or things that influence their individuality.

Who is or is not accountable for the benefits and advantages a person has is the central theme that ties together ideas about intentional implementation versus choice and chance. The idea of privilege being intentionally implemented implicates White people for their complicit role to embed social power into policies and practices that distribute unearned benefits to White people at the expense of people of color. On the contrary, the idea of choice rebuffs critical ideas about privilege by asserting that the acquisition of benefits was earned because of good choices made by an individual. Furthermore, when the idea of choice does not seem to

TABLE 3.1 Different Ideas and Shared Idea Categories About Privilege

Idea Category	Race Critical Knowledge Ideas Central to the Antiracism Discourse	White Racial Knowledge Ideas Central to the Whiteness Discourse
Manifestation	Social power	Situational
Accountability	Intentionally implemented	Choice and chance
Perception	Institutionalized superiority	Individual bias
Time	Situated in both the past and present	Ahistorical

be present, its sister idea of chance asserts that any acquisition of benefits must be coincidental and warrants no further consideration. An example of these ideas can be observed when individuals debate the success of high-profile personalities in society. While some people would say that their success was the result of unearned benefits associated with their social identities, others might suggest that they earned everything they have (which entitles them to success) or they were in the right place at the right time as a matter of chance. In short, these ideas operate to either implicate or absolve White people from their association with unearned benefits.

How we perceive social identities, including what influences these perceptions, is the category that connects ideas that privilege is either supported by institutionalized superiority versus individual bias. Both ideas share the notion that unearned benefits are connected to a favorable view of certain social identity groups over others. However, they differ in where these views are present and how they show up in society. The idea of institutionalized superiority posits that these favorable views are the result of a widespread belief in the superiority of White people and inferiority of people of color. Additionally, these views are situated within the collective consciousness of society due to the codification of these beliefs in policies and practices. On the contrary, the idea of individual bias situates favorable and unfavorable views of social identities within select individuals.

The individualization of these views suggests that the presence of unearned privilege is the result of individuals who made individual choices based upon their bias to favor certain people over others. Furthermore, this view of bias allows anyone to be biased toward anyone else, allowing White people to avoid considering their own bias that favors White people and instead focus on the bias people of color have against them. An example of how these ideas play out can be seen in the debate over police reform.

Some people argue that widespread revisions to policies and practices are needed to change the police culture that supports a view of people of color as inferior and more likely to be criminal than White people, which plays out in the overpolicing of Black and Brown people. Others argue that little changes are needed because there are only a "few bad apples" that do not reflect the broader police force. The extent to which favorable and unfavorable views are located in communal versus individual consciousness is the question before these competing ideas.

The relationship between privilege and time is the final category where the ideas of privilege as situated in both the past and the present versus ahistorical appear. The idea that privilege exists in both the past and the present supports structural notions about how certain social identity groups have retained similar benefits in two different time periods with distinct circumstances. On the other hand, the idea that privilege is ahistorical and only is relevant in the present narrows the focus to avoid any consideration of similarities to other situations of privilege as being irrelevant to the present context.

An example of these ideas emerges in discussions about home ownership. Owning a home is a path toward accumulating wealth, making it advantageous

94 Core Ideas About Privilege

for economic stability and success. However, the proportion of White people who own homes is higher than the proportion of Black people who own homes. Individuals who view privilege as ahistorical would only look at home ownership rates today and might speculate that the reason more White families own homes relative to Black families is explained by the unique circumstances of each family and the choices they have made such as how much each wants a home and is willing to work to acquire a home. Individuals who view privilege in both the present and the past would consider how home ownership today was influenced by home ownership in the past, noticing that White families have been and remain disproportionally more likely to own homes related to Black families due to racist housing policies and practices that have had a long-term affect noticeable today.

To only consider the ideas central to either race critical knowledge or White racial knowledge within their respective Discourse provides valuable insight about the internal logic, each set of ideas helps to produce and maintain that appear vastly different from one another. However, positioning individual ideas central to each type of knowledge from each Discourse in relationship to one another reveals the similarities between these seemingly different sets of ideas. For example, viewing the idea of privilege as ahistorical on its own makes invisible the way this idea operates with other ideas central to White racial knowledge when used by participants in the Whiteness Discourse toward a common purpose. Viewing this same idea solely related to the other ideas used by participants in the Whiteness Discourse might make it easy to dismiss these ideas and those who hold them as ignorant and uninformed even though it seems rational to that individual. However, to position the idea of privilege as ahistorical as one way to understand the relationship between privilege and time frames it as rational while offering an e idea that could reframe someone's understanding.

What These Ideas Offer Us

The utility of identifying these ideas, how they function, and how they relate to one another supports educators in their ability to influence students' understanding about social inequality. The ideas central to race critical knowledge that are used by participants in the Antiracism Discourse focus on privilege as structural and systemic. The ideas central to White racial knowledge that are used by participants in the Whiteness Discourse focus on privilege as individualistic and operate to distance White people from privilege. To oversimplify it, the ideas central to race critical knowledge focus on *White* people, whereas the ideas central to White racial knowledge Discourse focus on White *people*.

When educators can identify, understand, and engage these ideas central to White racial knowledge that are used by participants in the Whiteness Discourse, they will be better equipped to respond through localized and structural curricular and pedagogical interventions. A final example can help illustrate why educators benefit from being able to spot and engage these ideas. Ben Shapiro, a conservative media personality and speaker on college campuses, was videotaped after his *Young Americans for Freedom* lecture at Virginia Tech where he was engaging a student about the topic of institutional racism and White privilege. During the following interaction with a student, he leveraged all four ideas central to White racial knowledge commonly used by participants in the Whiteness Discourse (which are italicized for easier viewing) to dismiss the notion of institutional racism and White privilege while virtuously positioning himself as opposed to racism and racists:

Shapiro: Shouting institutional racism does not actually combat racism. *You have to find individual instances and you have to show me who the racists are* so that we can fight them together. I hate racism, I think it's evil, but if you are just going to say institutional racism every time something bad happens, there's no way to fight it. *I need a policy that you are proposing, or I need a person who is actually racist*, so that we can fight it together, or we can determine if the policy is good. What I find really problematic is the virtue signaling that I see by so many people on the other side, which is, I don't have to give you the racist, I don't have to tell you who he is or what measures that I am proposing, I just say institutional racism, everybody cheers for me because that's an approved point of view, and we move on with our lives.

Student: I would just say that there is kind of, again, you are painting a wide and diverse group of people with the same brush and saying that if you can't point to a policy or you can't point to a person then you are just wasting everyone's time. I think that a lot of people are trying to point to policies and the idea of pointing to a racist person is fundamentally in contrast with the idea of institutional racism because institutional racism grapples with implicit bias in society as a whole.

Shapiro: Unless you are connecting that to a policy then it's a cop-out. *Because now we are ghost hunting again*. If you said to me that we have a problem in American society . . . if you just gave me any problem and said well that's the Bilderberg's fault. . . .[7] you would say to me that's not useful because . . . what are you even talking about. When you say institutional racism it's too broad. *You at least have to name the institution. Which one is the racist one? Which institution is racist?* . . . I want to be on your side, I do, I think racist behavior is evil, I want to fight it with you, but I can't fight it if you're not showing me what it is, and we have to decide together if the policy you are proposing is alleviating racism or exacerbating racism, and it turns out that a lot of the policies proposed by the left, I think *institutional racism is a way, usually a lever, for proposing a policy that is actually unpalatable to freedom* and then castigating people on the other side of that policy as with being in league with institutional racism.[8]

During Shapiro's commentary, he repeatedly centered the situational idea about privilege by focusing on singular contexts of an individual person, group, or policy. He also relied on the idea of individual bias to position privilege and institutional racism as the result of "evil" people, even expressing his desire to join in the fight against these individual actors. However, his critique of proposals to end racism and privilege, which he framed as "unpalatable to freedom," invoked the idea of choice and chance by implying that they limit the ability of people to make choices that would lead to earned benefits. Furthermore, when he prefaced this view by stating that such proposals could "exacerbate racism," that suggested that anybody, including White people, could be hurt by racism. Finally, he leaned into the ideas of privilege as ahistorical when suggesting conversations about institutional racism without a singular focus were "ghost hunting." Overall, Shapiro's commentary provided a clear message that only a specific, locally contextualized view of privilege would be worthy of consideration, simultaneously positioning himself positively and against the evils of racism.

If educators took what Shapiro stated at face value, that it would take specific examples of privilege and institutional racism to convince him of their existence, the idea categories provide insight to approach this task persuasively. The core idea of privilege as situational is a response to the idea category of when privilege is manifested. Therefore, evidence of privilege must be clear and overwhelming across a multitude of "situations." These "situations" should consist of multiple policies and practices within institutions and across multiple institutions. This focus away from people could shift the focus of accountability from people to institutions.

Furthermore, having multiple examples that could point to the institutionalization of policies and practices that favor a racial group over others works to weaken the notion of bias as pervasive over being personal. Finally, these examples should stretch across time to highlight how the past is prologue, how policies and practices that exist today are connected to the past to shift the notion of what moments in time are and are not relevant to the question at hand. There is no guarantee this approach would be effective. Nevertheless, it does offer a blueprint for educational intervention that takes seriously the internal logic of ideas central to White racial knowledge that are commonly used by participants in the Whiteness Discourse.

Key Takeaways

1. There are two different views about privilege that are each supported by four key ideas.
2. The four key ideas central to race critical knowledge involve privilege being grounded in social power, being a manifestation of institutionalized superiority, being intentionally implemented, and being pervasive from the past into the present.
3. Ideas central to the race critical knowledge are commonly used by participants in the Antiracism Discourse.

4. The four key ideas central to White racial knowledge frame privilege as situational, occurring in the absence of choice and chance, grounded in individual bias, and being ahistorical.
5. Ideas central to the White racial knowledge are commonly used by participants in the Whiteness Discourse.
6. While each set of ideas central to race critical knowledge and White racial knowledge create different views about privilege, they are related to one another through idea categories regarding when privilege is manifested, who is accountable (or not) for privilege, the role and location of perception about social groups, and the nature of time.
7. The ability to notice these ideas and the idea categories into which they fall can support educators in understanding a student's logic to increase their effectiveness in their educational intervention.

Notes

1 This chapter is derived in part from an article published in *Whiteness and Education* on May 27, 2021, copyright Taylor & Francis, available online: www.tandfonline.com/10.1080/23793406.2021.1929426.
2 See TTPM Toy Reviews (2016) for an overview of this game and how to play.
3 See Rothstein (2017).
4 See Ogletree (1996).
5 See Soares (2020).
6 See Horsey (2014).
7 This is a reference to the annual Bilderberg Meeting that brings together world leaders in a private policy forum.
8 See Young America's Foundation (2016, 1:04:57).

References

Horsey, D. (2014). The American dream [Political Cartoon #142]. *The Los Angeles Times*. www.latimes.com/nation/la-tot-cartoons-pg-photogallery.html.
Ogletree, C. J. (1996, September–October). The case for affirmative action. *Stanford Magazine*. https://stanfordmag.org/contents/the-case-for-affirmative-action.
Rothstein, R. (2017). *The color of law: A forgotten history of how our government segregated America*. Liveright Publishing Corporation.
Soares, J. A. (Ed.). (2020). *The scandal of standardized tests*. Teachers College Press.
TTPM Toy Reviews. (2016, November 15). Outburst! From Hasbro. [Video]. *YouTube*. www.youtube.com/watch?v=lGZKRd2mGBg.
Young America's Foundation. (2016, April 1). Leftist lunacy | Ben Shapiro [Video file]. *YouTube*. www.youtube.com/watch?v=IQgvJMy48UM.

4
ANCHORING BELIEFS ABOUT PRIVILEGE

The ideas we have about privilege are only useful when they are organized and interpreted in meaningful ways. Our beliefs – the ideological stances used to explain and interpret ideas – play a critical role in the way we organize and interpret ideas about privilege. The metaphor of bricklaying highlights the relationship between ideas and beliefs. Ideas are like individual bricks that can be stacked together to form a structure. Free-standing bricks are not structurally secure and can be easily altered and knocked down. Beliefs are like mortar, an adhesive used to connect bricks together by creating a strong bond. Just as mortar is used to create strong and permanent structures, beliefs are used to create strong and resilient worldviews based upon a set of ideas to explain the cause of privilege. However, just as mortar and bricks require one another to build a strong wall, beliefs and ideas reinforce and sustain one another.

Ideological stances function in a second critical way beyond helping organize and interpret information. Ideological stances are epistemological: They are lenses through which we come to know our material reality and acknowledge the existence of phenomenon. Consider the historic debate about the relationship between the earth and the sun and which heavenly body revolves around the other. Prior to the Copernican Revolution of the 1500s, people believed in a geocentric view that the earth was the center of our solar system with the sun revolving around our planet. Afterward, a heliocentric view was adopted that believed the opposite, that the sun was the center of our solar system with the earth revolving around the sun. Both ideological stances were used to organize and interpret evidence through their distinctive lens, including which evidence to include or exclude from consideration, contributing to the fierce debate between these two opposing views. Therefore, ideological stances not only help to organize and interpret information, but also influence what empirical

DOI: 10.4324/9781003082378-5

evidence and conceptual ideas we choose to acknowledge in our explanations of our reality.

The White college students in my research study relied upon various beliefs that used different sets and combinations of ideas to understand privilege. Just as students used sets of ideas that framed privilege as either structural or individualistic, their beliefs similarly operated to explain the existence of privilege as structural versus individualistic. Sometimes these students used a race critical ideology often used by participants in the Antiracism Discourse to explain privilege as a structural phenomenon and critique individualistic views. Their race critical ideology drew upon many ideas expressed by Delgado and Stefancic's (2012) writing on critical race, including structurally oriented beliefs that (a) race is a social construction, (b) racial privilege and oppression are ordinary phenomena manifested through the normalization of Whiteness, and (c) racial privilege and oppression are knowable through the experiences of people of color.

Other times, these students used a White supremacist ideology often used by participants in the Whiteness Discourse to explain away a structural view of privilege as a phenomenon better explained at an individualistic level. Three specific variations of the White supremacist ideology that are consistent with Bonilla-Silva's (2014) exploration into color-blind ideology were used. These variations included (a) abstract liberalism, a reliance on political and economic liberalism to rationalize inequality, (b) naturalization, a reliance on pseudoscientific views that ascribe inequality to human traits and characters, and (c) minimization, a generic dismissal of privilege as structural without an alternative explanation. These variations were manifested through beliefs that (a) society is fair and therefore everyone has equal opportunity to succeed, (b) privilege and social inequality are natural parts of the human experience, and (c) privilege is not structural and is better understood as individualistic.

I present each of these beliefs in the context of their respective Discourses with examples from these White college students. What follows is a discussion about how these beliefs are used to reinforce or critique different worldviews about privilege in relationship to the specific core ideas discussed in Chapter 3. I continue with an exploration into how White students can and do use multiple and opposing beliefs. Finally, I conclude with implications for teaching and learning related to these beliefs.

Accurate Beliefs About Privilege

Anna, Jamie, Jane, and Scott all used a race critical ideology to explain and interpret the existence of privilege as a structural phenomenon. When identifying the existence and cause of privilege as a structural phenomenon, they often used beliefs about social identities as socially constructed, the ordinary nature of privilege and oppression resulting from the normalization of Whiteness, and the value of exploring privilege and oppression through the lens of those who are oppressed and denied privilege based on their social identities. Furthermore, these beliefs were used in conjunction with all four core ideas about privilege previously discussed.

Anna's response to the cause of privilege outlined how social inequality was socially constructed and infused into society on a structural level:

> Superiority complexes. . . . this belief system based on trivial things that were set up by someone who had all the answers already. Like just this idea of White people being better because they knew X, Y, and Z, but they freaking created X, Y, and Z. . . . Like the idea that people could come and try and colonize America, to come and move to America, almost starve to death and die, and literally only survive because Native Americans knew how to farm and like help them. . . . And then those White people could still feel superior because of the color of their skin.

According to Anna, socially ingrained beliefs were infused into social structures to create and maintain social power among Whites at the expense of people of color (specifically indigenous people). She explained that the belief that White people were superior was engineered because it was White people who created the social structures which perpetuate this belief in the first place. Furthermore, she articulated how White superiority is socially ingrained into systems to appear ordinary to the extent that White European colonists could almost die while maintaining a belief in their superiority relative to "Native Americans" they believed were inferior to themselves. Overall, Anna's explanation implicates the social structures and beliefs created by White people as the cause of privilege versus blaming a specific White person or set of White people.

Jamie similarly explained why people of color are denied privilege citing White colonialism. She stated that "Europeans kind of came over, they messed everything up in the Americas and Africa and a lot of Asia, and they kind of instilled a history of their own dominance that prevails in many ways today." In Jamie's statement, she described how privilege was manifested through the act of "instilling" ideas and beliefs that normalize Whiteness which have persisted into the present as an ordinary phenomenon. She later expanded on the pervasive and ordinary nature of privilege stating how privilege is "the way things have been done, it's the way things have always been done, and it's the way things continue to be done today." Her view of privilege as pervasive over time further underscores the notion that it is linked to social structures that last over time versus individuals who are limited to a single lifetime. Both Anna and Jamie emphasized how socially constructed power is ingrained into social structures as the means to manifest privilege.

Scott provided a similar explanation for privilege as being pervasive and ordinary because it is "very deep-rooted just in the whole race structure and like just the way society works . . . it's just ingrained into the way that things work." Later during his interview, Scott referred to a documentary about the prison system and stated how disproportionate arrests of Black people are an extension of slavery:

> [The documentary] was talking about how after slavery and with Jim Crow, and everything and all that, it was like law enforcement was looking for reasons to arrest Black people. It was like, almost like they weren't ready for their power trip to be over, so they wanted to continue it and find ways for [Black people] to be criminals.

Scott's desire to discuss this documentary when talking about the existence of privilege demonstrated a structural understanding about how Whites manifested their racial superiority through social institutions across time. He specifically named law enforcement as an entity versus individual law enforcement officers as the focal point for his explanation of privilege. His discussion of a documentary about Black people in the prison system also highlights how experiences from people of color illuminate the manifestation of privilege. His discussion of privilege was centered through the lens of marginalized social identity groups similar to the comments made by Jamie and Anna about colonization's impact on Black slaves and Native Americans.

Jane also applied a race critical lens when she discussed experiences of gendered privilege and oppression in her reflection paper. She reflected upon experiences of being reprimanded for similar behaviors her male peers exhibited without punishment during her childhood. Jane used a race critical lens in her meaning-making of these experiences:

> This example (one of countless I have in regard to my identity as a female), highlights two main concepts. One is that, as a female, I face oppression in my life. It generally is subtle, like when I receive different treatment from boys in school, but it still has an impact on my development and advancement in society. The boys in my example were treated with privilege. Because they are male, they got to continue the behavior that I was reprimanded for. The boys didn't do anything to earn that treatment, they simply existed in a system that granted it.

Jane used her experience as a marginalized group (females) to highlight male privilege. She stated how male privilege and female oppression are socially constructed conditions based on gendered social identity groups. However, she framed these moments as ordinary (i.e., "subtle") with a real material impact on her future life chances. In this excerpt, Jane invoked multiple aspects of a race critical framework to explain the nature of privilege as applied to gender.

How Accurate Beliefs and Ideas Work Together

It can be difficult to tease apart the differences between race critical ideas and a race critical ideology. While both share a structural view of privilege and are central to participation in an Antiracism Discourse, they operate in distinct ways. The beliefs related to a race critical ideology help to identify the cause of privilege and oppression on the basis of what is believed to be true about reality, such as the social construction of race, the ordinary nature of privilege, and how it can be identified through the lens of people of color or other marginalized groups. Once privilege is identified using these beliefs, the ideas related to race critical knowledge can be used to buttress these beliefs. While these beliefs and ideas may seem disconnected, they are purposefully connected to one another in particular ways.

The belief that race is a social construction is connected to the idea that privilege is a manifestation of social power. A belief in the social construction of race raises questions about why and for whom this social construction was created and maintained, which the idea of social power answers. Further, the idea that privilege is the manifestation of social power is sensible if one believes that social power is distributed based on social group identities that were created to benefit White people at the expense of people of color.

The belief that racial privilege and oppression are ordinary phenomena as a result of normalized Whiteness supports and are connected to the ideas that privilege is rooted in social power that was intentionally implemented and situated in both the past and the present. A belief that privilege is ordinary raises questions about how privilege came to be this way, which these three ideas help to answer. At some point in time, policies and practices that benefited White people were intentionally implemented into the fabric of our social institutions. However, these policies and practices have existed over time for so long that they both appear ordinary while simultaneously reinforcing a view that White people are better or more deserving than people of color. Further, these ideas about privilege are plausible if you are looking for ways in which privilege could appear ordinary to the general population since both the passing of time and our social institutions shape the way we see ourselves, others, and society as a whole.

The belief that racial privilege and oppression are knowable through the experiences of people of color connects to all four ideas central to race critical knowledge. A belief that those who are marginalized are well positioned to see and describe privilege and oppression opens the door to evidence that is based upon all four ideas. The experience of living life viewing the privileges others are given while being purposefully denied to themselves lends itself to see how this could happen. If race is a primary difference between received or denied benefits, the ideas of social power and institutionalized superiority help explain this reality. Furthermore, the ideas of privilege as intentionally implemented in both the past and the present help explain how the experiences of members of similarly oppressed racial groups could be similar over time and space.

One blatant example that illustrates how these beliefs and associated ideas are used to identify and explore privilege occurred as people discussed the armed siege of the United States Capitol on January 6, 2021.[1] One interpretation of these events situated the attack as an extension of White privilege and White supremacy as evidenced by White supremacist imagery and the softer response these perpetrators faced relative to the response received by Black Lives Matter protesters in the summer of 2020.[2] This view uses three beliefs within the race critical ideology to come to this conclusion. Based on the belief that race is a social construction, this interpretation uses a racial analysis that positions White people as a social group possessing privilege and benefiting from that privilege in the lax response from police as linked to their social power. Because of the belief that racial privilege is knowable through the experiences of people of color, the privilege experienced by White insurrectionists in January 2021 was more readily visible when contrasted against the violent police response to Black protesters in the summer of 2020, drawing upon idea that privilege persists over time. Finally, the belief that racial privilege has become ordinary through the normalization of Whiteness supports the view that the White insurrectionists could display their faces without fear of reprisal and more easily siege the United States Capitol because Whiteness, even in its most violent manifestations, is not viewed as threatening. This last belief draws upon the ideas that privilege is a reflection of institutionalized superiority that is intentionally implemented, such as when White police officers take pictures with White insurrectionists versus shooting Black citizens.[3] Collectively, these beliefs and ideas are used to explore and explain the existence of White privilege and its impact on our lived experiences in the United States.

Collectively, a race critical ideology illuminates the existence of privilege which is explained using ideas central to race critical knowledge. If one does not believe in a race critical ideology, it is less likely that someone would view privilege in relationship to the ideas central to race critical knowledge. If someone does not believe race is socially constructed, there is little reason to view privilege as a manifestation of social power. If someone does not believe that privilege is ordinary because of how it is normalized into society, there is little reason to look at policies and practices over time to view how and why social identity groups have different lived experiences and life chances. If someone does not believe that privilege is knowable through the lens of the oppressed, there is little reason to consider the existence of privilege at all because the only experience that matters is one's own experience. Without any race critical belief regarding the nature and existence of privilege, it is harder, although not impossible, to acknowledge the evidence of privilege that relates to ideas associated with race critical knowledge. In this way, these beliefs and ideas reinforce one another in the view of privilege as structural and operate to dismantle Whiteness as a worldview that perpetuates privilege.

Inaccurate Beliefs About Privilege

Carol, Lucy, Jason, and John all consistently used all three beliefs that (a) society is fair and therefore everyone has equal opportunity to succeed, (b) privilege and social inequality are natural parts of the human experience, and (c) privilege is not structural and is better understood as individualistic. These beliefs commonly found within a broader White Supremacy ideology were used to interpret or explain away the existence of privilege. Furthermore, Jane also occasionality used the belief that privilege and social inequality are natural to explain and interpret privilege, in addition to race critical beliefs. All three of these beliefs operate to dismiss structural explanations of privilege outright, evoke equality, or espouse claims that privilege and related social inequalities are natural.

Society Is Fair

The belief that society is fair, and therefore everyone has equal opportunity to succeed coupled with personal freedom to make their own choices, was most evident in students' reflections. This belief is associated with the abstract liberalism frame of color-blind racism that leverages liberal beliefs of fairness and equality to obfuscate inequitable racialized realities.[4] Carol, Lucy, Jason, and John used these beliefs in two particular ways: Through associated beliefs in meritocracy and color-blind equality. Often, meritocracy was related to the belief that privilege comes from personal choices while color-blind equality was evoked to describe privilege as situational when individuals acknowledge difference and thus fail to view everyone as universally human.

Meritocracy

The belief in merit or earning what one has in life as a mechanism through which life is fair was a salient across Jason's, John's, Lucy's, and Carol's explanations of privilege. All four students stated how something earned was not associated with privilege because they believed that everyone has equal opportunity to earn what they have in life. Carol provided an example of how earning something is the opposite of privilege:

> I did theatre in high school and [when] my director would do auditions for roles, she would have paper, like she would have your paper that you filled out with your information, and then she would put a sticky note on paper and then give you a number. And then she would have just a bunch of sticky notes on the stage while we were auditioning, and she would write based off of the sticky notes and then she would take notes. That's how she would assign roles. I mean there were males that got female roles. Like one guy got Queen of Hearts just because of the notes . . . there was no determination of looks just pure acting talent.

Carol described how her high school theatre director would host blind auditions to assign roles based on pure acting talent without any consideration of their social identity. She cited an example of how a male student was assigned a female role as evidence of how merit is a better fit to explain why people experience certain benefits. In Carol's view, merit negates privilege because she believed that a blind audition process treats all students equally and allows for merit to prevail. However, her belief that everyone has equal opportunity ignores the developmental experiences that are disproportionately available to individuals from privileged social groups that enhance their audition experiences under the guise of merit. For example, the ability to afford acting lessons or purchase tickets to watch live theatre may not be as accessible to lower-income families due to the costs associated with these activities.

Lucy invoked her belief in her own personal merit when asked if she had privilege:

> In some aspects of life yes, and in others no . . . I mean, I'm privileged but, once again, I still have to work for stuff, like not everything's handed to me . . . I am not judging other people who get everything handed to them either, like good for them. . . . I learn more life lessons, having to work for stuff.

Lucy acknowledged having privilege in a limited way before pivoting to a meritocratic defense of why she had any privilege at all. She explained how she had to "work for stuff" that used her belief that hard work negated privilege because it allows one to earn what they have. In Lucy's statement, she also asserted that she does not judge those who "get everything handed to them." However, earlier in her interview she expressed that "it kind of irritates me when people try to put the blame on others. Like if you don't like the situation you're in, do something about it." The juxtaposition of these two comments revealed how her belief in meritocracy operates to blame those without privilege yet shield those with privilege from any blame, working to protect privileged groups and blame oppressed groups.

John and Jason invoked a belief in personal merit more frequently. John repeatedly emphasized his belief that he earned what he has in life:

> Personally, I like to think that my achievements are my achievements. They aren't just because of the privilege that comes from my family or being White. I like to think that other people's achievements are the same. That it's not purely because of their [racial] privilege, which I think many people just forget. They forget that there is some achievement somewhere in what they are doing. Like, I'd like to think that I'm actually qualified for my job as a lifeguard, rather than they just needed a White guy.

During John's discussion of his own racial privilege, he disconnected privilege from identity on the basis of merit by describing how he earned his job as a lifeguard based on his qualifications but not because he was White. However, he also explained how what is earned from merit can be passed on within one's family. John explained what contributes to having privilege:

> [Privilege] comes from your family, and your ancestry, like the things they've done to what they've achieved that extends towards you. . . . People view me as privileged because they see the money my parents put into education for me. But they fail to realize that my parents somehow achieved that money. . . . My dad is the one that has provided for my family, and he has jumped around from job to job. . . . My mom started working too so that they could continue to provide for me and my two other siblings, and a lot of people don't know that . . . like they fail to realize that we do work for some of the things that we have.

John explained how familial achievement contributes to what is commonly seen as unearned privilege. While John acknowledged privilege is inherited, he attributed this inheritance to one's family based on their hard work, not their social group memberships. John's framing of privilege relied on his belief that the benefits resulting from individual hard work passed down within a family is a better fit for explaining privilege. However, John also adopted a hard work explanation for himself because of his "ancestral achievements." Before his interview ended, John again evoked ancestral achievement to explain his frustrations when discussing diversity during his first-year seminar course:

> The way that we were talking about [privilege] made it seem that straight White males, or just White people in general, had so much privilege that they didn't have the right to feel anything other than that privilege. They didn't have a right to feel oppressed or anything because they were so privileged, and I realized that I'm privileged, but . . . for that discussion, it was because I was a straight White male, and I didn't think it [should be] on account of that. I thought my privilege came from my parents, and I happened to be a straight White male in other's people's eyes, and they didn't [see it the same way]. So they're wrongly assuming my privilege comes from those things, rather than my immediate family

John expressed frustration because he believed that his classmates misattributed privilege to his social identities instead of his inheritance of the fruits of his family's hard work and accomplishments. For John, his peers' misunderstanding ignores hard work and merit. However, he maintained a belief in meritocracy for himself even though he acknowledged he inherited his family's achievements without naming evidence of any personal hard work. Additionally, John explained how he was denied the ability to express hardship because privilege was assigned to him based on his race and gender, but not merit. For John, merit includes achievement through hard work *despite* hardship. His comment reveals how a belief in merit through hard work legitimizes unequal benefits and advantages. Hard work as an explanation places personal effort to overcome obstacles in the foreground while relegating barriers to institutional access associated with social identities in the background to mask unearned benefits.

Jason expressed similar beliefs about merit eclipsing social identity. Jason explicitly contrasted merit and identity in his reflection paper:

> Nominal identity is not important; posterity will forget who you were, but your actions will resound throughout time. People don't remember Dr. Martin Luther King Jr. simply because he was Black, nor Sacagawea simply because she was a woman, or Mother Teresa simply because she was a Catholic. Identifying only as part of a group makes you just that, a unit in a whole whose uniqueness can't be easily distinguished by group membership alone. It is an exercise in futility. However, identifying with what you have done is the purest expression of uniqueness, only you have lived your life. So we remember Martin Luther King for his contribution to equality, Sacagawea for helping discover the American West, and Mother Teresa for her inspiring charity and selflessness. Regardless of who or what you may identify as, you won't be remembered for your identity, but for your ideas, your doings, the way you lived your life.

Jason positioned action over "nominal identity." His writing framed action as virtuous and identity as futile when he described the contributions of public figures as unrelated to their identities. His claim ignored how Rev. Dr. Martin Luther King Jr.'s social identities as a Black male Protestant minister influenced his actions, Sacagawea's social identity as an indigenous woman gave her a respected status within her tribal community, coupled with her local knowledge of the terrain and tribal languages, and Mother Teresa's status as a Catholic nun gave her access to resources within the Catholic Church to start a new religious order.[5] Jason's belief in merit was evident through his comments that devalued how identity facilitates access to opportunities that support an individual's capacity to achieve success in their lives. His final sentence that one's actions will be remembered over their identities perfectly encapsulates the way his belief operates to focus on what one has earned only through their actions.

Color-Blind Equality

Lucy and Carol expressed the belief that society is fair through a related belief that being color-blind was how to achieve fairness and equality. Color-blind equality rejects structural explanations of privilege by equivocating all racial experiences, shifting attention away from White people, and/or blaming people of color. After identifying "Caucasians" as having racial privilege, Lucy said she felt bad for saying that and offered the following explanation:

> I totally understand the whole like Black Lives Matter thing, but I also believe all lives matter, no matter what race. So, that's why I don't understand the whole Blacks Lives Matter argument, when they're trying to prove equality, to me that doesn't prove equality. They're trying to say that, okay, now they're privileged to other races, in a way. Sometimes I get the feeling that's how they are, what they're trying to get at.

Lucy's explanation for feeling bad about naming White people as having privilege involved focusing on Black oppression instead of White privilege. Her discursive shift focused on the Black Lives Matter movement to express her belief in color-blind equality that all lives matter, even after claiming to understand the rationale behind the movement. Her color-blind belief in equality ignores structural realities of discrimination that underpin the reason for naming Black lives as disproportionate victims of police brutality. However, at the very end of her commentary, the connection becomes clear. Lucy believed highlighting Black lives over all lives contradicted the goal of treating everyone the same because the act of acknowledging race works in opposition to her belief in color-blind equality. Similarly, her response to identify White people as having privilege similarly worked against her belief in color-blind equality. It is notable that her commentary about White privilege was instead centered on Black oppression, which she did not seem to view as contrary to her belief in color-blind equality that ignores race.

Carol similarly invoked a belief in color-blind equality to diminish notions of racial privilege. When explaining the cause of racial privilege, she described conversations about such as irrelevant:

> People are so aware of equality now in our generation that if something bad does happen, where privilege is a thing or even just racism, then it's all over the internet. And I feel like it's so big now that people overthink things and take things too far.

Carol used her belief in color-blind equality to claim that college students are sufficiently aware of privilege to render conversations about it unnecessary. However, she uses her belief to claim that "people," implying people of color, take conversations about privilege "too far." Carol implied that remaining silent about privilege is sufficient while discussing it is extreme. While Carol suggests "people" need not overemphasize privilege in this statement, earlier in her interview, she accused Black people of discriminating against her during a job interview. Her discourse reveals how her belief in color-blind equality operates to allow White people to name racial discrimination but prevents people of color from implicating White people with privilege.

Beliefs about meritocracy and color-blind equality within the broader belief that society is fair enable a dismissal of privilege, both overall and when it specifically implicates White people, based on the notion that individuals can control their reality through personal choices. However, these beliefs are connected because meritocratic beliefs grounded in color-blind equality benefit White people and maintain Whiteness as a worldview. If success results from hard work occurring on an equal playing field, structural explanations of privilege are seemingly unnecessary because all that a person has was earned fairly. These excerpts illustrate a synergy between beliefs in meritocracy and color-blind equality that collectively plays on notions of freedom and equality divorced from a structural analysis of reality.

Social Inequality Is Natural

The belief that privilege and social inequality are natural parts of the human experience was another common belief expressed among these White students. This belief, associated with the naturalization frame, was often grounded in biological, psychological, or sociological arguments that, respectively, emphasized genetic or physiological characteristics, cognitive traits, and social or cultural behaviors.[6] Jason, Lucy, and Jane used different versions of this ideological frame to assert their belief in privilege as natural.

Jason stated that privilege exists because "we have the tendency to compare ourselves to each other . . . all people . . . everyone likes to compare themselves." His statement asserted his belief that humans are psychologically predisposed to compare themselves to others. Additionally, he believed that people are innately different, leading him to conclude that "when there are innate differences, some people are going to have it better than others." When asked to provide an example, Jason hypothesized a person born as a quadriplegic. Linking these statements together illustrates his psychologically orientated belief that people are naturally physically different and naturally compare themselves to others. Therefore, the existence of privilege is a natural extension of the human experience. His belief operates to disconnect White people from any responsibility they have to racial privilege because he views human differences and its consequences as psychologically natural but not socially manufactured.

Lucy demonstrated the belief that social inequality is natural with a sociological view that privilege and social inequality are consequences of racial groups spending most of their time around other people like themselves as an assumed truth of human behavior. While discussing how segregated social spaces contribute to the existence of privilege, Lucy offered the following explanation:

> I've always just grown up around, you know, Caucasians, that's just my town. Like there's nothing bad about it, I don't think. Then there's other towns that are more, you know, more African American or more Latino, so

then everyone's just kind of growing up in that specific society . . . you're just growing up with those thoughts. I don't know.

Lucy explained how privilege resulted from the ideas people develop living within racially homogenous spaces. Her repeated use of the word "just" implied a natural view of these types of spaces as a taken-for-granted truth. Because Lucy did not question why racial segregation occurs, yet readily adopts its existence as a cause for privilege and social inequality, she seemingly assumes spatialized racial segregation is natural and warrants no further reflection. Her simplistic view of reality as existing "just" because it exists exhibits a circular logic that avoids structural explanations.

Jane relied on a biologically oriented belief that framed privilege as a natural result of that fact that "humans are inherently biased." She continued to explain that "people are inherently going to treat people that look like them better probably, which kind of sucks." Jane's belief that bias was an innate aspect of how people are born became clear through her verbal resignation to what she believes to be a physiological characteristic of humanity. Before our interview ended, I asked her to clarify her remarks about innate bias to ensure her beliefs were grounded in a physiological view of humans versus a characteristic resulting from social learning. Indeed, she reasserted her explanation and doubled down on her biological belief by stating that "I feel in human nature we are always a little bit judgmental. [That probably] harkens back to our primitive days." Her explanation of bias as an innate trait that persisted across years of evolution demonstrated how deeply ingrained a belief about social inequality as natural can be even though Jane expressed multiple ideas central to race critical knowledge and beliefs.

Even though these students infrequently expressed beliefs in privilege and social inequality as natural, the presence of these beliefs was apparent and useful. Framing privilege as biologically, psychologically, or socially innate operated to prevent students from considering structural elements of privilege. Notably, Jane used this belief alongside race critical ideological beliefs that social identities are socially constructed, privilege and social inequality becomes ordinary because of the normalization of Whiteness, and the exploration of privilege and oppression through the lens of those who are oppressed and denied privilege provides value. In her view, these beliefs seem to complement one another in that the structural reality and manifestation of privilege can be situated within innate biases. Therefore, these beliefs work together to employ a structural analysis of privilege as it exists while simultaneously situating privilege as the result of innate bias within individuals.

Privilege Is Individualistic, Not Structural

Jason, Carol, John, and Lucy also used a belief that privilege is not structural and better understood as individualistic to challenge assertions about privilege. The first portion of this belief is that privilege is not structural and therefore operates as a general refutation of privilege. The second aspect of this belief is that privilege is an individualistic phenomenon and therefore operates as a counter explanation.

Structural Refutation

Jason, Carol, John, and Lucy all expressed a belief that privilege is not structural. When asked to explain why some individuals have privilege during his interview, Jason deflected, stating, "I don't think there is really an answer to that question." While his reflection paper offered a structural definition of privilege being "caused by systemic, institutionalized bias against an identity group," his interview response demonstrated his inability to identify structural reasons people do not have privilege. In response to viewing the political cartoon during his interview, he also indicated that references to structural oppression (e.g., slavery) should be removed due to irrelevance.

Carol stated that "privilege has become such a narrow-minded [concept], like, privilege is only for White people, but they don't realize that privilege is for all races." Carol rejected a structural view of privilege as linked to specific social identity groups, including White people, and instead asserted that privilege is applicable to all races. Furthermore, she used "they" to refer to people of color, whom she claimed unfairly applied privilege only to White people. Her assertion simultaneously rejects structural explanations of privilege and denigrates people of color as ignorant about privilege.

John asserted a generic belief that privilege was not structural throughout his interview and reflection paper while continually claiming that focusing on structural and individual differences associated with privilege was the real problem that needed to be addressed. John wrote that he avoids viewing himself as a member of social identity groups because "I do not like to support the concepts of privilege and oppression." His dedication to this belief caused John to describe the root of privilege as "focusing too much on differences rather than similarities." While John accurately identified how focusing on differences "lead[s] to this separation of privilege and oppressed [groups]," he did not acknowledge how views about social identity groups have been institutionalized in society, reinforcing an individualistic view of privilege.

Lucy uniquely expressed the belief that privilege is not structural multiple times by offering anything but a structural explanation for privilege while attempting to avoid providing a direct response to my questions. In a memorable moment during our interview, Lucy struggled to explain who does and does not have privilege and why:

Tharp: Who has racial privilege?
Lucy: In the US, Caucasians. . . . I, I, I [giggles] feel so bad saying that . . . I just feel like, I mean coz just like I'm Caucasian, I don't wanna be like, I don't feel like I'm . . . mmm. The media just like, they like

	blow everything out of proportion, and then, I don't know . . . coz like I'm Caucasian, I don't, so I feel bad saying "Oh, I'm privileged coz I'm Caucasian."
Tharp:	So how does that relate to racial privilege in your mind, and feeling bad about saying Caucasian people have privilege?
Lucy:	Um, I guess again with the whole, I totally understand the whole like Black Lives Matter thing, but I also believe all lives matter, no matter what race. So, that's why I don't understand the whole Blacks Lives Matter argument, when they're trying to prove equality, to me that doesn't prove equality. They're trying to say that, okay, now they're privileged to other races, in a way. Sometimes I get the feeling that's how they are, what they're trying to get at.
Tharp:	So then, who does not have racial privilege in the United States?
Lucy:	If you're not Caucasian. . . . Yeah, once again I feel bad saying that. I don't know, I just feel like that's the society I grew up in, and I just, once again, I was just born into that, I don't know. Into the world where, I guess, but still racial equality is better than like back in the 1800s, you know. Like I don't know how much better, but I don't know whose job it is to make it better.
Tharp:	Why do non-Caucasian people not have privilege?
Lucy:	Once again, I feel like I hear and like read stuff online with people saying that.

In this extended exchange, Lucy expressed feeling bad when saying "Caucasian" people have privilege while "non-Caucasian" people do not have privilege. She attempted to explain herself by acknowledging how she is White and did not want to acknowledge her own privilege. Then she shifted to blame "the media" (e.g., news media, social media) while alluding to "people" or "they" (presumably people of color and allies) who promote Black Lives Matter online. Lucy stated that she believed the Black Lives Matter movement places Black lives above all others. She explained why people of color do not have privilege using multiple comments that either shifted accountability to a blameless cause (i.e., "that's the society I grew up in") or people of color (i.e., "it's what people online are saying") or minimized the extent of its existence (i.e., "racial equality is better"). Lucy's statements were reminiscent of disconnected sound bites that suggested her desire to attribute the cause of privilege to anything except a structural explanation caused by anyone except White people.

Individualistic Explanation

Jason, Lucy, and Carol also used this version of a belief that privilege is not structural but individualistic during their interviews and in specific reference to the political cartoon. Jason explicitly stated his individualistic belief about privilege when asked if racial privilege was still relevant today. He replied, "I think it'd depend on the situation . . . some situations might have it." He further stated that "privilege is more of an individual thing than, like, an entire race." His comments asserted both how privilege is not structurally linked to social identity groups but instead was based on the unique circumstances of each individual.

Lucy expressed her belief when describing the root cause of privilege as "probably just everyone's thoughts." She used this belief again when asked about any modifications she would want to make to political cartoon:

> I'd get rid of this wealth gap block because all races have wealthy people and have less fortunate people. I mean, I don't know certain statistics, but for example, there are Black celebrities who have a lot of money and there are White celebrities who have a lot of money. There are people who live in tiny apartments who are both races as well. So yeah, that's the only part I kind of disagree with. There's a wealth gap in America just period between everyone. I don't think it's a race issue.

Lucy's belief that privilege was individualistic was visible in her rejection of race as a structure through which privilege exists and operates. She specifically described similar economic conditions between Black and White people as the grounds to reject racial structures. Furthermore, her reliance on economics was done in a way to focus on what individuals can earn ("wealth") over social class identities that encompass elements such as education and occupational prestige that mitigate opportunities to accumulate wealth and also correspond with race. Furthermore, Lucy pointed to examples of wealthy Black celebrities and poor White people as individuals who supposedly disprove racial structures associated with privilege. Together, her approach to modify the cartoon uses her belief that privilege is individualistic to distance privilege away from White people and toward people of color, resulting in her final statement that "I don't think [wealth is] a race issue."

Carol went even further than Jason and Lucy when asserting her belief that privilege is individualistic multiple times throughout her interview. She offered the following response when asked who can experience privilege:

> I feel like White privilege is a saying in the world. But I feel like there are Black privileges but in a different sense. So, I feel like anyone can experience privilege. Like it's just a lot of stereotypes being put into actions and choices. People choosing things based off of stereotypes.

Carol expressed her belief that privilege is individualistic because "anyone can experience privilege" including Black people. She explained that privilege is linked to the choices made by each individual, including choices and actions based upon "stereotypes" about others. Carol not only believes that privilege is based on each person's experiences but also describes how decisions based on stereotypes can lead to "Black privileges."

This belief about privilege reemerged in other statements Carol made that worked to protect White people from being stereotyped as privileged while simultaneously stereotyping people of color as discriminating against all White people. While explaining the cause of privilege, Carol shifted to provide a commentary on the irrelevance of focusing on privilege that is used to harm White people and benefit Black people:

> People are so aware of equality now in our generation that if something bad does happen, where privilege is a thing or even just racism, then it's all over the internet. And I feel like it's so big now that people over think things and take things too far. [For example] when they you know, they see a White girl or something like that and they say to me, "Oh! You're White, like sure you've got nothing wrong, like, you're fine." I'm like, "Okay, take a step into my life for a minute." Yes, I understand that. Yes, your life isn't awesome, but mine isn't either, and I feel like it's building up such a thing, and now they're seeing it everywhere in everything. Like in some person's maybe innocent decision, now it could suddenly be twisted around to, "Oh, it's White privilege."

Carol never explicitly names Black people in her comments; however, she repeatedly blames "people"/"they" as opposed to White people for "taking things too far." She further claims that Black people blame all White people for racial privilege and oppression, citing herself as evidence of a White person not having privilege because her life was not "awesome." By connecting the notion of living well to the concept of privilege, she reinforced an individualistic belief about privilege that simultaneously attempted to frame Black people as using stereotypes about being oppressed into a privilege that allows them to blame all White people.

When asked to describe desired modifications she would make to the political cartoon during her interview, she again expressed her belief that privilege was individualistic to reject any structural notions:

> I think instead of saying all of these historical things, I would focus more on like, you know, "loses job" or something like that. Or "doesn't get position, move back a turn," . . . because I feel like this is just saying people are judging me, Black people, because of stuff that's happened in the past. It's not really focusing on the *real* things that happen in today's society. Or you know, "old White woman clutches a purse on train." . . . [I]f I were to look at this, I would just be like, "Oh, this means nothing." I don't, when I look at Black people, I don't see slavery, I don't see Jim Crow, I don't see the KKK. I just see it's a Black guy.

In her commentary, Carol explicitly rejects a structural view of privilege in favor of examples that happen to individuals versus entire racial groups. She even explained why, stating that a focus on racial groups allows Black people to judge her as a White person. What she did not say, but that could be implied based on her previous comments, is that focusing on *White* people versus her as a White *person* does not reflect what she believes to be true about herself as not having privilege and therefore is not relevant. Her belief is clearly summarized in her final sentence when she claims to only see a Black person but not any of the structural forces that impact their experience as a member of a Black racial group (even though she identified the person as being Black).

The ability to believe that privilege is irrelevant either because of a general rejection of it being structural or because it is better explained as individualistic was noticed repeatedly, likely because of the simplicity of this belief. To maintain a rejection of privilege as a structural phenomenon without any counter explanation requires little cognitive effort and can be used to provide distance from privilege. To believe that privilege is better understood as individualistic provides an easy path to maintain this belief by noting any number of observable differences regardless of how impactful those differences may be. Both iterations of the belief that privilege is not structural and better viewed as individualistic can be coupled together, as evidenced by these students, because once a person cannot reasonably maintain an argument to defend their belief that privilege is individualistic, they can pivot to a generalized rejection of privilege without further explanation, simply because that is what one wishes to believe.

How Inaccurate Beliefs and Ideas Work Together

Just as it can be difficult to tease apart the differences between race critical ideas and a race critical ideology, the same is true when differentiating between White racial knowledge and a White supremacist ideology. While both share an individualistic view of privilege, different combinations of these ideas emerge to support different iterations of this broader belief. Unlike how the beliefs central to a race critical ideology are used by participants in the Antiracism Discourse to identify and explore privilege, the beliefs central to a White supremacist ideology are primarily used by participants in the Whiteness Discourse to refute any structural notions of privilege, including the desire to explore it further, as a means to distance White people from being associated with privilege and social inequality. Once privilege is challenged upon the basis of beliefs that society is fair, social inequality is natural, and that privilege is not structural and instead individualistic, individuals tend to use the idea that privilege is situational in distinct combinations with other ideas central to White racial knowledge to bolster their beliefs.

The belief that society is fair and everyone has equal opportunities for success is connected to the ideas that privilege is situational, ahistorical, and a reflection of the personal choices we make. A belief that everyone has equal opportunities for success eliminates any structural view of privilege and positions it as variable relative to the situational context of each individual. Because the situational context is bounded by each individual, anything in the past is beyond the situational context of the individual and therefore irrelevant. Furthermore, the choices made by individuals, which they can control within their individualistic context, become the primary means by which social inequality is viewed to occur. As a result, the notion of color-blind equality explicitly centers the situational context of the person over their racial social group, which is beyond their scope of influence. Additionally, the notion of meritocracy and earning your success, or lack therefore, is viewed as deserving.

The belief that privilege is a natural extension of the human experience based on biological, psychological, or sociological reasoning is connected to the idea of individual bias along with the ideas of privilege as situational or based upon choice or chance. Biological and psychological iterations of this belief rely primarily upon the idea of individual bias as grounded in psychological differences or how people psychologically make sense of the world around them. However, this belief also draws upon the idea the privilege is situational because privilege is not believed to be present unless an individual acts upon that bias in any given situation. Sociological iterations of this belief position individual bias as shaped by our social and cultural situational contexts. However, privilege that arises from our individual bias within these social and cultural contexts is understood as an extension of rational cultural choices (e.g., White people choosing to live around other White people) or are the result of unexplainable chance (e.g., White people just happen to live together). Overall, the belief that social inequality is natural relies heavily upon the idea of individual bias in the situational context of the individual or their immediate sociocultural environment while remaining flexible regarding where to place the blame for privilege. Biological, psychological, and sociological iterations are used to position White people as blameless for their privilege because they cannot help the way they are or because that is just the way it is.

The belief that privilege is not structural but individualistic is primarily based upon the idea that privilege is situational as a way to generically refute any structural view. However, the ideas that privilege is ahistorical and based upon individual choices can be used together to create boundaries that only include individual controlled situations and choices in order to exclude any structural and historic evidence. Unlike the beliefs that society is fair and social inequality is natural, the belief that privilege is not structural and instead is individualistic does not have a strong internal logic because it primarily acts as a refutation. As such, it draws upon the ideas central to White racial knowledge in any number of ways to create distance between those ideas and privilege.

All three beliefs within the broader White supremacy ideology exist to prevent any critical examination of privilege as a structural phenomenon. These frames all share the same idea that privilege is situational because framing privilege as only true to a narrowly defined context allows these boundaries to be established

Anchoring Beliefs About Privilege   **117**

to reinforce this belief. In the process, the other ideas are evoked as secondary supports once the situational context is established. The result is that the core idea of privilege being situational establishes parameters under which privilege is irrelevant and uses the remaining ideas to reinforce the different iterations of its irrelevance as either explainable (i.e., choice, innate bias) or unexplainable (i.e., chance). Therefore, these three frames use different sets of ideas to defend beliefs which operate with the common goal of reinforcing Whiteness as normative.

An example of how one of these beliefs and associated ideas are used to resist a structural view of privilege can also be seen in how some people discussed the armed siege of the United States Capitol on January 6, 2021. A different interpretation of these events reflected a mixture of surprise and disavowal. Those who shared this reaction to the siege on the United States Capitol displayed a range of disconnected beliefs that relied upon distinct ideas in order to avoid any association between these White insurrectionists and other White people. Some individuals used the belief that privilege is not structural but individualistic. Senator Pat Toomey expressed surprise stating that "I don't think that this unbelievable behavior . . . could've been reasonable expected" to minimize views that this was avoidable as a structural problem.[7] Similarly, Donald Trump's former Chief of Staff, Mick Mulvaney, described how the events at the United States Capitol were in no way connected to previous rhetoric and views espoused by Trump,[8] rhetoric and views that proposed racists ideas and beliefs while also expressing affection toward White supremacist groups. This belief operates to protect Whiteness by using the ideas that privilege is situational, ahistorical, and related to chance. By interpreting these events as unforeseeable, it suggests that they happened as a matter of chance, positioning it as a unique situation divorced from anything in the past. Adopting this stance both distances the White insurrectionists from other White people, including Trump and other elected officials who have been permissive toward racism, while protecting them from any accountability for their actions and thus preserving their own innocence.

Traces of the belief that society is fair are evident in the reactions of other individuals to the events at the United States Capitol. For example, Congresswoman Marjorie Taylor Greene adamantly distanced the White insurrections from Trump supporters and conservatives: "What happened at the capitol does not represent Trump supporters, it does not represent the make America great again movement . . . it has nothing to do with the past 4 years."[9] Additionally, the President of the Chicago Police Union, John Catanzara, defended the White insurrectionists as "a bunch of pissed off people" who were "individuals" that "get to do what they want. Again, they were voicing frustration. They're entitled to voice their frustration."[10] Both of these comments reflect the belief that people are individuals free to make their own choices because individual choices matter more than shared social group membership. These comments use the ideas that privilege is situational and ahistorical to bracket out any past events or rhetoric along with seemingly tandem events and comments among GOP politicians who spoke at the rally immediately preceding the siege on the capitol. The idea of choice is used to emphasize that these individuals have the right to make their own choices, and it is implied that it is their choices that further distance them from others who may share similar beliefs. While these comments are not directly tied to a rebuttal of White privilege and its relationship to White insurrectionists, these beliefs operate to reject and alternatively interpret the same situation that participants in the Antiracist Discourse view as another example of White privilege.

Similarly, faint traces of the belief that social inequality is natural are visible in reactions that view the White insurrectionists as uniquely bad. Congressman Markwayne Mullin described the White insurrectionists as "a different group of individuals" who "had evil in their eyes."[11] The belief that these people were different based on a psychological characteristic (i.e., evil) draws upon the ideas of situational and innate bias that draw contextual boundaries around each individual and are explained by an internal deficiency. This same framing is reminiscent of explanations used to explain away mass shootings as a problem caused by mentally ill individuals versus structural policies and practices.[12] While it is also not directly engaging the view of the United States Capitol siege as an iteration of White privilege, it shifts the focus away from any race critical analysis.

Because Whiteness is the status quo in our society, the beliefs central to a White supremacy ideology are used by participants in the Whiteness Discourse to adopt a defensive position. As a result, these frames are not often used with one another because they emerge when needed to defend against a structural view of privilege. Furthermore, because these frames rely on the contradictory ideas of choice and chance, it would be challenging to form beliefs that use both of these ideas at the same time. For example, it is not likely for someone to argue in the same breath that privilege is irrelevant because people are free to make their own choices in a free society, yet rational because we are hard-wired to discriminate against others and cannot be changed. Therefore, while the ideas central to White racial knowledge support various beliefs to reject a structural view of privilege, there is a danger to the internal logic of these frames and how their supporting ideas intersect with one another.

Acknowledging and Engaging Different Beliefs and Ideas

These students provided evidence of using specific beliefs central to either a race critical ideology or White supremacy ideology. However, these students also demonstrated a familiarity with beliefs or their associated ideas outside of the ideologies they most strongly used themselves. While Anna, Jamie, Jane, and Scott predominantly used beliefs central to a race critical ideology, they were able to identify and engage with the beliefs central to a White supremacy ideology used to refute the structural nature of privilege. However, Jane and Anna offered the most explicit acknowledgment and refutation of beliefs central to a White supremacy ideology.

Jane identified all three frames central to a White supremacy ideology. She recognized, and rejected, a common belief that everyone regardless of their race is equal while discussing the political cartoon. She volunteered the following description of the cartoon:

> It's attempting to depict the struggle of African American people in this country since its inception, as compared to White people, and the overarching idea of, "Oh, you have the same [rights], we are all American citizens. We are all equals, we all have equal rights. So, don't complain. Don't say you have these problems because we are equal citizens." When in reality that's not exactly true and hasn't been true.

Jane demonstrated her awareness of a false belief that everyone is equal as grounding to dismiss privilege through her impersonation of the White character in the cartoon. She clearly identified, and rejected, this belief in favor of a structural view that she expressed throughout her interview. Jane also identified other beliefs when she described why people from privileged social identity groups struggle to acknowledge privilege and its structural nature:

> It's hard for people to accept their privilege when it sort of seems negative to them to have it . . . wherein privilege inherent is discrimination. So, and I even find this with myself sometimes, where I'm like, "Well I don't feel privileged in this situation, I'm just being me, I can't help who I am. I can't help how I was raised, who I was born as." And it's sort of because you don't want to blame yourself.

Jane's comments identified one reason people with privilege, including herself, reject claims of privilege because it implicates them as beneficiaries at the expense of others. She explicitly identified the idea of privilege being situational, a core idea within White racial knowledge, as it is connected to both beliefs that privilege is not structural but individualistic or that privilege is a result of biological, psychological, or sociological differences. Overall, Jane demonstrated an awareness of these beliefs and was able to empathize when an individual choose to use them.

Anna also demonstrated a depth of awareness and frustration with beliefs that reject the structural nature of privilege when discussing the political cartoon. While examining the cartoon, she focused her attention on the White character who says, "Are you just slow or what?" to the Black character who is farther behind. She shared her views through a hypothetical conversation between these two characters in the cartoon:

> I think the caption of "are you just slow or what," is not funny. . . . [W]hen you see such a clear disadvantage where it's so obvious. And then having that [White character] be like, "Why are you not here yet? Like that's

crazy" is sort of a funny like twist to it. And then like the Black [character] is just like, "Are you kidding me? No, like I'm not slow, like I'm doing my best!" . . . I think it is trying to convey a very, very real [sentiment].

Anna's reflection on this portion of the cartoon demonstrated her awareness of the false belief that everyone is equal and their success or lack thereof reflects an individual's personal choices. Through the embodiment of the Black character, she expressed her view that such a belief is ridiculous because it is divorced from her belief that social inequality is the result of structural obstacles.

Anna then turned her attention to another part of the cartoon that identified affirmative action as one of the only benefits the Black character received. She describes how affirmative action is commonly used as evidence to reject structural privilege among White people:

The idea of affirmative action and the "get one free turn" [space] is kind of an interesting thing to add there, because it's true and people are using [it] today as like, "Oh boy, you have affirmative action, you're fine, like you'll probably get the job over me because you're Black and I'm White. My life is now at a disadvantage" . . . [However] they do get one free turn. But then compared to the number of turns that other people [get], the other things that have been put in place like lots and lots of turns as opposed to getting one free turn.

Anna's reflection again demonstrated her awareness of the generic belief that privilege is structural that points out situational advantages received by people of color as evidence that privilege is not structurally linked to White people. She further demonstrated a keen insight to how this belief is also used to blame people of color as perpetrators of social inequality against White people, regardless of how much structural advantages White people have.

Carol, John, Lucy, and Jason also were able to recognize opposing ideas used to acknowledge and explore the structural nature of privilege even though they primarily used beliefs central to a White supremacy ideology. When doing so, they would offer a temporary concession to a structural view of privilege. Carol acknowledged the relationship between privileged social group memberships in her reflection paper, writing that "the White race still holds a 'better' [position in] society" because people are discriminated against because of "their race or sexual orientation." Her statement explicitly identified all White people as having privilege at the expense of people of color. However, she used the remainder of her reflection paper to offer arguments about reverse discrimination occurring when "White privilege" is taken too far. Overall, Carol seemingly provided what she believed to be a socially desirable response before offering her alternative view of the topic.

John also acknowledged the relationship between privileged social group memberships in a single moment during the latter half of his interview. While describing and critiquing the political cartoon as negatively portraying White people and not including any barriers that they face, he offered a single, half-hearted concession of privilege as a structural phenomenon:

> I do believe that White people in our society have some sort of privilege that non-White people don't have. I just didn't think, or I guess I didn't want to believe, that it was so drastically different, that it was so drastic of a privilege. I don't think that this image is like entirely honest. It doesn't have the full picture, but it is showing valid points of argument.

John's commentary briefly acknowledged that White people have some amount of privilege relative to people of color. He also named that it is difficult to acknowledge the existence of privilege. Even though he conceded that the political cartoon had some "valid points of argument," he ultimately concluded that the political cartoon is not "entirely honest" and reverted to his previous beliefs. John's comment was the first and only time in his interview when he used a racial lens to consider racial differences compared to repeatedly rejecting the significance of social identities in reflection paper and the remainder of his interview.

Lucy momentarily acknowledged that privilege is linked to social group memberships and is intentionally implemented to retain social power. Her acknowledgment came while interpreting the gap between the White and Black characters in the political cartoon:

> Um, in a way both sides are responsible. Well no. (pause) I would say the Caucasians are more responsible for all of this. I mean they're the ones that made all those Jim Crow laws and segregation like the Bla –, African Americans didn't ask for that. I mean, who would?

Lucy initially wanted to attribute responsibility for racial inequality to both White people and Black people before momentarily acknowledging White people as solely responsible. Contrary to her consistent belief that privilege was based on choices regardless of social identity, she briefly conceded that White people contributed to privilege because it benefited them. In her explanation, she even used the race critical belief that social inequality is knowable through experience of people of color to acknowledge that Black people would not have chosen to create Jim Crow laws or segregation.

Jason acknowledged structural ideas about privilege twice, once in his reflection paper and once during his interview. In his reflection paper, he acknowledged the institutional nature of privilege when he wrote "inequality is caused by systemic, institutionalized bias against an identity group." Similarly, he used an institutional understanding of inequality to describe the gap between the Black and White characters in the political cartoon:

> Many of the marked squares on the Black path imply government... [pounding noise] slavery was government, Jim Crow laws were also government,

voting rights [were] government, segregation [was] government, and cops also [are] government, poor schools [are] government. And on the other hand, the White side has free land [from Indians which] also [was] the government and [free labor from] slavery again was also the government.

Jason was particularly animated when offering this explanation of the cartoon and repeatedly touched the paper copy of the political cartoon with enough force to hear an audible thud against the table when pointing to each government influenced space. He identified multiple structural causes of inequality and was adamant in blaming the government for inequality. However, Jason then pivoted when he declared the political cartoon was not an accurate reflection of his view of privilege because it is "more of an individual thing than [associated with] an entire race." Jason momentarily conceded that government, a social institution, was responsible for social inequality and privilege, only to revert to his dominant stance that privilege is an individualistic phenomenon.

It is important to note the difference in how opposing views were acknowledged by these students. Students who predominantly espoused beliefs central to a race critical ideology identified opposing beliefs and associated ideas central to a White supremacy ideology and White racial knowledge. Students who predominantly espoused beliefs central to a White supremacy ideology retained these beliefs even after they identified and conceded to opposing ideas central to race critical knowledge.

Exposure to All, Adherence to Few

The White college students in my study demonstrated different levels of awareness about the beliefs (and associated ideas) commonly used among participants in *both* the Whiteness and Antiracism Discourses. Within the United States, everyone is originally socialized into the Whiteness Discourse. Related to the topic of privilege, everyone is socialized around a White supremacy ideology that includes beliefs that privilege is not a structural phenomenon and is better understood as individualistic, that privilege is the result of naturally occurring biological, psychological, or sociological differences, and that privilege is individualistic because we live in a fair society where people have freedom to make choices and determine their own success. These beliefs are embedded in the foundation of the United States through policies and practices traced back to chattel slavery and the creation of the US Constitution.[13] These beliefs are also reinforced by thought leaders, such as Bill O'Reilly, Tucker Carlson, and Ben Shapiro, who participate in the Whiteness Discourse and work to legitimize these beliefs as accurate.[14] Therefore, it is sensible that all these students would either adopt the beliefs central to a White supremacy ideology or at least demonstrate a keen awareness of them.

Even though everyone in the United States is originally socialized into the Whiteness Discourse, there are multiple Discourses which individuals are exposed to and may choose to participate in throughout their lifetimes. The students in my study demonstrated the possibility of rejecting the beliefs and associated ideas central to a White supremacy ideology used by participants in the Whiteness Discourse. Some of these students demonstrated a stronger rejection of the ideas and beliefs that dismiss privilege as structural and adopted beliefs central to a race critical ideology in order to fully acknowledge and examine privilege. Other students only momentarily conceded that some ideas and beliefs central to race critical knowledge and a race critical ideology were valid before returning to their beliefs central to a White supremacy ideology. Beliefs play an important role in acknowledging and organizing information used to interpret our reality. While these beliefs become harder to change over time as ideas and beliefs operate to reinforce one another, these beliefs are susceptible to change.

A useful analogy to highlight the relationship between individuals, beliefs, and various Discourses can be found when examining how an individual shops for shoes over time. When first looking for shoes, an individual will go to a store and try on multiple pairs of shoes to determine which shoes to buy. While trying on different pairs of shoes, they consider multiple factors such as the purpose of the shoe (e.g., casual, dress, walking/running, athletic, outdoor), the aesthetic of the shoe (e.g., color, style, brand), and of course the shoe size. Over time, this individual learns what type of shoe works best for them based on their lifestyle, what is popular or trendy, and which brand they come to trust as being a reliably good fit. Eventually, individuals may not try on shoes again because they know what works best for them and repeatedly buy the same type of shoes. However, a time may come when this individual's lifestyle changes, such as starting a new job that requires a dress shoe they do not have. This individual may return to the shoe store once again to try on shoes to find a good pair, repeating the process all over again.

The way individuals shop for shoes is similar to how individuals relate to their beliefs over time. Individuals are exposed to multiple beliefs based on the many Discourses in which they participate. However, individuals ultimately decide to adopt certain beliefs that are both a good fit for themselves and simultaneously allow them to participate in select Discourses. Every time an individual uses a belief, they reinforce their participation in a particular Discourse that simultaneously influences them to maintain such beliefs. Eventually, using these beliefs becomes second nature and requires little thought. However, when life circumstances change, such as going away for college, individuals become exposed to different beliefs and, depending on the Discourse in which they wish to participate, may decide to adopt different beliefs.

While these students were aware of the beliefs and associated ideas central to both a White supremacy ideology and race critical ideology, they tended to adopt one view of reality. Carol, Jason, John, and Lucy consistently expressed beliefs within a White supremacy ideology to reject the structural nature of privilege and provide alternative explanations. Anna, Jamie, Jane, and Scott expressed varying degrees of rigor when using beliefs within the race critical ideology to explore the structural nature of privilege. Anna, Jamie, and Scott were the most consistent in their adherence to race critical beliefs. However, Jane specifically offers a unique glimpse into individuals who use both sets of beliefs to understand privilege.

Jane's comments provide evidence regarding how an individual straddles both the Whiteness and Antiracism Discourses while in the process of unlearning beliefs central to White supremacy ideology. She adopted a race critical view that examines the structural and sustained nature of privilege. In her commentary, she acknowledges and explicitly rejects beliefs that society is fair and privilege is not structural central to a White supremacy ideology and commonly used by participants in the Whiteness Discourse. However, she also adopts a belief that privilege was a fated outcome because people are psychologically prone to bias. Her adoption of the belief that social inequality is natural is distinctive because she does not view it as contradicting to her structural views of privilege. Instead, she seemingly contends that privilege is a structural phenomenon that is perpetrated by individuals who cannot help themselves due to their predisposition toward bias. The totality of her beliefs about privilege reveals that unlearning various beliefs and their associated ideas central to a White supremacy ideology and White racial knowledge may be harder or easier based on how incongruent they seem to be with one another. Overall, everyone may choose to adopt any number of beliefs about privilege based on where they find themselves in relationship to participation in the Whiteness or Antiracism Discourses.

What These Beliefs Offer Us

Ideological stances are used by individuals to make meaning of their reality. However, ideologies both exist and are shared within the Discourses in which individuals participate.[15] Therefore, ideologies are simultaneously social and individualistic because the multiple Discourses in which individuals participate socializes them around a multitude of beliefs they may choose to adopt or reject. The beliefs an individual chooses to adopt simultaneously influences the extent to which they can participate in certain Discourses that either embrace or reject those same beliefs. Over time, individuals may choose to alter which beliefs they adopt or reject, influencing the extent to which these individuals participate in various Discourses over others.

The beliefs individuals adopt to interpret privilege simultaneously draw upon and reinforce select ideas about privilege. A belief that privilege is knowable through the experiences of marginalized communities is built upon the idea of social power unequally distributed based upon social group memberships. Furthermore, the idea that social power is unequally distributed based upon social group memberships suggests that those groups without power are better situated to view the benefits they are purposefully denied. Similarly, a belief that privilege is individualistic is based upon the idea that privilege is situational relative to a localized context of any individual. Additionally, the idea that privilege is situational relative to a localized context of any individual suggests that some level of equality must already exist and that individual circumstances better explain social inequality than social group memberships. Beliefs help individuals see reality in a particular way that supports their existing view through select ideas.

The specific beliefs central to both a White supremacy ideology and a race critical ideology reveal the specific ways individuals use various ideas in the service of maintaining a particular understanding of privilege. While beliefs are not merely the sum of an individual's ideas, beliefs are easier or harder to maintain depending on the presence of these ideas. Therefore, understanding the specific frames within the ideologies central to the Whiteness and Antiracism Discourses illustrate different paths to adopt or reject privilege as either a structural or individualistic phenomenon. By understanding what these beliefs are, and which ideas are pivotal to their utility to explain reality, it is possible to leverage different ideas to reinforce or challenge beliefs as part of the process of unlearning views within the Whiteness Discourse and internalizing views central to the Antiracism Discourse.

For example, consider the belief that society is fair and therefore all people have equal opportunity to succeed as individuals. This belief is propped up by ideas that privilege is situational, ahistorical, and based upon the choices made by individuals. Because our beliefs inform what information we acknowledge, these three ideas act as filters through which evidence is screened relative to our beliefs. If an educator wanted to influence a student who adopted a belief that society is fair, it is important to know that referencing history would not likely be effective since it would be detected as irrelevant based on both the ideas of privilege being ahistorical and situational because the past exceeds the boundaries of an individual's situation relative to having privilege. Therefore, one strategy might entail identifying numerous contemporary "situations" where individual White people from similar backgrounds have privilege and individual people of color from similar backgrounds are denied privilege. This approach would use examples of privilege that are not historical and minimize the variability between these individuals' "situations," leaving the student to consider how rational it is to believe that people are sufficiently able to make choices to be successful. If educators are able to identify these beliefs and their associated ideas, they may have a greater chance of successfully being able to cultivate cognitive dissonance between what a student believes and what evidence they are willing to consider.

Key Takeaways

1. There are two different ideological stances that rely upon and are reinforced by select ideas used to interpret the nature and relevance of privilege.
2. A race critical ideology consists of three beliefs that operate to acknowledge and explore the existence of privilege as a structural phenomenon.

3. The three beliefs common with a race critical ideology include beliefs that (a) race is a social construction, (b) racial privilege and oppression are ordinary phenomena manifested through the normalization of Whiteness, and (c) racial privilege and oppression are knowable through the experiences of people of color.
4. The belief that race is a social construction is connected to the idea that privilege is a manifestation of social power.
5. The belief that racial privilege and oppression are ordinary phenomena as a result of how Whiteness is normalized is connected to the ideas that privilege is intentionally implemented and situated in both the past and the present.
6. The belief that racial privilege and oppression are knowable through the experiences of people of color connect to the ideas that privilege is a manifestation of social power, intentionally implemented, rooted in institutionalized superiority, and situated in both the past and the present.
7. A White supremacist ideology consists of three beliefs that operate to reject the notion that privilege is a structural phenomenon and offer counter explanations that privilege is better understood as individualistic.
8. The three beliefs common with a White supremacist ideology include beliefs that (a) society is fair, (b) social inequality is natural, and (c) privilege is individualistic, not structural.
9. A belief that society is fair and everyone has equal opportunities for success is connected to the ideas that privilege is situational, ahistorical, and a reflection of the personal choices we make.
10. The belief that privilege is a natural extension of the human experience based on biological, psychological, or sociological reasoning is connected to the ideas that privilege is linked to individual bias, is situational, and is based upon choices to be biased or random chance.
11. The belief that privilege is not structural and is better understood as individualistic is connected primarily to the idea that privilege is situational and secondarily to the ideas that privilege is ahistorical and based upon individual choices.
12. Because all individuals within the United States are socialized into the Whiteness Discourse, everyone has some level of familiarity with the beliefs central to the White supremacist ideology; however, it is possible for individuals to unlearn these beliefs and adopt beliefs central to a race critical ideology.
13. The ability to notice these ideas and the idea categories into which they fall can support educators in understanding a student's presenting logic to increase their effectiveness in their educational intervention.

Notes

1 See Mascaro and Daly (2021).
2 See MSNBC (2021), Simon and Sidner (2021).
3 See Warren (2021).
4 See Bonilla-Silva (2014).

5 See Dyson's (2001) writing about how Rev. Dr. Martin Luther King Jr.'s male privilege and his status as a Christian preacher indelibly shaped his actions for Civil Rights; See Summitt's (2008) biography that discusses Sacagawea's life.
6 See Bonilla-Silva (2014).
7 See NBC News (2021).
8 Ibid.
9 See NewsmaxTV (2021, 11:20).
10 See Mitchell (2021, paras. 3, 13).
11 See Keleher (2021, para. 7).
12 See Bhuyan (2019).
13 See Feagin (2013).
14 See Allan (2015), Comedy Central (2014), and Fox News (2017, 2020).
15 See Althusser (1971, 2003), Gee (1996), and Hall (1996).

References

Allan, J. (2015, November 28). *Ben Shapiro destroys the concept of White privilege* [Video file]. *YouTube.* www.youtube.com/watch?v=rrxZRuL65wQ.

Althusser, L. (1971). *Lenin and philosophy* (B. Brewster, Trans.). Monthly Review Press.

Althusser, L. (2003). *The humanist controversy and other writings* (F. Matheron, Ed. and Trans., and G. M. Goshgarian, Trans.). Verso.

Bhuyan, N. (2019, September 18). Don't blame mental illness for mass shootings. [Blog post]. *American Academic of Family Physicians.* www.aafp.org/news/blogs/freshperspectives/entry/20190918fp-massshootings.html.

Bonilla-Silva, E. (2014). *Racism without racists: Color-blind racism and the persistence of racial inequality in America* (4th ed.). Rowman & Littlefield Publishers.

Comedy Central. (2014, October 16). *The daily show: Bill O'Reilly extended interview* [Video file]. *YouTube.* www.youtube.com/watch?v=8raaT7SRx18.

Delgado, R., & Stefancic, J. (2012). *Critical race theory: An introduction* (2nd ed.). New York University Press.

Dyson, M. E. (2001). *I may not get there with you: The true Martin Luther King, Jr.* Touchstone.

Feagin, J. R. (2013). *The White racial frame: Centuries of racial framing and counter-framing* (2nd ed.). Routledge.

Fox News. (2017, February 2). *Dyson: Whites should open individual reparations accounts* [Video file]. http://video.foxnews.com/v/5308799067001/?#sp=show-clips.

Fox News. (2020, September 9). *Tucker: Critical race theory is a lie from start to finish.* [Video clip]. https://video.foxnews.com/v/6188946152001?playlist_id=5198073478001#sp=show-clips.

Gee, J. P. (1996). *Social linguistics and literacies: Ideology in discourses* (2nd ed.). Taylor & Francis.

Hall, S. (1996). The problem of ideology: Marxism without guarantees. In D. Morley & K. Chen (Eds.), *Stuart Hall: Critical dialogues in cultural studies* (pp. 25–46). Routledge.

Keleher, K. (2021, January 7). Rep. Markwayne Mullin describes coming face-to-face with rioters in Capitol. *KJRH News.* www.kjrh.com/news/local-news/rep-mullin-describes-coming-face-to-face-with-rioters-in-capitol.

Mascaro, L., & Daly, M. (2021, January 7). Capitol siege by pro-Trump mob forces questions, ousters. *Associated Press.* https://apnews.com/article/election-2020-joe-biden-donald-trump-media-elections-73dacf9bc0d906f4efe358279520eeac.

Mitchell, C. (2021, January 7). Chicago police union president defends those who stormed the U.S. Capitol. *WBEZ.* www.wbez.org/stories/chicago-police-union-president-defends-those-who-stormed-us-capitol/6842fa80-3b83-4396-af05-a5f15f4ac740.

MSNBC. (2021, January 6). *Joy Reid: If this was a BLM protest, 'there would already be people shackled, arrested or dead'*. [Video file]. www.msnbc.com/msnbc/watch/joy-reid-if-this-was-a-blm-protest-there-would-already-be-people-shackled-arrested-or-dead-98978373607.

NBC News. (2021, January 10). *Meet the Press: Jan. 10 – Mick Mulvaney, Rep. Hakeen Jeffries, Sen. Pat Toomey*. [Video file]. www.nbcnews.com/meet-the-press/video/jan-10-mick-mulvaney-rep-hakeem-jeffries-sen-pat-toomey-99229765546.

NewsmaxTV. (2021, January 8). *Spicer & Co*. [Video file]. www.newsmaxtv.com/Shows/Spicer-and-Co/vid/1_6f31l0z6.

Simon, M., & Sidner, S. (2021, January 11). Decoding the extremist symbols and groups at the Capitol Hill insurrection. *CNN*. www.cnn.com/2021/01/07/opinions/capitol-rioters-contrast-with-june-2020-black-lives-matter-jones/index.html.

Summitt, A. R. (2008). *Sacagawea: A biography*. Greenwood Press.

Warren, D. (2021, January 7). Capitol police treatment of Trump rioters underscores America's racist reality. *NBC News*. www.nbcnews.com/think/opinion/capitol-police-treatment-trump-rioters-underscores-america-s-racist-reality-ncna1253293.

5
COMPELLING FEELINGS ABOUT PRIVILEGE

Ever since I was old enough to vote, I have treated election days as a holiday. There is something special and sacred to me about influencing society by exercising the right to vote, a right that was and still is denied to various groups of people based on their social group memberships.[1] I find myself compelled to absorb as much information as possible before voting which contributes to very strong emotions once the results are projected and finalized.

My emotional investment in politics contributes to a roller coaster of emotions, especially around presidential elections. When Barack Obama was projected to become the first Black man elected President of the United States back in 2008 (and again in 2012), I was ecstatic and filled with hope for the country and the world. I loved walking around and noticing the number of people wearing Obama-related apparel. These were my people and when we would make eye contact, we would exchange a knowing smile to confirm this connection we shared.

When I awoke the day after the 2016 election to discover Donald Trump was projected to become the next President, I felt numb, anxious, and angry. Under the new administration, I often felt angry whenever I spied red baseball hats, even before I could verify that they were MAGA hats, a symbol of those who shared Trump's values and convictions. At the same time, I would actively look for signs that read "hate has no home here" or "Black Lives Matter" to feel like I was around others who shared my values. During his administration, I sought solace from others who shared my concerns and worked with them to double our efforts for social change through political activity and organizing. When I would encounter someone who thought Trump was not as horrible as I evaluated him to be, I questioned their commitment to values of social justice and the common good.

When I look back on the emotional roller coaster related to these presidential elections, I am reminded of the powerful role emotion plays in our relationships.

DOI: 10.4324/9781003082378-6

My emotional journey was a combination of feelings that were a reaction to stimuli (e.g., the outcome of an election) that were directed toward someone or something (e.g., myself, others, institutions, the president) for a particular purpose (e.g., to create change, to connect with others). However, these feelings did not exist on their own but were deeply connected to my ideas and beliefs about what was good for society. While my emotions felt like mine alone, emotions are simultaneously internal and social, reflecting how I viewed myself, others, and society.[2] My emotionality operated to create connections with others similar to myself while interrupting any desire to form connections with others who did not share my feelings. In total, my emotional journey was connected to my ideas and beliefs that actively shaped how I related to myself and others in society.

Our feelings related to privilege and social inequality are equally influential to our ideas and beliefs. These feelings are also connected to the social groups in which we actively participate, shaping how we view and relate to others and ourselves.[3] The White college students in my research study expressed a multitude of feelings in regard to privilege. These feelings were expressed through explicit language (e.g., "I feel . . .") or through a collection of verbal and nonverbal discursive cues (e.g., facial expressions, gestures, posture, word choice, vocalization). Their feelings were uniquely expressed, purposefully directed, and intentionally used for particular outcomes that coincided with participation in the Antiracism or Whiteness Discourses. In the context of privilege and social inequality, their feelings demonstrated how emotions are sites of social control and political resistance which we are socialized to adopt.[4]

I present a range of purposive feelings and the ways in which they are expressed in the context of their respective Discourses. While I continue to use examples from these White college students, their emotional responses did not align as neatly as their ideas and beliefs shared in the previous chapters. What follows is a discussion about these feelings, including the ways in which they are expressed, directed, and used to expose and dismantle or deflect and sustain privilege in relationship to various beliefs and ideas discussed in Chapters 3 and 4. Finally, I explore how these feelings relate to one another and expose the challenges of shifting participation from the Whiteness Discourse to the Antiracism Discourse.

Racial Emotional Resiliency: Emotionality That Facilitates Social Change

Central to the Antiracism Discourse is racial emotional resiliency. Racial emotional resiliency refers to a set of feelings, as well as the allowance to experience and express those feelings, that are primarily directed toward unjust systems to fuel social change. Consistent with the purpose of the Antiracism Discourse, racial emotional resiliency operates to dismantle privilege and social inequality and uses emotionality for this goal. A core set of feelings central to racial emotional resiliency includes feeling upset, shame, anger or frustration, and determination.

Allowing oneself to experience emotions is central to racial emotional resiliency for two reasons. First, emotion is pivotal to the development of knowledge and skills as part of embracing social justice.[5] Second, emotionality is viewed as antithetical to Whiteness, which minimizes emotionality in favor of a supposed objective rationality.[6] When individuals lean into emotions, including challenging painful emotions, it is possible to uncover uncomfortable truths that are critical to growth. In the context of privilege and social inequality, exploring emotions can help individuals recognize and let go of harmful ideas and beliefs that position them as superior to others.[7] For example, feeling ashamed when confronted with the ways we personally reinforce privilege can reveal ways we let others down along with opportunities to make different choices in the future.

Feeling upset, shame, anger or frustration, and determination are all emotions that have been identified as common among those who work for social change. When individuals "wake up" from the belief that social groups are superior to others, it is common for them to experience many of these feelings as they reconcile their newfound awareness about the privilege they receive from their social identities juxtaposed with their prior knowledge and experience.[8] Individuals may feel ashamed for having believed they were superior to others, along with their actions that perpetuated privilege and social inequality. They might feel angry or frustrated with other people who share these beliefs and with the existence of social inequality and privilege overall. It is common to feel upset when faced with the fact that privilege and social inequality are so deeply ingrained into our social institutions and cultural ways of being even though it is false. However, as individuals come to recognize the magnitude of systemic privilege, feelings of determination are cultivated in order to sustain themselves in a long-term effort to challenge and dismantle social inequality. The range of feelings coupled with the long-term goal that they help produce are why I discuss them as part of racial emotional *resiliency*. Simply experiencing these emotions is not enough, but they must be joined with a resiliency to persevere in the uphill fight against privilege.

The concept of racial emotional resiliency presented above is imperfectly reflected in the discourse of the White students in my study. As Bobbie Harro's cycles of socialization and liberation make clear, the process of "waking up" from systemic dominance is difficult because it happens in direct opposition to our de facto socialization into the Whiteness Discourse that begins at birth.[9] While the students in my study do reflect all these aspects of racial emotional resiliency, they more readily illustrate White students in the process of developing this third aspect of participating in the Antiracism Discourse.

Vulnerability Through Emotional Expression (I Feel)

One core feature of racial emotional resiliency is the ability and willingness to express one's emotions. The act of sharing feelings makes them visible to others and ourselves, making it possible to be supported (e.g., "it's okay to feel afraid.") or challenged (e.g., "You have no right to feel angry at me."). Sharing feelings contributes to a sense of vulnerability because in doing so we open ourselves up to be held accountable by others for those feelings. In the context of privilege and social inequality, exploring and expressing emotions are equally critical to our development when working toward social justice.[10]

Anna, Jane, and Scott all explicitly used the signal phrase "I feel" to describe their feelings and associated experiences and thoughts related to privilege. Anna explicitly stated feeling uncomfortable, ashamed, and upset when reflecting on past conversations about privilege in class. She also theorized how she would feel if a faculty member used the political cartoon in one of her classes.[11] Anna stated the following:

> I would feel maybe a little uncomfortable . . . the idea of discussing race [also] makes me a little uncomfortable. But not in a bad way, like in a way where I get upset and [recognize] I do have this privilege and I shouldn't . . . I think that if you're having a good conversation you can feel uncomfortable because you want to apologize for having this privilege. You feel bad for that and well, that's a step. But feeling bad about it isn't going to change anything in the sense of like, "Darn, I have privilege. I'm so sad about it. Someone comfort me." Like that's not going to produce any results. It's more [about] listening to people who are oppressed and hearing from them.

Anna described how racial conversations make her feel uncomfortable. She continued to reflect about how discomfort should help to acknowledge one's own privilege and consider different ways of acting. Anna also clarified that her discomfort was not a desire to be comforted by others, something that was a "bad way" to feel uncomfortable because it did not contribute to reflection or social change. In her comments, she used the phrase "a little" to intentionally quantify her level of discomfort.

Jane also explicitly verbalized her feeling uncomfortable when discussing privilege. Jane shared her feelings when reflecting on her experience participating in our interview:

> It's a little bit uncomfortable to talk about. I feel like there is almost a taboo to talk about [privilege]. I don't want to say the wrong thing, you know? Because I don't want to sound like an idiot, but also because I don't want to hurt people, even if it's just you and me in the conversation, I just don't want to be mean, you know? So, I felt a little nervous to talk about it just because I don't want to say the wrong thing. You know? Not that I don't believe [it's important], but I feel like I just don't want anything I say to be perceived the wrong way.

Jane confessed feeling uncomfortable during our interview for two reasons. First, she wanted to preserve her perception in the eyes of others by not sounding "like an idiot" or saying the "wrong thing." Second, she shared her concern for negatively impacting others by saying things that might be "mean" and "hurt" them. She also repeatedly sought affirmation from me, presumably as a White person she perceived to participate in the Antiracism Discourse, by asking "you know?" Her desire for affirmation from me suggests how emotions are one way in which individuals share a connection as participants in a similar Discourse. Like Anna, she also used the phrase "a little" repeatedly to quantify her feelings during her reflection.

Scott described feeling ashamed in response to viewing the political cartoon and feeling hopeless and sad during past conversations about privilege in class. Scott also theorized how he would feel if a faculty member used the political cartoon in one of his classes:

> I don't really have that much individual ability to change [privilege]. I wish I could just go right to the Supreme Court and do something really effective. It kind of makes me feel a little bit hopeless because I feel like no matter how hard people are going to try, there is always going to be this whole setback [such as] the losing 50 turns, lose 100 turns [for the Black character] that was in this image.

Scott expressed feeling hopeless about his ability to change privilege because he views it as an institutionalized phenomenon that is bigger than himself as a single individual. Contrary to Anna's previous quote, Scott's feelings of hopelessness did not inspire social change but instead was paralyzing. His analysis of the institutionalization of privilege withered his determination and prevented him from considering ways in which he could take action. Like Anna and Jane, he quantified his feelings as "a little" hopeless and his perception that he did not "have that much" ability to influence change.

All three of these students demonstrated a willingness to share their emotions, as is the case with racial emotional resiliency. However, it is critical to note that all three students also intentionally quantified their feelings to a lesser degree using variations of the phrase "a little." Using this common modifier worked to provide some distance between themselves and their feelings. Distancing oneself from one's emotions makes it harder to be held accountable and inspire social change. Therefore, these students demonstrated limited racial emotional resiliency in this regard.

Being "Upset"

When people express feeling upset, it tends to capture moments when the stability or peacefulness one is accustomed to becomes destabilized. Feeling upset regarding privilege aligns with racial emotional resiliency because these feelings destabilized individuals from feeling complacent with the status quo that sustains Whiteness. Anna, Jane, and Scott all expressed feeling "upset" when faced with the realities of privilege and social inequality.

Anna verbalized feeling "upset" repeatedly throughout her interview. She expressed feeling upset in response to viewing the political cartoon, saying "It's a very upsetting because there is no reason for [social inequality]. The fact that these disadvantages are put on people for very, very literally no reason at all. It's just, it's ridiculous and it's upsetting." In her response, she was able to connect her emotional reaction to the "ridiculous" existence of social inequality that was not justifiable. Anna later confessed feeling upset when reflecting on her experience during the interview:

> [Privilege is] upsetting. Not as much for me firsthand, but especially to talk about race relations, I just don't get it. Not to say that I don't hold any ingrained racism or biases that have been put in me, and not to say that I am a perfect example of someone, I like to think that I try and that I work on it. . . . I want other people who have experienced this type of oppression to tell me how to be better all the time. I would love that because I'm not [perfect]. But it is just something that when consciously thought about, I just cannot fathom this belief that certain people are better than other people based on race.

Anna verbalized feeling upset because of privilege in general and racial privilege in particular. She specifically cited feeling upset that some White people believe they are superior to people of color solely based on race. However, her commentary connected her feeling upset with a desire to grow in her own awareness, citing her ingrained racism and biases. She stated a desire for, and openness to, feedback from people of color to help her be better as a way to resolve her feeling upset because of the existence of privilege. While her desire could be interpreted as wanting to take the lead from people of color, a stance that would be consistent with participating in the Antiracism Discourse, it is more likely that she shifted responsibility to people of color to educate her about social change versus taking responsibility for that work herself.

Jane also verbalized feeling "upset" in response to viewing the political cartoon:

> It's upsetting for sure. . . . The fact that everyone knows about slavery, and Jim Crow, and the Civil Rights [movement] . . . but I think currently there are people that like to deny [these things] after this turn, all the new stuff [including poor schools, a wealth gap]. . . . I feel like people don't really talk about that as being in the same [category]. Also, just the fact that it's [called] the American dream game when it should be all of us lifting each other up versus playing a game and competing. It shouldn't be a competition; it should be lifting up the people that need the help.

Jane verbalized feeling upset for two interconnected reasons. First, she was upset because White people deny contemporary manifestations of racial oppression even though she believes everyone knows about historical racial oppression. Her feeling upset was directly connected to the idea of privilege as ahistorical, an idea central to White racial knowledge. Second, she expressed feeling upset because the political cartoon depicted social inequality as a competitive game, a notion supported by the belief that society is fair, central to a White supremacy ideology. Instead, Jane felt that society should work collaboratively to "lift up" those who are oppressed. Collectively, Jane connected her feeling upset to common ideas and beliefs used by participants in the Whiteness Discourse while simultaneously articulating a more socially just vision.

Scott expressed feeling upset when discussing contributions to oppression:

> The fact that people who are privileged aren't really doing anything about it, can kind of continue [oppression] and just keep it as the same old way that things are . . . definitely. Honestly the whole idea of privilege is so annoying to me because it's so annoying that people are even mistreated, it just really irks me. So, when I am thinking about the reasons, it's really hard to even understand why. Because for me I don't really see a reason for it, you know?

While Scott verbalized feeling "annoying" and "irked," phrases more commonly associated with frustration and anger, his demeanor appeared upset as he reflected on privilege. He expressed feeling upset with the phenomenon of privilege because it is unjustifiable. While he understood how privilege operates, he was emotionally unsettled when attempting to reconcile how individuals created and continued to sustain a system that benefits some through the mistreatment of others. He seemed unable to reconcile his belief in equality with a reality where people justify privilege and oppression.

Anna, Jane, and Scott all demonstrated or verbalized feeling upset when faced with the reality of privilege. A common cause of feeling upset stemmed from either (a) reconciling their views about a just society relative to the realities of privilege or (b) the ways in which people who participate in the Whiteness Discourse express their views about privilege. While all three students felt upset in ways that could have inspired a commitment to social action, only Anna indicated a desire to increase her awareness as an extension of her feelings. Jane's feeling upset helped her to articulate her vision of a better society but not ways in which she was willing to take action to work toward her own vision. Scott identified the lack of action for change among White people as a source of feeling upset; however, he did not talk about ways in which he was willing to act himself. Overall, the destabilization related to feeling upset can be useful when individuals are resilient enough to be compelled to act for change. However, if individuals are only destabilized without a commitment to act, it only partially aligns with racial emotional resiliency.

Feeling Shame

Feelings of shame (or guilt) arise when individuals feel distressed by their own actions. When the shame a person feels contributes to internalized accountability and a desire to do better in the future, it can align with racial emotional resiliency. Anna was the only White student who expressed feeling ashamed in the context of conversations about privilege, specifically when discussing racial privilege with others.

Anna verbalized feeling ashamed when reflecting on a classroom activity where students depicted their social identities relative to one another in a pie chart, including how they experience privilege or oppression related to each. Specifically, she felt ashamed when discussing her privileged identities with another peer in her class:

> When you talk to someone who had more privileges than you, or that you had more privileges than them and vice versa. I don't know if like ashamed is the right word, but feeling almost ashamed based on certain things . . . and seeing what some people didn't put on their wheels felt weird. To see people not put their ability status on there, because they didn't think about it, and then to be someone who's chronically ill and have that be a larger thing was an affirmation that people aren't thinking about the privileges that they have . . . acknowledging the fact that people don't think about the privileges that they hold over you and being forced to think about the privileges that you hold over other people.

Anna's feelings of shame arose when noticing how much privilege someone had relative to someone else and also when that privilege was invisible to them. She specifically recalled feeling "weird" noticing how her peers failed to acknowledge their able-bodied privilege when she herself identified as a person with a disability. Anna was able to connect this experience to her other privileged identities, which inspired her to reflect about "the privileges that you hold over other people." Overall, the conversation about privilege was a catalyst for awareness, and that awareness inspired her feelings of shame. However, she later expressed how feeling ashamed contributed to "this feeling of needing to do something . . . that need or want for change and that feeling for activism." For Anna, shame was potentially productive in its ability to motivate her to take action to redress racial inequality.

Feeling Anger Toward Systems

Feelings of anger, or its milder counterpart frustration, arise when individuals feel some degree of irritation. When these feelings arise, they are directed toward what is perceived to be the cause, typically something or someone. When individuals exhibit racial emotional resiliency, they tend to direct feelings of anger and frustration toward systems where privilege is institutionalized or people who, through their participation in the Whiteness Discourse, maintain social inequality.

For these feelings to align with racial emotional resiliency, they would need to serve as fuel to act for social change.

Jane and Scott both verbalized their anger toward systemic privilege and oppression in their written reflection papers. Jane wrote about her privilege as a cisgender woman, comparing it to her high school transgender classmate's experience of oppression. Jane offered the following conclusion after retelling her classmate's challenges:

> This glaring societal oppression still gets me angry. All she wanted was equal access to things allotted to her gender, but that was denied. I would have never been in a situation where my entire school experience is a never-ending battle for my identity and rights, and it is all due to my privilege of being cisgender.

Jane explicitly verbalized her anger toward the systemic inequality related to gender that privileged herself and oppressed her classmate. She concluded her paper with a desire to "fight for the rights of others" as "a listener and participant [instead of] a leader in social change in groups that I did not represent." While Jane did connect her anger toward social inequality to a desire for action, she qualified her commitment as a follower of others in this work.

Scott also reflected on his White privilege relative to racial oppression experience by Black people in his reflection paper:

> Watching the news and hearing about the all too frequent oppression of mainly African Americans really makes me grateful for my Whiteness, but it also makes me angry. Angry that I am put on a higher pedestal for only a fraction of my social identity while so many others suffer in their oppression. Being from an arguably "elevated" social position, it can sometimes be awkward to bring up race-related issues with minority groups. Sometimes when I am talking to a Black person about racism in America and the oppression of African Americans, I am nervous that I'm stepping on toes or being out of line. The most important thing I can do to better race relations is to continue being an ally of the BLM movement and other equalizing forces, in an attempt to achieving social justice.

Scott simultaneously expressed gratitude for his racial privilege and anger toward racial inequalities that privilege White people at the expense of people of color. While he confessed feeling "awkward" and "nervous" when discussing race with people of color in general and Black people in particular, he decided that he needed to work for social change by supporting social movements led by the Black community. While it is important for White people to support communities of color in their efforts for social change, his admitted hesitancy suggested that his commitment to social change was through a more passive role similarly expressed by Jane.

138 Compelling Feelings About Privilege

Unlike feelings of anger that were directed toward systemic inequality, feelings of frustration were primarily directed toward individuals participating in the Whiteness Discourse. Anna, Jamie, Jane, and Scott all verbalized or exhibited behaviors consistent with being "frustrated" or "irritated."

Anna expressed frustration when discussing privilege generally, racial privilege specifically, and the political cartoon. She expressed her frustration in the form of impersonating individuals who participate in the Whiteness Discourse, and those impersonations appeared to make individuals participating in the Whiteness Discourse seem arrogant and ignorant. She did this once while describing institutional supremacy, stating "this idea of just a difference and then relating that difference to being superior, and being like, 'Oh, well *I* am *civilized.*' But the idea of being civilized was literally just created to demean other cultures." Anna performed another impersonation when discussing the political cartoon previously discussed in Chapter 4:

> The idea of affirmative action and the "get one free turn" [space] is kind of an interesting thing to add there, because it's true and people are using [it] today as like, "Oh boy, you have affirmative action, you're fine, like you'll probably get the job over me because you're Black and I'm White. My life is now at a disadvantage" . . . [However] they do get one free turn. But then compared to the number of turns that other people [get], the other things that have been put in place like lots and lots of turns as opposed to getting one free turn.

Both of Anna's impersonations were rhetorical moves to draw attention to what she found to be unfounded and absurd views common to the Whiteness Discourse.

Anna demonstrated feelings of frustration through her tone and word choice. Her voice sounded fatigued when describing how often her peers claim, "We live in a post-racial America, which is such a tough saying." Later in her interview, her tone and word choice expressed agitation when explaining the root cause of racial privilege as previously discussed in Chapter 4:

> Superiority complexes . . . this belief system based on trivial things that were set up by someone who had all the answers already. Like just this idea of White people being better because they knew X, Y, and Z, but they freaking created X, Y, and Z. . . . Like the idea that people could come and try and colonize America, to come and move to America, almost starve to death and die, and literally only survive because Native Americans knew how to farm and like help them.

Anna was very expressive when identifying a belief in White supremacy and critiquing it using the idea that privilege is built upon institutionalized superiority that was "freaking created" by White people. She was visibly frustrated with both a belief in White supremacy and those who adopt these irrationally false views that oppress others.

Jamie verbalized how "annoying and frustrating" she found the political cartoon. She specifically directed her feelings toward the individuals who participate in the Whiteness Discourse as embodied by the White character in the political cartoon:

> Just the smug way that the White guy is saying, "Are you just slow or what?" because, I know he doesn't realize that this path was that bad. And the Black guy is looking at him like, "Really, are you serious right now?" but yeah, they are clearly on very different wavelengths.

Jamie provided an imaginary conversation between the characters in the political cartoon to express her frustration with the absurdity of the White character's comment. While she acknowledged how the White character failed to recognize his privilege, it was the lack of awareness among White people about their racial privilege that was the focus of her frustration.

Jane expressed frustration when discussing gender inequalities in her reflection paper. She described how her teachers in school were permissive toward her male peers who were talkative and "class clowns" while punishing her for the same behaviors. While summarizing what she learned from these differences in treatment, she stated, "I learned to reign in my behavior later in my elementary years, but those wise-cracking boys never did." Her description of the "wise-cracking boys" revealed her frustration with them and her teacher for maintaining unequal treatment that privileged boys over girls. Jane more directly expressed this same frustration toward individuals who participate in the Whiteness Discourse when imagining how she would explain privilege to a White male peer. She verbalized how "annoying" both that peer would be as well as the need to explain privilege to them. After offering a thoughtful explanation, she expressed frustration toward her peer because she assumed he would not accept her reasoning:

> I feel like it would be really easy for someone to brush that off, and say "Well that's not true, slavery is over. So, it's over" you know what I mean? I mean, like the argument's been made a billion times if you will, annoyingly.

Jane's frustration was directed toward her White male peer because of his rejection of privilege. Similar to Anna and Jamie, Jane performed an impersonation of her peer as part of her frustration with his "annoying" rebuttal. Collectively, she expressed frustration with individuals who participate in the Whiteness Discourse because of how they fail to understand, yet benefit from, privilege.

Scott verbally and nonverbally expressed frustration when also imagining how he would explain privilege to a White person. When asked to imagine that his peer did not understand his first explanation and he would have to try again, he scrunched his face and explained how he was feeling:

> I was just thinking seriously, you don't get it by now? I've made it crystal clear. But that's just a big frustration, the fact that people don't understand it. People don't really get the fact that they are so lucky for what they have. It's kind of hard to kind of break that wall and to kind of get into that level where they can understand.

Scott explained the source of his frustration as individuals who do not "get" the concept of privilege, alluding to individuals who participate in the Whiteness Discourse. He acknowledged that such individuals fail to see how they benefit from privilege, making it hard to effectively explain privilege to them which he found frustrating.

Anna, Jamie, Jane, and Scott all expressed frustration directed toward others who do not understand privilege, such as individuals who participate in the Whiteness Discourse. Most of them verbalized their feelings or performed impersonations as part of expressing their feelings. Unlike feelings of anger which seemed to motivate a desire for social change, feelings of frustration directed toward individuals who participate in the Whiteness Discourse seemed to make it harder to want to engage others in conversation as a vehicle for bringing about social change.

Feeling Determination

Racial emotional resiliency entails emotions that contribute to social change. However, feeling compelled to act despite obstacles, a feeling of determination, is also possible without a mediating emotion. Individuals who participate in the Antiracism Discourse feel determined to challenge and dismantle Whiteness despite its deep and pervasive entrenchment across social institutions and hegemonic norms. Feeling of determination for social change can arise based on an individual's conceptual or ideological view. Anna and Jane were the only two students who demonstrated a feeling of determination for social change.

Anna expressed her determination for social change when describing her feelings associated with conversations about race and racial privilege:

> [I have] this feeling of needing to do something which I feel rings true in all matters of privilege or oppression. Because even if I'm talking about something that I have experienced personally, there is that need or want for change and that feeling for activism.

Anna verbalized feeling compelled to act for social change in the context of conversations about race and racial privilege. She explicitly connected her desire for activism to both dismantling oppression and privilege. While Anna previously expressed other emotions that contributed to her desire for social change, here she explicitly expressed determination for change on its own.

Jane wrote about her determination for social change in her reflection paper. Her expression of determination arose when writing about her response to witnessing sexism:

> When I see sexism, I call it out. It may make men uncomfortable, but that temporary discomfort pales in comparison to the discomfort countless women face daily when men catcall them, when they get paid less than men for the same work, when they don't receive adequate maternity benefits in America, and when they are perceived as "bossy and bitchy" instead of a leader.

Jane demonstrated a feeling of determination by explicitly describing her reaction to witnessing gendered privilege and oppression. Her writing illuminated her desire for social change as a result of the reality of sexism without any intermediary emotions. Jane's ability to name multiple iterations of sexism as a reason for her desire to "call out" gendered privilege and oppression connects her determination to her view of sexism as wrong based on her conceptual understanding.

Expressions of determination were the least commonly observed emotion among the students in my study. Anna and Jane expressed feeling determined to act for social change based on their understanding of privilege and oppression as unjust. In both Anna's and Jane's comments, their feeling of determination seemed personal. Anna expressed an internalized sense of responsibility for action. Jane's desire for action seemed grounded in her personal experience around gendered oppression. Collectively, a feeling of determination may arise when privilege and oppression is made to feel personal.

How Feelings That Facilitate Social Change Work Together

Allowing oneself to be emotionally vulnerable, along with feeling upset, ashamed, angry, and determined may, seem to reflect a disparate grouping of feelings and expressions. It may seem intuitive for feelings of shame to align with emotional expression that appears vulnerable. However, feeling determined or angry hardly seem an intuitive fit with emotional vulnerability. Similarly, it may seem instinctive for feelings of determination and anger to contribute to social change but not necessarily feelings of shame. While these emotions and their expression are not the same *categorically*, they are similar in their *functionality*.

Musical instruments provide a useful analogy for how emotions may be categorized differently yet function in a similar way. In a full orchestra, instruments can be classified as woodwinds (e.g., flute, clarinet), brass (e.g., trumpet, trombone), strings (e.g., violin, cello), or percussion (e.g., snare drum, xylophone). Instruments are categorized based on the way sound is produced by blowing (woodwinds), buzzing (brass), rubbing (strings), or striking (percussion). Even though there are important differences in how sound is produced, they all share the same function of producing sounds as part of music. In the same way, emotions differ categorically in their expression yet function similarly to support social change.

Emotional vulnerability, feeling upset, ashamed, angry, and determined are all avenues toward social change. This group of feelings and expressions are functionally similar in that they facilitate social change directed either internally toward the self or externally toward other people or institutions. Feeling upset is primarily directed inward as individuals lean into the dissonance between the world as it is and the world they aspire to create, creating a healthy tension that can lead to action. Feeling ashamed is primarily directed internally as individuals reflect on their privilege and what actions they can take to minimize the ways they actively or passively sustain privilege in their lives. Feeling angry is primarily directed externally toward either systems of inequality or those who sustain these systems in order to change those systems or persuade those individuals. Feeling determination can be directed internally or externally for social change depending on the impetus for one's sense of resolve. Emotional vulnerability does not directly contribute to social change; however, the ability to be vulnerable increases the likelihood that an individual is open to growth. Therefore, emotional vulnerability can lead to either internal or external change depending on whether someone uses their vulnerability to examine themselves (e.g., how they personally benefit from privilege) or their external reality (e.g., how their economic decisions sustain Whiteness).

The relationship between these four feelings and expressions to racial emotional resiliency is analogous to distinct lanes on the same highway. While each lane has boundaries that separate one from the others, these boundaries are permeable and all travel to the same destination. Just as cars may change lanes multiple times while driving down a single stretch of road, an individual who embodies racial emotional resiliency may exhibit multiple feelings along with emotional vulnerability in order to arrive as their ultimate destination of a more socially just reality.

Consider the following examples of these feelings and expressions and how they are used to facilitate a commitment to social change. Cheryl Strayed, a White female author and advice columnist in the *New York Times*, offered the following response to a writer named "Whitey" who felt paralyzed with feelings of shame about being White:

> Your race granted you privileges that were and are denied to people who are not white. . . . Every white person should be ashamed of that injustice. Which is different than being ashamed of being white. You don't have to relinquish your heritage to be an ally to people of color, Whitey. You have to relinquish your privilege. And part of learning how to do that is accepting that feelings of shame, anger and the sense that people are perceiving you in ways that you believe aren't accurate or fair are part of the process that you and I and all white people must endure in order to dismantle a toxic system that has perpetuated white supremacy for centuries.[12]

Strayed's commentary offers a critical distinction between feeling shame for one's racial identity versus the privilege and oppression distributed based upon one's racial identity. She explicitly states that feelings of shame ought to serve as a catalyst for social change, specifically actions that relinquish privilege and dismantle social inequality.

Tim Wise, a White antiracism educator who is an author, public speaker, and podcast host, provides multiple examples of how these feelings are manifested in ways that work toward social change. He does not shy away from emotional expressiveness and has explicitly stated the importance of emotional expression as a central part of a commitment to antiracism.[13] Fittingly, he is rather emotionally expressive himself. He demonstrates feelings of anger and frustration directed toward systemic inequality and individuals who participate in the Whiteness Discourse. His emotional intensity is clear through his louder volume, quicker pace, hand gestures, and the way he peppers swearing into his comments. For example, consider the following expert from a Black History Month keynote address critiquing "all lives matter" and connecting it to the US Constitution:

> When White people say all we never meant it. Black people know that. Brown people know that. Most White people never really had to learn that so we said all men are created equal and we didn't mean that shit. See, we said it but we didn't mean it. We said it, and we wrote Black people and Brown folks out of "all" so in fact when people of color hear, when Black and Brown folks hear "all lives matter" what they hear is the same thing they heard with all men are created equal . . . so if you want to actually make it clear that all lives matter a) you gotta act like all lives matter and you gotta really treat people like all lives matter, and b) you have to proclaim that the lives that you denigrated for centuries actually matter because that is the part that gets left out.[14] [12:34]

In the video of his remarks, Wise speaks with intensity and a fast tempo. He uses repetition to drive home his frustration with the existence of social inequality that exists in opposition to both the language of the US Constitution and the way White people proclaim to value all lives. However, he ends this segment of his comments with a clear call to action, making it clear that anger and frustration with social inequality can and should be challenged into actions that demonstrate a commitment to caring for all people, including acknowledging the historical and contemporary realities of social inequality.

Wise also demonstrates feelings of determination in his steadfast commitment to racial justice work and unwavering ability to articulate a vision for social change including what he can and should do as part of this work. For example, consider the last paragraph of his autobiography *White like Me*, as he reflects on the need to act for social change:

> I have no idea when (or if) racism will be eradicated. I have no idea whether anything I say, do, or write will make the least bit of difference in the world.

> But I say it, do it, and write it anyway, because as uncertain as the outcome of our resistance may be, the outcome of our silence and inaction is anything but. We know exactly what will happen if we don't do the work: nothing. And given that choice, between certainty and promise, in which territory one finds the measure of our resolve and humanity, I will opt for hope . . . if we are committed to the struggle because we know that our very humanity depends on it, that the fight for human liberation is among the things that give life meaning, then burnout is far less of a threat. We do the work to save our lives morally and ethically, if not physically.[15]

In his concluding remarks, Wise expressed determination for social action. His deliberate word choice confessed uncertainty for success while remaining adamantly convinced that he must remain committed to social action. His determination was explicitly connected to his view that social action is not only necessary but also critical to liberate both oppressed and privileged social groups alike.

While it may seem obvious that emotions can lead to social change, it is far from guaranteed. The students who embodied elements of racial emotional resilience felt and expressed emotions without always leading to social change. For some students, their emotions seemed to act like a road bump upon which they found themselves stuck. Emotions are also just as likely to lead to resistance of social change, as evidenced by students who embodied an emotionality of Whiteness.

Emotionality of Whiteness: Feelings That Resist Social Change

Central to the Whiteness Discourse is an emotionality of Whiteness. An emotionality of Whiteness refers to both feelings and how feeling language is used to divert attention away from privilege and Whiteness as an institutionalized phenomenon from which White people benefit at the expense of people of color. Instead, an emotionality of Whiteness uses feelings and feeling language to either shift attention to oneself as an emotionally distraught victim or toward people of color who are framed as perpetrators of injustice. Consistent with the purpose of the Whiteness Discourse, an emotionality of Whiteness works to reinforce the hegemonic nature of Whiteness by shifting attention away from itself and toward individuals.

Scholars have explored racialized emotions and their impact on protecting Whiteness. Cheryl Matias examined how White people use emotion and discursive maneuvers to protect their self-perception while simultaneously asserting their own dominance.[16] In particular, she discussed the "narcissism of Whiteness" when White people position their own feelings above both the reality of social oppression and any associated feelings expressed by people of color.[17] Unlike conventional interpretations of narcissism that refers to individual self-centeredness, a narcissism of Whiteness centers White racial knowledge, White supremacy, and an emotionality of Whiteness as normative and socially acceptable ways of understanding reality. Robin DiAngelo examined White fragility, the phenomenon that occurs when White people react to their discomfort when confronted with racial inequality.[18] White fragility focuses on defensive maneuvers, including a range of emotionally and ideologically driven reactions, White people employ to maintain Whiteness. An emotionality of Whiteness brings together both of these ways of framing racialized emotions that seek to maintain and defend Whiteness.

The purpose of an emotionality of Whiteness is to defend against acknowledging or critiquing the institutionalization of dominance, including its manifestation among individuals. When faced with the reality of social inequality, individuals may feel discomfort rooted in the dissonance between how an individual feels about themselves relative to how they ought to feel when benefiting from the oppression of other people. Instead of manifesting a desire for social change, they may withdraw to avoid the topic entirely.

Other times, an emotionality of Whiteness entails expressing other feelings to shift attention away from institutions and toward individuals. Individuals may express feeling sad about the world in general when faced with the reality of privilege. Feeling sad normally gets coupled with a fatalistic sentiment of "that's just the way things are." Feeling sad may be an authentic reaction; however, it also allows an individual to cultivate a perception as caring while not demonstrating any capacity or desire to challenge social inequality. It reflects an emotional response that ultimately is a performance of empathy without any intention to commit to social change. Sadness works to minimize the extent to which inequality is structurally embedded in our social institutions as an unfortunate occurrence.

Similarly, feeling bad for oneself is a choice that seeks care and support from others because the focus is on how horrible someone feels versus the reality and consequences of privilege. The desire to focus on one's own struggles and feelings is common among privileged groups that makes the situation about an individual versus an intuition.[19] Feeling bad for oneself is used to draw the focus away from the horrible nature of social inequality and toward an individual who seeks to paint themselves as innocent. The concept of "White women's tears" refers to White women who are challenged about their racist behaviors and respond by demonstrating performative regret or sorrow (e.g., crying, apologizing), and this provides a clear example of how emotional discomfort manifests itself to avoid accountability. Expressions of sorrow and regret cultivate sympathy from others that ultimately shield the person from further challenge by shifting the focus away from holding them accountable and instead offer support to that individual to make them feel better. In total, such feelings and expressions of discomfort might *appear* to resemble an intention for social change without any actual commitment.

Other times, being confronted with privilege and social inequality contributes to feelings of anger that are externally directed toward individuals who are believed to have created the discomfort. Sometimes the external target of this anger is a specific individual. For example, when a White person is confronted with their own racist behavior, this White person may lash out against the messenger instead of accepting and reflecting on that feedback. Other times, the external target of this anger is a collective group, specifically people of color. For example, if a White person does not get a job they felt entitled to and instead discovers a person of color was hired, they might express anger toward all people of color as perpetrators of "reverse discrimination." In both cases, how an individual feels about themself is challenged by the material reality of social inequality, creating discomfort that is dealt with through expressions of anger toward others. By diverting attention away from oneself or social inequality, Whiteness is maintained while simultaneously blaming people of color.

Individuals also use an emotionality of Whiteness by co-opting emotional language to express thoughts and beliefs instead of their personal feelings. Consider the difference between the following two statements:

Statement 1: Privilege makes me feel angry.
Statement 2: Privilege feels like a false concept.

The first statement uses feeling language to connect a feeling to the speaker. This statement could lead into a conversation about why the speaker feels angry and how they channel those feelings of anger for social change. The second statement uses feeling language to assert an idea. Substituting the word "seems" in place of "feels" would allow the speaker to convey the same message. However, the second statement would not lead to an emotional conversation but instead focuses on why the speaker *thinks* or *believes* privilege is a false concept. While the co-option of emotional language may seem benign, it operates as another mechanism to defend against assertions of privilege. Conventional wisdom suggests that everyone is entitled to their feelings. By co-opting emotional language, individuals can frame conceptual or ideological arguments as "how they feel" to assert their views while avoiding being challenged. It becomes a socially acceptable way for individuals to shut down conversation and withdraw without being held accountable for their views and behavior.

Carol, Lucy, Jason, and John all demonstrated elements consistent with an emotionality of Whiteness. They co-opted emotional language to assert their views and resist acknowledging privilege and social inequality. They also specifically demonstrated feeling bad, sadness and pity, upset, and anger and contempt in response to the concept of privilege or social inequality.

Co-opting Emotional Expression to Assert Dominance

The inability and unwillingness to express emotions is a core feature of an emotionality of Whiteness. Instead of sharing feelings which would make them vulnerable and susceptible to challenge, the phrase "I feel" is discursively used in two distance ways. Sometimes, it is used to express ideas and beliefs under the guise of emotional expression. Other times, it is used to share one's own feelings as a victim while diverting attention elsewhere toward a perpetrator of harm. In the context of privilege and social inequality, emotional language is used either to neutralize conversations or to shift the focus toward White victimhood at the hands of people of color.

Carol, John, and Lucy all used variations of the signal phrase "I feel" to assert their ideas and beliefs through emotional language. John reflected on a previous classroom experience that focused on privilege to express that he was "oppressed" by his peers:

> They're wrongly assuming my privilege comes from [social identities] rather than my immediate family. I remember being very upset and being told that I didn't have a right to feel oppressed because of being [a] straight White male, and in a sense, that's a form of oppression, being told you can't feel a certain way because of something else that's out of your control.

John described feeling upset when he was denied the "right to feel oppressed" by his peers during a conversation on privilege. While John described how he felt in this situation, he primarily focused on blaming his peers for "oppressing" him by regulating his feelings, which he felt was wrong and therefore the cause of feeling upset. While John could have focused on how not being able to claim being oppressed made him feel and exploring those feelings, he used emotional language to cast blame on his peers while asserting his belief that privilege is not based on social identity.

Lucy also used the "I feel" phrase to shift attention away from herself and toward others as the cause of her feelings multiple times throughout her interview. She expressed feeling bad while struggling to explain who does and does not have privilege[20]:

Lucy: In the US, Caucasians. . . . I, I, I [giggles] feel so bad saying that . . . I just feel like, I mean coz just like I'm Caucasian, I don't wanna be like, I don't feel like I'm, . . . mmm. The media just like, they like blow everything out of proportion, and then, I don't know . . . coz like I'm Caucasian, I don't, so I feel bad saying "Oh, I'm privileged coz I'm Caucasian."

[Lucy goes on a short tangent]

Tharp: So then, who does not have racial privilege in the United States?

Lucy: If you're not Caucasian. . . . Yeah, once again I feel bad saying that. I don't know, I just feel like that's the society I grew up in, and I just, once again, I was just born into that, I don't know.

While engaging this line of questioning, Lucy struggled throughout her reply. She was noticeably stuttering and said "I don't know" repeatedly which appeared to be a manifestation of feeling shame in her response. She kept stating how "bad" she felt every time she spoke about who did and did not have privilege. However, she navigated her emotional reaction to shift the conversation away from exploring why she felt bad and instead focused on the external forces that caused her to feel bad (the media, the society in which she grew up). Like John, Lucy did not take ownership for and explore her own feelings and cast blame on others for causing these bad feelings.

Carol most frequently used the "I feel" phrase to assert her ideas and beliefs about privilege, such as when she stated early in her interview that "I feel like, honestly, especially in my experience, I feel like White privilege is a saying in the world. But I feel like there are Black privileges." She also regularly used her feelings to divert the focus away from herself. Sometimes her diversions included other White people who were insincere or racist (unlike her view of herself), such as when she stated, "I feel like people don't want to admit to themselves that they would feel safer around a White guy than they would with a Black guy." However, Carol most often used emotional language to frame her personal experiences as generalized truths used to cast blame on people of color for allegedly mistreating White people. During her interview, she offered the following reflection when asked about her personal experiences related to privilege:

> I feel like White privilege is being taken to the next level, because, yes, maybe I'm White, but that doesn't mean I'm necessarily going to judge other people. It doesn't mean I, you know, have a right to other things. I mean my parents they have money, I am sorry. Like, yes, I lived a very happy life and I'm okay with that, but that doesn't mean I'm going to judge you and that doesn't mean I want you to judge me because I might be privileged. That's not my fault that other people see me like that, and I try and not hang out with those people or to you know feel like that. But I feel like people are, instead of fixing the problem, they are just flipping the coin and being like, "How dare you be privileged." [laughing].

During Carol's extended commentary, she exhibited an observable emotional reaction. She was noticeably alert and expressed through a higher-pitched tone, quicker speech speed, and upright posture. In her heightened emotional state, she used emotional language to assert her belief that people of color took the concept of White privilege too far, by assuming all White people, including herself, feel entitled to have more resources than others. She went on to accuse people of color of wrongfully perceiving her to have privilege and using that perception to discriminate against White people ("flipping the coin"). Carol also used emotional language to direct the focus of privilege to bad White people whom she tries not to associate with. If it were possible to give her the benefit of the doubt and take her comments at face value, her laughter after impersonating a person of color as chastising her as a White person suggested a strong emotional reaction toward people of color that she was unwilling to explicitly name.

All three of these students used emotional language as a vehicle to assert their ideas and beliefs, frame themselves as victims at the hands of people of color, or shift the focus away from themselves by blaming others, all of which fail to acknowledge and take ownership for their own feelings. While Lucy sometimes expressed glimpses of guilt by minimizing the strength of her feelings ("I don't know..."), John and Carol were not apologetic and did not attempt to minimize their feelings. On the contrary, John and Carol seemed to feel entitled to and justified in their reactions. Discursive decisions to use emotional language to assert their views and cast blame seem to require such convictions in order to effectively divert the focus away from privilege overall and themselves as embodiments of privilege and how Whiteness operates to obfuscate privilege in reality.

Feeling Sad

Sadness is a common feeling that arises when individuals feel distressed or discouraged by reality (e.g., coping with grief or rejection). Feelings of sadness that arise when individuals are faced with the reality of privilege and social inequality can be accompanied by a sense of hopelessness and resignation. Other times, individuals may *perform* feeling sad about social inequality because it is a socially acceptable response that portrays a veil of compassion without any commitment to social change. In this way, sadness is congruent with an emotionality of Whiteness because it centers the emotions of the individual, which subverts any efforts for accountability or social change. Carol and Lucy stated, demonstrated, or performed feelings of sadness when faced with privilege.

Carol stated feeling sad in response to the reality of oppression and privilege twice in her reflection paper. She first expressed feeling sad regarding the existence of oppression, stating, "The fact that some people are still being turned down from job opportunities or certain benefits, just because of their race or sexual orientation, saddens me." She expressed feeling sad a second time later in her paper when reflecting on her racially privileged experiences relative to racially oppressed experiences of Black people:

> I never had to fear that people were afraid of me, and I was always looked upon as a trustworthy young girl. Until I came to GLC, I never saw the sadness behind that fact. I never thought about how unfair it was that I was treated like that, but an African-American girl in the same position would not get that same treatment.

In this second excerpt, Carol described feeling sad because of the unfair treatment Black people face relative to White people. She inferred that her feeling sad was a reaction to becoming aware of social inequality. While Carol explicitly stated feeling sad in both excerpts, her emotional reaction appeared to remain shallow and performative. The reflection paper was an assignment read by her faculty member, raising the possibility that Carol stated feeling sad as a means to be perceived as caring about social inequality. However, during her interview, she never demonstrated feeling sad and also expressed multiple ideas and ideologies that more strongly point to her vigorous rejection of racial privilege as a legitimate phenomenon.

Lucy also identified a feeling of sadness when discussing the realities of privilege and social inequality. During her interview, she commented how it is "kind of sad" seeing "a lot of people on the streets who're homeless." Her expression of sadness was accompanied with a sense of resignation when she asserted that "it's a sad thing to say, but in today's world if you have money, you go further, I think." This same sense of resignation, coupled with identifying a feeling of sadness, arose again when reacting to the political cartoon. Upon viewing the cartoon for the first time, she reacted in the following way:

> [Whispers] Whoa, okay. [Long pause]. It's interesting how the African American side is just so long, you keep losing turns, you keep going back spaces. It's sad to see because all of it is so, you know . . . and then the Caucasians we just got free land and free labor.

Lucy's eyes became wide upon first viewing the political cartoon when she whispered a vocalization ("whoa"), indicating a visceral emotional reaction. After a long pause, she again named a feeling of sadness when faced with the oppression experienced by African Americans and privilege experienced by White people. Lucy seemed to want to acknowledge the truth of the political cartoon but instead inferred that we shared an unspoken understanding of its truth ("it is so, you know"). Interestingly, in all three excerpts when she named sadness, she never said that she herself felt sad. Taken together, all three times she identifies feelings of sadness are reactions to privilege and an underlying notion that social inequality is something that cannot be changed. Furthermore, her comments about sadness are situated externally. She never expressed feeling sad, but described social inequality as "sad to see," suggesting her sadness may be performative.

Lucy acknowledges an emotional reaction; however, she does not claim that emotion for herself. She affirmed this interpretation when later asked how she felt viewing the cartoon, stating, "it's just sad that they had to, the Africans had to go through all of that, and then like, I don't know what that's like. I'm Caucasian, I have never felt that kind of pain I guess." In her second comment regarding the cartoon, she expressed sadness as the limit of her emotional range because Whites have not experienced oppression, suggesting she cannot empathize with the Black experience. Both Lucy's and Carol's reactions reveal that oppression is a sadness they cannot empathize with because of their privileged identities. Furthermore, their framing of oppression as sad to see suggests they would rather not see it, thus preventing them from feeling sad.

Feeling Bad

Shame normally entails feeling personally responsible for one's actions coupled with a desire for restoration. However, when a person does not feel a desire for restoration because they are focused on how they feel about themselves, this emotional reaction could be described as feeling bad for oneself. Unlike feelings of shame that are motivations for social change, feeling bad for oneself both prevents social change and centers attention on oneself. Both Lucy and Scott demonstrated feeling bad for themselves when faced with privilege.

Lucy verbalized "feeling bad" when identifying "Caucasians" as receiving privilege and "non-Caucasians" as not receiving privilege. She struggled to articulate herself when identifying White people as having privilege, saying "I, I, I [giggles] feel so bad saying that . . . I just feel like, I mean coz just like I'm Caucasian, I don't wanna be like, I don't feel like I'm" Lucy's emotional response of feeling bad was linked to implicating White people, including herself, as having privilege. Her stammering response coupled with her circuitous explanation revealed her desire to avoid being associated with White privilege.

Lucy again verbalized feeling bad when identifying people of color as not receiving privilege. She followed her reply by explaining, "Once again, I feel bad saying that . . . I just feel like that's the society I grew up in, and I was just born into that . . . I don't know whose job it is to make it better." Lucy expressed feeling bad only after identifying people of color as being denied privilege. In her explanation, she attempted to defend herself using the belief that societal inequality is a natural phenomenon (see Chapter 4). She ended her comment by distancing herself from any commitment to social change ("I don't know whose job it is to make it better."). Taken together, Lucy's statements and expressions made clear that she did not feel she should be blamed neither for having racial privilege nor for people of color being denied racial privilege. However, as a White person associated with privilege, it appeared to be her association with privilege that made her feel bad about herself.

Scott repeatedly expressed feeling "guilt" throughout his interview. He confessed feeling "a lot of guilt for sure" when looking at the political cartoon "because it's so easy for me to sit here and talk about how this is so bad. But like I said before, this isn't really affecting me." In addition to feeling bad for his privilege (stated as a lack of oppression), he verbalized feeling bad about having the advantages privilege provided him as well as being associated with ignorant White people like the White character, stating "it makes me feel guilty that people actually act like this for sure. It also makes me feel guilty because the White board is straight and like nothing is setting us back." Scott again expressed feeling bad for being associated with White people who are unaware of their privilege when describing an experience during a class discussion on privilege:

> [Another White student] was clearly just in disagreement with a lot of the class, because a lot of the class [believed] people are clearly privileged, and

> Black people are clearly oppressed. And [the White student] was saying that he feels oppressed. So, me as a White person and him also as a White person, me seeing that some people actually act like that and continue to perpetuate the whole concept makes me feel guilty that I am in the same boat as that person, that we are associated.

Scott explicitly named how being associated with White people unaware of their privilege contributed to feeling bad about himself. Collectively, these statements from Scott's interview highlight how he felt bad because he does not experience oppression and also because of his shared racial identity with other White people ignorant about their own privilege.

Both Scott and Lucy felt bad about themselves because of their association with having privilege. Instead of feeling a sense of responsibility or desire to contribute to social change, they focused on how *they* felt for having privilege. By focusing on their association with racial privilege or supposedly bad White people, they used an acknowledgment of privilege to recenter the conversation about their feelings, which drew attention away from privilege as an institutionalized phenomenon.

Feeling Anger Toward Others

Experiencing irritation contributes to feelings of frustration and anger toward the perceived source of the irritation. Unlike racial emotional resiliency that focuses frustration and anger toward systems of privilege, an emotionality of Whiteness focuses these same feelings toward people. Sometimes individuals direct these emotions toward people who are naming or highlighting privilege and oppression. At other times, individuals direct their emotions toward social groups whose existence is a constant reminder of social inequality. Sometimes feeling angry toward oppressed social groups manifests itself in contempt for these social groups and is expressed through mockery. In all these instances, feeling anger that is directed toward individuals who focus on privilege and oppression is an attempt to deflect acknowledgment and responsibility regarding privilege to oneself, privileged social groups, or systemic privilege in general. Lucy, John, and Carol all expressed some combination of frustration, anger, and contempt.

Lucy verbalized her frustration twice during her interview. The first time occurred when she was articulating why people should blame themselves for not having privilege:

> It kind of irritates me when people just try to put the blame on others. If you don't like the situation you're in, do something about it. For example, when my parents stopped giving me money when I was about 16, they were like "Okay, you need to get a job." I went out and got a job so I could continue like going out with my friends, pay for my gas. I did that myself.

Lucy expressed feeling "irritated" when people who claim to be denied privilege are perceived to not help themselves. She expressed her view that people should demonstrate a commitment to self-improvement through hard work, citing a personal example of getting a job to earn resources instead of relying on her parents. Her comments highlighted how her feelings of frustration are directed toward others who she believes ought to work harder.

Lucy expressed frustration a second time when discussing the political cartoon. Her frustration arose because she did not see "White struggles" portrayed in the image:

> I feel like I still have struggles in life. [The cartoon] just kinda makes it seem like, oh I get to do whatever I want, but no . . . I mean I'm in college, it's pretty hard and [I'm] not just like riding through. I still have loans to pay off when I'm done. I'm not just getting a free ride here.

Lucy's comments about the cartoon began with her typical tone and demeanor. However, when describing her struggles with student loan debt and how difficult college is for her, her tempo and pitch increased indicating an emotional response. Her focus on how hard she is working without extra help coupled with her nonverbal cues indicated she was irritated by the assumption that the challenges White people face were ignored. Specifically, she seemed irritated that people assume White people have an easy time, which does not match her experience.

Both of Lucy's excerpts illustrate how her frustration occurred due to how White people, including herself, are perceived because of their privilege. What Lucy seems to want is recognition for the challenges she faces along with how hard she works to face these challenges despite any racial privilege. As a result, she directed her frustration toward those individuals who assume White people as a privileged group face no challenges. Her reaction to these perceptions is to share a hard work explanation to defend against being viewed as privileged, both in general and as a White person. While she never named who these people are who she believes falsely accuse her of an easy life, it is implied that they are people of color. In total, her expression of frustration operates to shift attention away from privilege as an institutionalized phenomenon by framing herself as a virtuous hard worker. Her emotional response both decenters privilege and attempts to center the focus on undeserving people of color.

John's multiple expressions of anger, frustration, and contempt during his interview were more animated relative to Lucy. The first time he calmly verbalized feeling angry was while describing his reaction if a faculty member used the political cartoon to teach students about privilege. He stated he would get "heated and angry trying to clarify that [the political cartoon] isn't exactly how it is." Not only did John connect his anger to the political cartoon, but he also explained that his anger would compel him to speak up against the political cartoon:

> I'd make sure that I'd have my input and show that this isn't necessarily the truth, because not all people believe, or will be influenced to believe that

154 Compelling Feelings About Privilege

that is the case. And I wouldn't want the professor to continue trying to teach people that this is the truth because that would influence people to believe that, and thus allow this to be the truth.

John explained that he viewed the political cartoon as "untrue" and wanted to prevent other students from believing in its content. In this instance, he directed his anger toward the faculty member in this hypothetical scenario to stop the conversation about privilege. Further, he explained how his emotional reaction would motivate him to challenge notions that privilege is institutionalized and connected to social identity groups. His anger about the political cartoon manifested itself again when he said that he would "want to cross the whole thing out" when invited to modify the political cartoon to reflect his views about privilege.

John's expression of anger grew larger when reflecting on a past conversation about privilege in one of his courses:

> The way that we were talking about [privilege] made it seem that straight White males, or just White people in general, had so much privilege that they didn't have the right to feel anything other than that privilege. They didn't have a right to feel oppressed or anything because they were so privileged, and I realized that I'm privileged because I was a straight White male, and I didn't think it was on account of that. I thought my privilege came from my parents and I happened to be [a] straight White male in other's people's eyes, and they didn't. So they're wrongly assuming my privilege comes from those things rather than my immediate family. I remember being very upset and being told that I didn't have a right to feel oppressed because of being [a] straight White male.

John attributed his frustration with being told he had privilege because of his social identities when he instead views privilege as coming from one's family. He further shared how the conversation about privilege made him feel that privileged groups, specifically "straight White males," were denied the "right" to express their own challenges in life. For John, being told he had privilege was a source of irritation that was magnified when the label of privilege felt like it prevented him from expressing his own challenges in life. He verbalized how these views made him feel "upset." He continued his comments by describing how his anger motivated him to assert his own views about privilege in his reflection paper:

> That was the paper that I wrote the night of because I was like, "This is, this is dumb." We're focused so much on I'm a straight White male and that's out of my control, like we can focus on the similarities that I'm a person, that I'm working presumably just as hard as everyone else, even though you might not see it that way, to achieve the same things. I want happiness. I want love. I want success. It doesn't always have to come easy to me just

because I'm straight, White, and male. The class seemed to push this idea that we're diverse and that privilege exists, rather than trying to abolish that diversity and that privilege.

John's demeanor shifted while describing how he felt while writing his reflection paper. He leaned toward me while speaking faster and with greater intensity. He verbalized his anger at being accused of having privilege and relatedly only being "allowed" to "feel" privilege when stating how "dumb" such views were. His emotional intensity peaked when challenging the sentiment that he could only feel privilege by emphatically stating his wants for happiness, love, and success. Taken together, John's anger was a reaction to his view that the label of privilege is used to limit his "right to feel oppressed" as a human being, a view that caused him emotional distress. While he did not state this directly, he seemed to direct his anger toward those who accuse him of having privilege, undoubtedly people of color. His emotional reaction directed his anger through his reflection paper to challenge these notions of privilege. His anger at being denied the right to express his feelings not only recentered the conversation about privilege around himself but also minimized feelings experienced by people of color in order to not allow his own feelings to be minimized.

John's anger toward what he perceived as a faulty view of privilege that prevented him from emotional expression contrary to a life of ease morphed into feelings of contempt channeled through his reflection paper:

> Since I am apparently the stereotypical definition of "privileged" is it ok for me to feel "oppressed"? Is a conflict going to start between me and another "oppressed" person simply because, no matter how I feel about my situation, they will think they are more "oppressed"?

John's expression of contempt is manifested through his use of quotation marks and voice when challenging notions of privilege and oppression. He used quotation marks around "privilege" and "oppression" to highlight his disagreement with these terms as used in his course discussion. His discussion included a passive aggressive voice that challenged these terms indirectly by positioning him as a victim instead of directly stating his view or how it made him feel. This excerpt seems to mock the way privilege is framed and diminishes those who make these claims against privileged groups in general and him in particular. All of John's expressions of anger collectively operate to shift attention away from institutional privilege and toward his own emotional needs while actively lashing out against those who talk about privilege.

Carol expressed frustration, anger, and contempt the most in her reflection paper and interview. Similar to John, she viewed conversations about privilege as problematic and that they made invisible the feelings and challenges faced by people who happen to be White. Overall, she felt privilege was weaponized by

156 Compelling Feelings About Privilege

people of color to inflict harm upon White people. A passage from Carol's reflection paper makes this point explicit:

> A common phrase I hear in my life is "White privilege." I feel as if this phrase is used lightly among people my age, but it really is an offensive term. I find it embarrassing and degrading to my social identity.

In her paper, she explicitly stated that being labeled with privilege is "offensive," "embarrassing," and "degrading." For Carol, privilege is not simply a description of an institutionalized phenomenon but an attack used against White people.

Throughout her interview, she returned to this same theme while expressing frustration toward people of color. Early in her interview, she confessed her "honest" thoughts about privilege:

> If I'm being honest with you, I don't think I've been more aware of my race until I came [to GLC], and not necessarily in a good way . . . I feel like instead of finding a balance, people my age especially are kind of twisting it the other way. I've had instances where people judge me because they see that I'm White, and it's like I almost don't have the right to struggle, or I don't have the right to, you know, have hardships in life. Just because I'm White and female, and my parents are upper class like.

Carol was fairly calm while simultaneously scrunching her face when discussing how "people" judge her because she has privilege. Even though she did not explicitly ascribe the origins of this judgment from people of color, she implied it because she felt judged as a White person. Throughout her interview, Carol repeatedly directed her emotion toward people of color as it grew from frustration into anger and contempt.

Carol expressed anger toward people of color for judging White people once again when reacting to the political cartoon. Upon seeing the political cartoon, Carol's face became expressive and her initial comments were abrupt. When invited to share what she was feeling, she verbalized her feelings:

> This makes me mad, the "are you just slow or what?" Like I get it, but I think it just makes me mad because it's putting a stereotype on White people as well. Because not everyone thinks like this, but I feel like now, instead of saying that Black people are beneath us, we're just saying White people are pretentious jerks.

Carol confessed feeling "mad" because the cartoon portrayed a Black character saying something negative to the White character. In addition to expressing anger toward Black people for judging White people, she also expressed anger with being generalized with all other White people. She described some White people as "jerks" multiple times in her interview and used it again here to distance herself as virtuous, relative to some bad people who happen to be White. Again, she used her anger to distance herself from other White people with privilege while simultaneously casting blame on Black people for stereotyping all White people as privileged.

Lucy, John, and Carol expressed anger when they believed they were being falsely judged by other people because of having privilege. Lucy's and John's anger fueled their desire to assert their counter views about privilege, using personal or familial hard work narratives, respectively. Lucy, John, and Carol all felt angry because they felt that being labeled with privilege implied they lost their right to voice the challenges they faced and overcame, including the "right" to *not* feel privileged. Furthermore, they all directed their anger toward other people who draw attention to privilege, either in general or as it applied to themselves. Their anger was commonly directed toward people of color through attempts to paint them as perpetrators of discrimination and to frame themselves as victims.

Feeling Discomfort

Individuals may feel emotional discomfort when they have an experience that generates dissonance. In the context of privilege and race, emotional discomfort may arise when conversations involving privilege and race create dissonance between the topic and how they perceive or feel about themselves. If White students are not used to talking about race and perceive themselves to be raceless, a conversation about race and racial privilege both makes visible their White racial identity and stirs feelings about what it means to be White that may be unfamiliar. Such dissonance generates emotional discomfort that may inspire reactions that minimize the dissonance someone experiences. Common reactions may involve withdrawing from the experience or assertively engaging the experience to alter the focus. In both cases, the reaction operates to protect the person by stopping the source of their discomfort. Lucy, Carol, and Jane all expressed feeling discomfort in relationship to conversations involving privilege that led to engagement or withdrawal.

Lucy verbalized feeling discomfort in the form of "awkwardness" when confessing how she felt during her interview. She attributed feeling uncomfortable because of the interview's focus on privilege, stating, "I'm White . . . I guess it makes it seem like I'm privileged regarding race." She continued her reflection by distancing herself from privilege using the same hard work narrative she previously articulated when expressing frustration:

> I mean I'm privileged but, once again, I still have to work for stuff. Not everything's handed to me. I am not judging other people who get everything handed to them either, like good for them. I feel like I learn more life lessons, having to work for stuff.

158 Compelling Feelings About Privilege

Lucy's discomfort inspired her to speak up and refute her association with having absolute privilege on the grounds that she works hard and does not judge other people for the benefits they have in life. While she conceded having White privilege, she framed herself as hardworking and therefore less privileged. Her comment operated to provide distance from White people with more privilege and frame herself as virtuous.

Carol verbalized that she would feel uncomfortable if a faculty member used the political cartoon as an example of privilege in a class discussion. She explained how her comfort level varied based upon her perception of how "open" the environment appeared:

> If I felt comfortable enough to speak my opinion, I would mention that it only focuses on one aspect of privilege. . . [that] we're more privileged because we're White. Now that irritates me. [Laughs]. . . . If I was in a class that was open and there is different, there is different, it doesn't really . . . to me it doesn't really matter if I was the only White one in the room. Yes, I would be uncomfortable. But if it was, even if there was a half and half mix or even there was five of us that were White, it just kind of, that doesn't matter. To me it just matters how close I am with class. . . . You know, there are some classes where you just sit and you listen to the professor, and you learn and you don't talk to the people and it's not a group discussion class. Then there are other classes where there's lots of group discussions, and you're very open in your conversation and sharing your opinions. I feel like that matters.

Carol provided an insightful train of thought regarding what influences her level of comfort, inspiring her to either engage or withdraw from conversations about privilege. The content of the political cartoon, that only White people have privilege, caused her to feel frustration. The hypothetical situation where this content was being taught in a class was the cause of her discomfort. On the surface, she identified needing an environment where she perceived everyone to be "open" in order to feel comfortable enough to engage. However, a deeper analysis of her comment deconstructs what she means by an "open" environment.

Carol began describing an environment that had a certain "mix" of White people to people of color. She pivoted away from her initial stance involving racial demographics to instead emphasize the importance of her relationship to the class. Even though she concluded aloud that the racial makeup of the class ultimately does not matter, her stream of consciousness revealed that her perception of an "open" class depends upon how close she is to other students which depends upon how many other White students are present. She likely assumed that other White students would share her views on privilege, allowing her to feel supported in expressing her views and contributing to an "open" environment. However, if there were fewer White students, she would be less likely to feel close to the class and perceive the class as a space not "open" for discussion. Her views about the "openness" of a classroom environment implies how "open" she perceives other students to be to her views on privilege.

Jane verbalized feeling uncomfortable engaging in conversations about privilege when reflecting on how she felt during her interview. She ascribed her discomfort to a concern with saying the right thing:

> It's a little bit uncomfortable to talk about [privilege]. . . . I don't want to say like the wrong thing, you know. Because I don't want to sound like an idiot, but I also because I don't want to hurt people, even if it's just you and me in the conversation, I just don't want to be mean, you know. I don't want to be mean. So, I felt like I was a little nervous to talk about it just because I don't want to say the wrong thing. You know? Not that I don't believe or anything. But I feel like I just don't want anything I say to be perceived the wrong way.

Jane's "nervousness" when talking about privilege stemmed from not wanting to hurt other people with her words and her desire to protect how others perceive her. However, she primarily focused on not wanting to be misperceived, frequently seeking affirmation from me as another White person. While a desire to not harm other people may appear virtuous, her primary desire to not harm herself operates to silence her engagement in conversations about privilege without challenging notions of privilege rooted in Whiteness.

Lucy, Carol, and Jane all expressed discomfort associated with a concern with how they were perceived by others. Carol's comment about needing her peers to be "open" to engage coupled with Jane's concern about saying "the wrong thing" is a form of withdrawal that operates to avoid being labeled as a stereotypical White person, just as Lucy herself described. Overall, these three White students' discomfort influenced their decision to withdraw unless they felt more secure and less vulnerable in expressing themselves.

How Feelings That Resist Social Change Work Together

Co-opting emotional language, along with feeling bad, sad, angry, and uncomfortable, all share a common purpose to divert attention away from notions of privilege as an institutionalized phenomenon. However, these emotions and uses of emotional language work together to provide two common functionalities to achieve this purpose. One functionality operates to draw positive attention to the speaker as a victim. Another functionality operates to redirect negative attention toward people of color. Both functionalities ultimately work to protect Whiteness as a dominant, hegemonic force in how we view ourselves, others, and society.

Feeling uncomfortable when faced with privilege may inspire White people to withdraw from conversations or educational experiences in order to minimize attention to themselves. Ideally, White people participating in the Whiteness Discourse may prefer to quietly wait until topics on privilege and social inequality pass, like extinguishing a fire by denying it oxygen. However, if an uncomfortable White person is invited to engage, they may express feeling sad or bad for themselves. Public expressions of sadness channel unwanted attention away from their privileged social identities by framing themselves as kind, caring, or empathetic. Similarly, public expressions of feeling bad about having privilege often expressed as iterations of feeling ashamed for being White and having privilege, which is beyond their control. Expressions of feeling bad and sad are attempts to steer attention toward themselves as White *individuals* based on how virtuous they appear while diverting attention away from themselves as *White* people and the privilege they receive based on their racial identity.

One example of expressing feeling bad and sad after being critiqued around their own privilege involves Megyn Kelly, a White female media personality. In October of 2018, she hosted a segment on her morning talk show where she demonstrated frustration and contempt toward others about how "political correctness has gone amok" related to Halloween costumes, arguing that "the costume police" are not allowing offensive costumes including those involving blackface and cultural appropriation.[21] After being challenged about her views, she issued two apologies. She emailed a written apology to her colleagues the same day as her televised segment:

> Today is one of those days where listening carefully to other points of view, including from friends and colleagues, is leading me to rethink my own views.... I realize now that such behavior is indeed wrong, and I am sorry. The history of blackface in our culture is abhorrent; the wounds too deep. I've never been a "P.C." kind of person – but I understand that we do need to be more sensitive in this day and age. Particularly on race and ethnicity issues which, far from being healed, have been exacerbated in our politics over the past year.[22]

Kelly's written apology focused on what she learned and how she has evolved in her views. Her decision to highlight her commitment to "listening carefully to other points of view" that lead her to "realize now that such behavior is indeed wrong" is a form of feeling bad about oneself in order to draw attention to how they have changed for the better. Kelly ended her email by expressing feeling bad about how racial issues continue to be challenging and require "more sensitivity" in order to "heal." Her verbalization of the challenges related to racism operate to demonstrate how she too is sad about the state of racism, a discursive move that again diverted attention away from her complicit behavior and toward herself as someone who feels terrible about racism like any good person should. Kelly offered a second on-air apology on her talk show the following day. Her apology expressed sadness that involved verbally stating "I'm sorry" with a noticeably somber tone and a pained look on her face.[23]

Kelly's public apologies collectively reflect how expressions of feeling bad and sad can successfully deflect attention away from institutionalized privilege and those who carry its message. Her original feelings of frustration and contempt regarding race have been expressed previously throughout her career as a media personality on Fox News. Her ability to shift to authentically feeling bad and sad within 24 hours strongly suggested these feelings to be performative to rehabilitate how others viewed her versus any commitment to social change.

If a White person who participates in the Whiteness Discourse is feeling comfortable engaging others regarding privilege and social inequality, they are likely to co-opt emotional language and use expressions of anger. Sometimes they might be willing to offer their views directly and explicitly about privilege. In expressing themselves, it is possible they may express frustration, anger, and contempt as they frame the topic of privilege as a weapon used by people of color to discriminate against White people. Other times, they might co-opt emotional language to proactively frame their views as equally deserving of validation as anyone else's because it's "just the way they feel." In either case, their willing engagement is driven by a desire to challenge notions of institutionalized privilege and offer another explanation for who is to blame *other* than White people.

Multiple examples of White people expressing anger toward a person of color when privilege is challenged were evident during the NFL "kneeling controversy" that began in 2016. Colin Kaepernick, a Black male professional football player, knelt during the national anthem in protest of police brutality against Black people in the United States. In response, many public figures expressed variations of anger that redirected the focus away from institutionalized racism and toward Kaepernick as a disrespectful and ungrateful individual. Alex Boone, a former teammate of Kaepernick's, stated "You should have some fucking respect for people [in the military]. . . . We're out here playing a game, making millions of dollars. People are losing their life, and you don't have the common courtesy to do that."[24] Sports broadcaster Rick Monday reacted to the decision to kneel during the national anthem saying that "I was shocked . . . I don't like it, and I don't respect it."[25] US Senator Ted Cruz reacted on Twitter by writing, "stop insulting our flag, our nation, our heroes."[26] Donald Trump reacted to any athletes who protest the anthem by declaring "get that son of a bitch off the field."[27] All of these reactions reflect a range of angry emotions from plain anger to contempt that purposefully ignores the topic of institutionalized racism and individualized the issue around a "bad" person of color.

An emotionality of Whiteness exists to divert attention away from privilege and social inequality through absorption or deflection. Absorbing attention channels the focus onto an individual as a victim or someone who is a good person at heart. Deflecting attention channels the focus on people of color to cast blame on them for being a mirror for privilege and social inequality through the reality of their lived experiences. In both instances, an emotionality of Whiteness recasts attention to individuals who are good or bad versus institutions and systems.

Similarities and Differences

Racial emotional resilience and an emotionality of Whiteness are quite different in their purpose and manifestation yet surprisingly similar in their emotional stimuli. Broadly speaking, both racial emotional resiliency and an emotionality of Whiteness are responses to the existence of privilege and social inequality. Both versions of emotionality have similarities in doing the following:

1. Inspire individuals to use feeling language to express themselves.
2. Arise when an individual feels destabilized.
3. Arise when confronted with the material realities of social inequality.
4. Arise when an individual feels blame.
5. Arise when an individual interprets a situation to be unjust.

What all five stimuli have in common are situations where individuals are somewhere connected to privilege and social inequality. However, the way individuals express their emotionality diverges based on how they interpret that connection.

Individuals who engage in racial emotional resiliency interpret their connection to privilege and social inequality as a by-product of their social identity group membership which they cannot control. They also interpret themselves as able to alter the social institutions that maintain privilege, which inspires an ability to act. However, individuals who engage in an emotionality of Whiteness interpret their connection to privilege and social inequality as a false notion that makes invisible the merits and actions of every individual. They interpret claims of having privilege as a version of an accusation or insult, inspiring them to adopt a defensive position. These two diverging interpretations shape the reaction to each common stimulus.

Everyone uses feeling language to express themselves. Individuals who engage in racial emotional resiliency embrace feeling language to express vulnerability because they are willing to be held accountable for both their behavior and their emotional expressions that may reinforce Whiteness. Individuals who engage in an emotionality of Whiteness use emotional language to assert their views and defend themselves. While the words may sound alike, the way they are used to preface their comments are quite different.

Facing the existence of privilege and social inequality can destabilize what we assume to be true about ourselves, others, and society. Being socialized into a Whiteness Discourse by default includes beliefs and accompanying ideas about the superiority of White people, the inferiority of people of color, and the way society rewards those who work hard. These views create a foundation for our relationship with social institutions, our family and friends, and our sense of self. The destabilizations of these powerful views are akin to an earthquake that rattles the structural foundations of a city. Individuals who engage in racial emotional resiliency feel upset as they lean into the experience because they acknowledge it is important to continually disrupt deeply internalized assumptions that reinforce Whiteness. Individuals who engage in an emotionality of Whiteness feel deeply uncomfortable as they more tightly embrace their internalized assumptions while waiting for the discomfort to pass. As a result, they withdraw physically, mentally, and emotionally to protect themselves, knowing that eventually they can return to other spaces and places that will affirm and reinforce their views once more.

The existence of privilege and social inequality raises the question of whether we wish to change the systems that create these conditions. Individuals may decide that privilege and social inequality are either (a) problematic and ought to be dismantled or (b) unfortunate and just the way things are. Individuals who engage in racial emotional resiliency will express an emotional commitment to change these systems. The path to dismantling privilege is difficult, and likely hard to imagine, yet that does not deter those with an emotional commitment to social change. Individuals who engage in an emotionality of Whiteness will not share this same desire to change privilege and social inequality because, at some conscious or subconscious level, they enjoy the benefits they receive regardless of the cost to society, others, and even themselves. However, in a world where a blatant embrace of privilege and social inequality is out of fashion, such sentiments are seldom expressed. Instead, these individuals express sadness about the realities of privilege as a permanent fixture of society. While their sentiments may not necessarily be sincere, these expressions of sadness allow them to perform empathy for those less fortunate than themselves and garner positive attention as virtuous individuals despite their privileged status.

It is reasonable for individuals to feel some level of fault when they are confronted with having benefits purposefully denied to others based on their social identity group membership. Unlike situations where someone intentionally takes something from another person in a society that agrees such actions are wrong, privilege involves institutions that unevenly distributes resources in a society that agrees such action are just. Reconciling how it feels to have something that was denied to others, relative to how we view ourselves as good people, is not easy. Individuals who engage in racial emotional resiliency feel ashamed or guilty for their unearned benefits while reminding themselves they have a responsibility to acknowledge and challenge these unjust systems. Individuals who engage in an emotionality of Whiteness feel bad about the whole situation and may struggle with "privilege paralysis" as they focus on being blamed, without any capacity to see ways to challenge social equality. This emotional reaction feeds feelings of helplessness and acquiescence because institutionalized privilege to far too big for them to change.

When individuals are irritated, they commonly express frustration and anger toward what they perceive to be the source or cause of irritation. When the source of irritation is privilege and social inequality, individuals who engage in both forms of emotionality experience frustration and anger alike at what they perceive to be the cause of the injustice. Individuals who engage in racial emotional resiliency direct their frustration and anger toward concrete examples of institutionalized privilege or individuals who participate in the Whiteness Discourse whose ideas, beliefs, and feelings reinforce the hegemonic dominance of social inequality. Individuals who engage in an emotionality of Whiteness direct their frustration, anger, and contempt toward individuals who participate in the Antiracism Discourse who point out the existence of privilege or people of color who, by their lived experiences, are examples of social inequality. Often, expressions of anger directed toward people of color are misdirected as individuals blame them for their own lack of privilege and oppression.

When examining the similarities between individuals who engage in either racial emotional resiliency or an emotionality of Whiteness, the differences between one form of emotional expression and another become more apparent.

- Both sets of individuals use feeling language to express themselves, yet they differ based on the extent to which they value emotional expression. All individuals are capable of emotional vulnerability if they give themselves permission and practice such forms of expression.
- Both sets of individuals are destabilized by the existence of privilege, yet they differ in their willingness to explore the source of their destabilization. All individuals are capable of introspection and reflection if they allow themselves to do so and practice such behaviors.
- Both sets of individuals will be confronted with the material reality of privilege and oppression, yet they differ in their willingness to change these social systems. All individuals are capable of embracing and working toward social change if they examine how everyone, including themselves, benefits from social equity and allow themselves to feel hopeful about a socially just society.
- Both sets of individuals feel some level of blame for receiving benefits purposefully denied to others based on their social identity group memberships, yet they differ in how they personalize that blame. All individuals are capable of learning new ways of being to avoid replicating privilege if they allow themselves to make mistakes and continually learn how to be better.
- Both sets of individuals are irritated by injustices related to privilege and social inequity, yet they differ in who and what they perceive to be the cause of these injustices. All individuals are capable of appropriately directing their frustration and anger at the systems and individuals that created and sustain inequity if they are brave enough to examine the circumstances and not allow themselves to lash out to silence the messenger.

Individuals who engage in both racial emotional resiliency and an emotionality of Whiteness are more alike than different at their core.

Much of what differentiates these individuals are the Discourses in which they participate that reinforces their respective emotionality. As stated at the start of this chapter, emotions are more than expressions of feelings but are ways of connecting to social groups. Expressing emotions related to privilege not only works to dismantle or protect privilege, but it also helps bind us to other individuals who participate in the same Discourse. There is a certain currency within the Whiteness Discourse for blaming people of color for their own oppression: It helps bind those individuals together around a common target. Similarly, there is a certain currency within the Antiracism Discourse for a commitment to social change. In that case, it helps bind those individuals together around a common goal.

Connecting Emotionality to Beliefs

The relationship between emotionality and beliefs is evident when exploring how the purpose of both racial emotional resiliency and an emotionality of Whiteness connects to the broader ideological stance central to a race critical ideology and White supremacist ideology, respectively. The central stance within a race critical ideology is that privilege exists as a structural phenomenon that is worthy of exploration. The structural nature of privilege permeates our institutional and cultural ways of being. Therefore, racial emotional resiliency supports this ideological stance by encouraging emotional vulnerability and exploring how we feel about privilege as a mechanism to fuel reflection and motivation for social change.

On the contrary, the central stance within a White supremacist ideology rejects privilege as a structural phenomenon and offers multiple counter explanations. An emotionality of Whiteness supports this ideological stance by using emotional language to challenge structural views of privilege and encourages emotional expression that align with counter explanations. Consider a range of examples of how beliefs and feelings may support one another. Feeling uncomfortable and choosing to withdraw from discussions about privilege is a sensible option if someone does not know how to defend their view. Feeling bad about their privilege and seeking comfort and positive attention from others allow an individual to view themselves as an exception to privilege that reinforces the belief that privilege is individualistic. Feeling sad in the face of privilege in order to frame the self as compassionate and caring aligns with a belief that privilege is a natural phenomenon that does not warrant further reflection or action, only the equivalent of "thoughts and prayers" that affected individuals may experience comfort in the future. Feeling angry when believed to be wrongly accused of something aligns with beliefs that individuals are responsible for their (mis)fortune, supporting attacks against the marginalized themselves. Overall, these emotional reactions are purposeful ways to support beliefs by directly challenging structural notions of privilege or indirectly diverting arguments to individuals versus structures.

Beliefs underpin our feelings and their expression, and feelings provide motivation to adhere to certain beliefs. This relationship between feelings and beliefs is underscored by the labels for these two types of emotionality. To believe that privilege is a structural phenomenon that we are all implicated by requires resiliency in order to stay committed to social change. The belief that privilege is not structural and better understood through alternative explanations reflects the slippery and chameleon-like nature of Whiteness as a worldview. While Robin DiAngelo accurately describes how participants in the Whiteness Discourse express emotion because of the fragility of their views,[28] I contend that it is important to acknowledge the constructed rationality that maintains Whiteness as an internally logical worldview.

What Insights Into Emotionality Offer Us

Emotions play a powerful role in how we understand and react to privilege and social inequality. Privilege is a manifestation of unequally distributed social power. Therefore, the way individuals feel related to privilege is linked to how they feel power: The power that benefits them, the possibility of losing that power, and the power to facilitate social change.[29] If educators want to help individuals learn to participate in an Antiracism Discourse, they must help students come to recognize, understand, and harness their own emotions to avoid reinforcing Whiteness while working for justice.

Everyone is socialized into the Whiteness Discourse by default, which includes engaging an emotionality of Whiteness. To unlearn the ideas, beliefs, and feelings associated with participation in the Whiteness Discourse requires White students to relinquish how they feel about themselves as part of shedding their ideas and beliefs. The process of leaving our self-perceptions and the worldviews that help maintain these perceptions is similar to a grieving process that should be taken seriously.[30]

Accepting the reality of privilege as bad and harmful can become misinterpreted through the lens of individualism, causing a belief that all White people are bad and harmful because of their social identity group receiving privilege.[31] This belief reasonably may produce strong feelings that must be engaged to continue unlearning the ideas, beliefs, and feelings that anchor participation in the Whiteness Discourse. However, there is a critical difference between blanket responsibility for all past, present, and future iterations of privilege versus responsibility for the choices we make to repair past transgressions and stop the perpetuation of privilege in the present and future. There is a difference between viewing privilege as something to do with only "me" versus a collective responsibility taken by "we."

There is something useful to be learned in efforts to educate the public around climate change. Like privilege, climate change is a real phenomenon that is rooted in cultural and institutional processes and decisions. There are views that you are either part of the problem or the solution, views that similarly frame individuals as all good or bad. Even when individuals reduce their carbon footprint, they may still make choices that harm the environment that may feel as if they negate their efforts, making them feel they cannot meaningfully contribute to change (e.g., "One person who recycles won't save the planet."). However, to work for climate change involves embracing individual agency over all of our choices to be environmentally sustainable based on the belief that social change is possible and necessary. Similarly, individuals committed to climate change must become resilient enough to acknowledge mistakes and not become paralyzed when feeling bad in order to learn and continue to do better. The same approach can be taken with helping students unlearn Whiteness by engaging their emotions as part of the learning experience.

Emotions simultaneously reinforce our beliefs and ideas while also being motivation to challenge them. If students can be engaged on an emotional level to explore their feelings, including how privilege and social inequality makes them feel, it may reveal examples of the psychological, social, and material ways White people are also harmed by sustaining social inequality and privilege.[32] Once students' emotions are engaged in learning process, it opens the door for revisiting their ideas and beliefs that fuel an emotionality of Whiteness. Practicing emotional vulnerability, reflecting on their discomfort related to privilege, envisioning ways to contribute to social change that helps everyone including themselves, learning to become resilient when they make mistakes and not judge themselves as universally good or bad, and directing their anger toward systems versus individuals are all avenues for education.

Key Takeaways

1. There are two different types of emotionality that simultaneously are manifestations of, and fuel for, our beliefs regarding the reality of privilege.
2. Racial emotional resiliency consists of vulnerability through emotional language and feelings of upset, shame, anger, and determination work together to hold a person accountable and sustain efforts for social change.
3. An emotionality of Whiteness consists of co-opting emotional language to assert counter arguments coupled with feeling bad, sad, angry, and uncomfortable to divert attention away from institutional privilege and toward individuals.
4. Both racial emotional resiliency and an emotionality of Whiteness have commonalities that suggest individuals who engage in an emotionality of Whiteness are capable of developing racial emotional resiliency through reflection and practice.
5. Practicing emotional vulnerability, a willingness to make and learn from mistakes to avoid sustaining privilege, introspection when they feel destabilized, reflection about their own emotional habits related to privilege, and examination of the benefits of or hopefulness about social equity are elements that can contribute to racial emotional resiliency.
6. Because all individuals within the United States are socialized into the Whiteness Discourse, everyone engages with an emotionality of Whiteness and needs to relinquish the feelings and associated emotional habits that sustain Whiteness and its associated beliefs and ideas.
7. The ability to engage students through their emotions provides critical avenues to learn new ideas, beliefs, and feelings that are central to participation in an Antiracism Discourse.

Notes

1 See Al Jazeera (2020).
2 See Matias (2016).
3 See Gee (1999).
4 See Boler (1999).
5 See Adams (2016).
6 See Wise (2019).
7 See Matias (2016).
8 See Hardiman and Jackson (1997).
9 See Harro (2013a, 2013b).
10 See Adams (2016), Goodman (2011).
11 See Horsey (2014).
12 See Strayed and Almond (2018).
13 See Wise (2019).
14 See WSUTV (2016, 12:34).
15 See Wise (2011, p. 287).
16 See Matias (2016).
17 See Matias (2016, pp. 69–81).
18 See DiAngelo (2018).
19 See Goodman (2011).
20 This same quote was featured in Chapter 5 but is featured again here to help the reader see how emotionality operates.
21 See Today (2018, 0:10).
22 See Robinson (2018).
23 See Winsor (2018, 1:41).
24 See Goessling (2016).
25 See Walker (2016).
26 See Cruz (2016).
27 See Graham (2017).
28 See DiAngelo (2018).
29 See Boler (1999).
30 See Matias (2016).
31 See Goodman (2011).
32 Ibid.

References

Adams, M. (2016). Pedagogical foundations for social justice education. In M. Adams, L. A. Bell, D. J. Goodman, & K. J. Yoshi (Eds.), *Teaching for diversity and social justice* (3rd ed., pp. 27–53). Routledge.

Al Jazeera. (2020, August 18). *Who got the right to vote when?* https://interactive.aljazeera.com/aje/2016/us-elections-2016-who-can-vote/index.html.

Boler, M. (1999). *Feeling power: Emotions and education*. Psychology Press.

Cruz, T. [@tedcruz]. (2016, September 16). *To all the athletes who have made millions in America's freedom: Stop insulting our flag, our nation, our heroes* [Tweet]. Twitter. https://twitter.com/tedcruz/status/775348594060562432.

DiAngelo, R. (2018). *White fragility: Why it's so hard for White people to talk about racism*. Beacon Press.

Gee, J. P. (1999). *Introduction to discourse analysis: Theory and method*. Routledge.

Goessling, B. (2016, August 28). Alex Bone on ex-teammate Colin Kaepernick: 'Show some respect.' *ESPN*. www.espn.com/nfl/story/_/id/17411286/alex-boone-minnesota-vikings-calls-ex-teammate-colin-kaepernick-decision-sit-national-anthem-shameful.

Goodman, D. J. (2011). *Promoting diversity and social justice: Educating people from privileged groups* (2nd ed.). Routledge.

Graham, B. A. (2017, September 23). Donald Trump blasts NFL anthem protesters: 'Get that son of a bitch off the field.' *The Guardian*. www.theguardian.com/sport/2017/sep/22/donald-trump-nfl-national-anthem-protests.

Hardiman, R., & Jackson, B. (1997). Conceptual foundations for social justice courses. In M. Adams, L. A. Bell, & P. Griffin (Eds.), *Teaching for diversity and social justice* (pp. 16–29). Routledge.

Harro, B. (2013a). The cycle of liberation. In M. Adams, W. J. Blumenfeld, C. R. Castaneda, H. W. Hackman, M. L. Peters, & X. Zúñiga (Eds.), *Readings for diversity and social justice* (3rd ed., pp. 618–625). Routledge.

Harro, B. (2013b). The cycle of socialization. In M. Adams, W. J. Blumenfeld, C. R. Castaneda, H. W. Hackman, M. L. Peters, & X. Zúñiga (Eds.), *Readings for diversity and social justice* (3rd ed., pp. 45–52). Routledge.

Horsey, D. (2014). The American dream [Political Cartoon #142]. *The Los Angeles Times*. www.latimes.com/nation/la-tot-cartoons-pg-photogallery.html.

Matias, C. E. (2016). *Feeling White: Whiteness, emotionality, and education*. Sense Publishers.

Robinson, J. (2018, October 23). Megyn Kelly hastily walks back blackface costume argument: "I am sorry." *Vanity Fair*. www.vanityfair.com/hollywood/2018/10/megyn-kelly-blackface-apology.

Strayed, C., & Almond, S. (2018, August 14). How can I cure my White guilt? *The New York Times*. www.nytimes.com/2018/08/14/style/white-guilt-privilege.html.

Today. (2018, October 23). Are these Halloween costumes too controversial to wear? | Megyn Kelly Today. [Video] *YouTube*. www.youtube.com/watch?v=VY1Hf2taOPY.

Walker, R. (2016, August 30). Kaepernick supports, haters and everyone in between. *The Undefeated*. https://theundefeated.com/features/a-comprehensive-aggregation-of-colin-kaepernick-supporters-haters-and-everyone-in-between/.

Winsor, M. (2018, October 24). NCB's Megyn Kelly apologies for comments about blackface. [video]. *ABCNews*. https://abcnews.go.com/Entertainment/nbcs-megyn-kelly-apologizes-comments-blackface/story?id=58713638.

Wise, T. (2011). *White like me: Reflections on race from a privileged son*. Soft Skull Press.

Wise, T. (Host). (2019, November 27). Facts don't care about your feelings, but decent people do: The dangerous emotional detachment of the right (Episode 59) [Audio podcast episode]. In *Speak out with Tim Wise*. Speak Out. www.podomatic.com/podcasts/speakoutwithtimwise/episodes/2019-11-27T12_09_06-08_00.

WSUTV. (2016, March 10). Time Wise – Black history month keynote speech [Video]. *YouTube*. www.youtube.com/watch?v=oV-EDWzJuzk.

6

AN IRON TRIANGLE

How Ideas, Beliefs, and Feelings Collectively Inform Our Understanding About Privilege

Ideas, beliefs, and feelings are equally powerful factors toward student learning. Traditional educators may focus on most of their efforts around factual content to influence students' ideas. However, educators may be equally, if not more, successful in cultivating understanding by engaging students' beliefs and feelings.

Consider the educational effort involved with encouraging someone to stop participating in a Smoking Discourse and start participating in a Non-Smoking Discourse. Focusing on conceptual information, such as the harmful chemicals in cigarettes, the statistical chances of chronic illness and death associated with smoking, and the financial costs associated with smoking, may appear to offer compelling evidence to dissuade some individuals. Such information may be compelling to some but not all. New ideas alone may not be sufficient or effective at persuading many individuals, including those who have smoked for many years, to ditch this habit.

Some individuals who choose to smoke have strong beliefs about smoking. Some people may believe that smoking is an effective way to reduce stress, enhance their concentration, or have an easier time socializing with others.[1] Other people may believe that once you are a smoker, there is no benefit to quitting.[2] Individuals may reject new ideas that seem contradictory to their existing beliefs. After all, if someone believes smoking is an effective treatment for stress, they might claim that smoking is beneficial to their health.

Individuals who choose to smoke may also have strong feelings associated with smoking. Some people may describe themselves as feeling happier and more relaxed when smoking.[3] Other people may suggest that smoking makes them feel "cool" and more confident.[4] Individuals may reject new ideas that seem inconsistent with how smoking makes them feel within themselves or about themselves.

DOI: 10.4324/9781003082378-7

After all, if someone feels happier and more relaxed when smoking, they might rationalize that their happiness is worth a few dollars per pack of cigarettes.

Notice how beliefs and feelings can operate to reject new ideas. Imagine if an educator also engaged beliefs and feelings in addition to ideas. Exploring what individuals believe about smoking offers a different path to examine where these beliefs come from and what evidence they have to support their beliefs. Exploring how smoking makes individuals feel offers insight into the types of feelings that are most persuasive to smoking that could be maintained through healthier and less expensive alternatives. To primarily focus on ideas threatens educational efforts because beliefs and feelings are independent, yet interconnected, factors that reinforce ideas.

Engaging ideas, beliefs, and feelings are equally important when educators want to help students stop participating in a Whiteness Discourse and begin participating in an Antiracism Discourse. This chapter synthesizes the insights about core ideas, beliefs, and feelings shared in Chapters 3 through 5 to describe how they collectively reinforce an understanding of privilege associated with participation in either a Whiteness or Antiracism Discourse. I begin with a presentation about how ideas, beliefs, and feelings relate to one another. I follow this presentation with an application of how specific ideas, beliefs, and feelings relate to one another central to the Whiteness and Antiracism Discourses.

How Ideas, Beliefs, and Feelings Reinforce One Another

Participating in a Discourse helps build and sustain relationships with others. Participation in the same Discourse creates a shared understanding about ourselves, others, and society that help bond people together. Ideas, beliefs, and feelings are elements that influence this shared understanding. When people express certain ideas, beliefs, and feelings, they reinforce both a particular understanding and a relationship to others who also share this same understanding within any given Discourse.

A triangular prism provides a useful visual to illustrate the relationship between ideas, beliefs, and feelings that revolve around participation in any given Discourse. Imagine looking down upon a triangular prism (see Figure 6.1). Ideas, beliefs, and feelings make up each side of the prism. These three sides serve as the externally facing "walls" of participation in the Discourse which resides at the center.[5] Just as all three sides are needed to externally represent a triangular prism, ideas, beliefs, and feelings are all needed to externalize our participation in a Discourse.

The triangular relationship between ideas, beliefs, and feelings is purposeful. Architects frequently use triangles because of how all three sides work together to maintain structural integrity. When one part of a triangle is under stress, the remaining parts help redistribute the weight. Anthropomorphically speaking, when one side comes under attack, the remaining two sides come to its aid. The same is true

172 An Iron Triangle

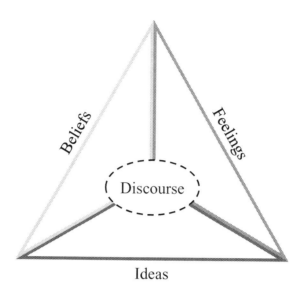

FIGURE 6.1 Visual Representation of Ideas, Beliefs, and Feelings Related to a Discourse

for ideas, beliefs, and feelings. When someone is exposed to new and contradictory ideas, existing beliefs and feelings intervene to reinforce existing ideas.

The circular relationship between ideas, beliefs, and feelings can be oversimplified in the following way. Working around the triangle clockwise (see Figure 6.2), we see that (a) our ideas help to anchor our beliefs, (b) our beliefs are used to justify our feelings, and (c) our feelings serve as fuel to sustain our ideas. Similar functions exist when working around the triangle counterclockwise (see Figure 6.3) where we see that (a) our ideas help to anchor our feelings, (b) our feelings serve as fuel to sustain our beliefs, and (c) our beliefs are used to justify our ideas. In short, (a) ideas help anchor beliefs and feelings, (b) beliefs are used to justify our ideas and feelings, and (c) feelings act as fuel to sustain our ideas and beliefs.

The way ideas, beliefs, and feelings collectively reinforce one another can be seen using the same example about educating someone to stop smoking. Imagine that someone who participates in the Smoking Discourse expresses the following idea, belief, and feeling:

Idea: Smoking is a personal choice.
Belief: Smoking has health benefits.
Feeling: Smoking makes me feel happier and more relaxed.

These assertions collectively operate to reinforce one another. If this individual adopts the core idea that smoking is a personal choice, that idea may anchor their belief that smoking has health benefits that they *choose* over other health benefits.

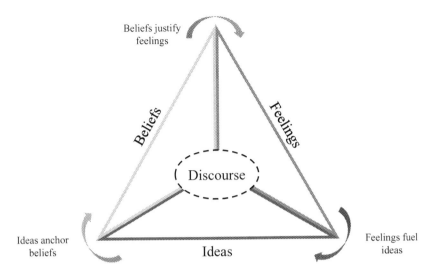

FIGURE 6.2 Clockwise Visual Representation of How Ideas, Beliefs, and Feelings Reinforce One Another

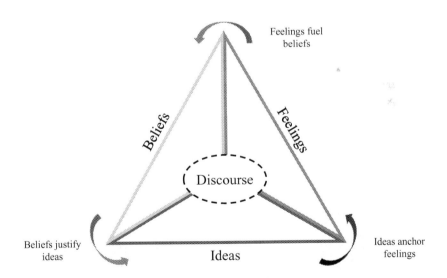

FIGURE 6.3 Counterclockwise Visual Representation of How Ideas, Beliefs, and Feelings Reinforce One Another

The belief that smoking has health benefits can be applied to their feelings to justify why they feel happier and more relaxed while smoking. Every time they feel happy and more relaxed while smoking, those feelings make fuel for their idea that smoking is a personal choice, making them feel grateful for choosing to smoke.

In addition to their ideas, beliefs, and feelings working together, participating in a Smoking Discourse also provides additional fuel for this shared understanding. Interactions with other people who participate in the Smoking Discourse can reinforce these ideas, beliefs, and feelings. Casual conversations that involve someone saying "I could quit anytime I wanted to" reinforces the idea that smoking is a personal choice. Hearing other people who smoke describe how healthy they believe themselves to be reinforces a belief that smoking may not be dangerous and potentially have health benefits. Commiserating with other people about how they smoke when feeling stressed to help them relax reinforces how they feel when they themselves smoke. It is for this reason that support groups to help people quit smoking happen in social spaces not typically where participating in a Smoking Discourse occurs.

The relationship between ideas, beliefs, and feelings is equally powerful when considering how individuals understand privilege relative to participation in an Antiracism and Whiteness Discourse. It is critical to examine how these ideas, beliefs, and feelings operate together if educators want to maximize their chances to facilitate learning about privilege and social inequity.

Participating in the Whiteness Discourse

White students who participate in a Whiteness Discourse and reject the existence of privilege as a structural phenomenon do so from a rational place. They have been deeply socialized into Whiteness Discourse since birth. Part of their socialization involved adopting ideas, beliefs, and feelings related to privilege. These ideas, beliefs, and feelings are reinforced by other participants in the Whiteness Discourse. As demonstrated by the triangular prism analogy, these ideas (White racial knowledge), beliefs (a White supremacist ideology), and feelings (an emotionality of Whiteness) buttress one another (see Figure 6.4).

White racial knowledge consists of four core ideas that revolve around the notion that privilege is an individualistic phenomenon. These ideas frame privilege as situational, occurring in the absence of choice and chance, grounded in individual bias, and existing ahistorically. A White supremacist ideology consists of three belief frames that revolve around a broader belief that privilege is not structural or unjust. These include beliefs that society is fair and everyone has equal opportunities for success; privilege is a natural extension of the human experience based on biological, psychological, or sociological reasoning; and either a generic refutation that privilege is not structural or a counter explanation that privilege is individualistic. An emotionality of Whiteness consists of five different feelings and ways of using emotional language that operate to divert attention away from manifestations of privilege. Specifically, it entails co-opting emotional language to assert counterarguments coupled with feeling bad, sad, angry, and uncomfortable. (see Figure 6.5). These reinforce one another in a bidirectional manner.

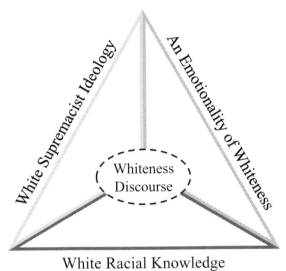

FIGURE 6.4 Visual Representation of Ideas, Beliefs, and Feelings Related to the Whiteness Discourse

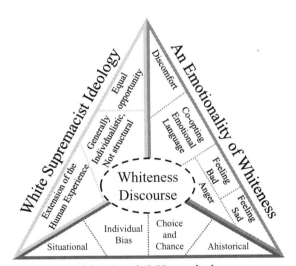

FIGURE 6.5 Visual Representation of Specific Ideas, Beliefs, and Feelings Related to the Whiteness Discourse

Moving clockwise around the triangle, ideas that position privilege as individualistic anchor a belief that privilege is not structural. A belief that privilege is not structural justifies emotional language and emotional reactions that deflect attention away from privilege. Emotionality that deflects attention away from privilege by making it about specific individuals, either oneself as a victim, specific "bad" White people, or vengeful persons of color, serves as fuel for ideas that privilege is individualistic (see Figure 6.6).

Moving counterclockwise around the triangle, ideas that position privilege as individualistic anchor feelings that defect attention about privilege toward specific individuals. Feelings that deflect attention toward specific individuals fuel the belief that privilege is not and cannot be structural. A belief that privilege is not structural is used to justify the notion that privilege is therefore an individualistic phenomenon (see Figure 6.7).

Specific ideas, ideological frames, and feelings support one another similarly as the broader categories of White racial knowledge, a White supremacist ideology, and an emotionality of Whiteness. As an example, consider the comments made during an episode of the radio show *The Breakfast Club* by Rush Limbaugh, a White male conservative radio personality. During a conversation about the murder of George Floyd, Limbaugh replied, "I don't buy into the notion of White privilege" when asked how he would use his White privilege to help challenge racism. He explained his stance that rejects White privilege by stating that White privilege is "designed to intimidate and get people to shut up and admit they are guilty for doing things they haven't done." He returns to this same viewpoint later in his comments by declaring, "I'm not denying that there are certain individuals out there that think they are better than other people. But structurally, institutionally, white supremacy, that's a [false] construct."[6]

Limbaugh expressed three specific ideas, one belief, and two feelings to reject the idea of privilege. Ideas about privilege being situational, ahistorical, and connected to individual bias are all present in his comments. He explicitly expresses the idea that privilege is situational when declaring that privilege is not structural or institutional. His reference to privilege being related to "things [White individuals] have not done" relies on the idea that privilege is ahistorical because racism perpetuated by White people in the past is separate from White people today. His statement that "there are certain individuals out there that think they are better" uses the idea that bias resides in specific individuals. Limbaugh expressed a White supremacist ideology through the use of the belief that privilege is not structural but individualistic when he generically rejected the structural existence of privilege in his concluding comments. He also expressed an emotionality of Whiteness related to feeling bad and uncomfortable when describing how privilege makes White people feel "intimidated" and admit "guilt."

These three ideas, one belief, and two feelings work together to reinforce his understanding of privilege in a particular way (see Figure 6.8). Limbaugh's ideas about privilege as situational, ahistorical, and rooted in individual bias collectively

An Iron Triangle 177

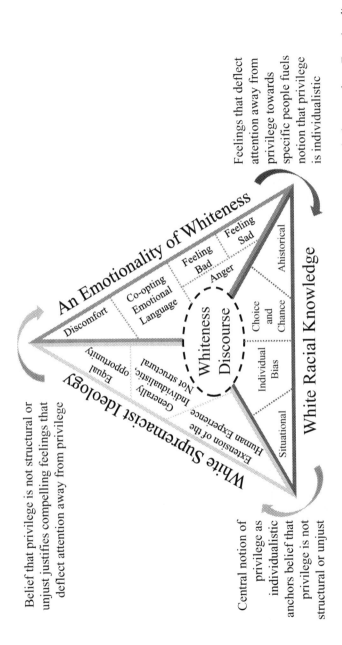

FIGURE 6.6 Clockwise Visual Representation of How White Racial Knowledge, a White Supremacist Ideology, and an Emotionality of Whiteness Reinforce One Another

178 An Iron Triangle

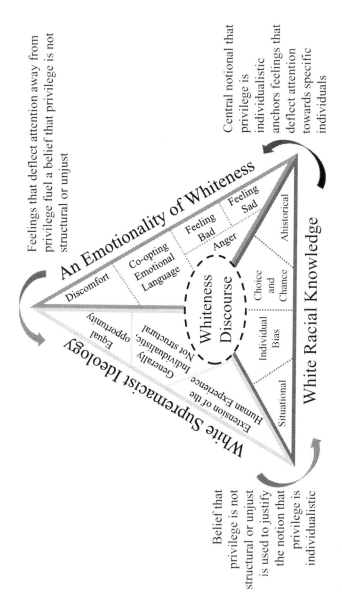

FIGURE 6.7 Counterclockwise Visual Representation of How White Racial Knowledge, a White Supremacist Ideology, and an Emotionality of Whiteness Reinforce One Another

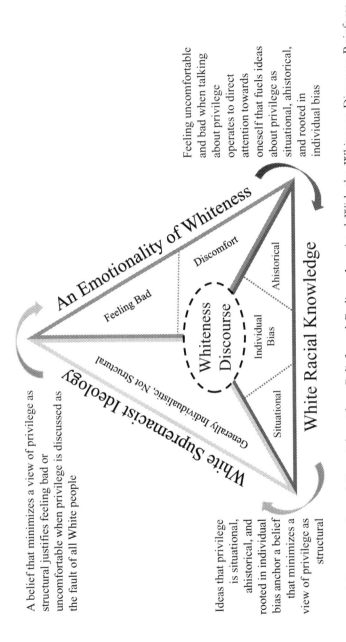

FIGURE 6.8 Visual Representation of How Select Ideas, Beliefs, and Feelings Associated With the Whiteness Discourse Reinforce One Another

reinforce a view of privilege as individualistic. A view of privilege as individualistic provides sufficient anchors to generally minimize views of privilege as structural, reinforcing a belief that privilege is not structural. The idea that privilege is ahistorical helps reject structural claims by separating the White people "in the past" from those who exist today. The idea that privilege is rooted in individual bias singles out "bad" White people versus White people as a collective group across structures and institutions. Both of these ideas are grounded in the idea the privilege exists in select situations. All of these ideas provide no specific rejection of a structural view of privilege but seem sufficient to retain Limbaugh's belief. Furthermore, his general minimization of privilege as structural is used to justify alternative explanations about the term itself. Specifically, privilege is a weapon to harm individual White people. Therefore, it is rational that White people would feel uncomfortable or bad when privilege is bought up. Finally, feeling bad and uncomfortable about privilege directs attention to oneself as a White victim who is bullied by a person of color who chooses to bring up privilege. The realization of this dynamic of people of color harming White people further fuels ideas that privilege is not structural. Bringing up the past to "guilt" White people is a smoke screen, fueling ahistorical ideas. Admitting that some White people are bad fuels ideas that individual bias is to blame over structures. Both of these ideas rely on situational ideas that bring us to the beginning of the process all over again.

The ideas, beliefs, and feelings central to participation in a Whiteness Discourse reinforce one another in ways that can be difficult to change. However, it *is* possible to adopt different ideas, beliefs, and feelings that are associated with participation in an Antiracism Discourse. Evidence from people who participate in the Antiracism Discourse, including the White college students in this study, provides insight into what these new ideas, beliefs, and feelings ought to be and how they may become adopted.

Participating in the Antiracism Discourse

White students who participate in the Antiracism Discourse acknowledge the existence of privilege as a structural phenomenon and embrace a commitment to its dismantlement. Even though they were also originally socialized into the Whiteness Discourse, they adopted new ideas, beliefs, and feelings that emerged from having their existing understanding effectively challenged, coupled with opportunities to master this new understanding around other people who participate in the Antiracism Discourse. As demonstrated by the triangular prism analogy, these ideas (race critical knowledge), beliefs (a race critical ideology), and feelings (racial emotional resiliency) buttress one another to sustain this new view about privilege (see Figure 6.9).

Race critical knowledge consists of four core ideas that commonly operate together to sustain the view that privilege is structural and rooted in the creation and maintenance of social power. These ideas frame privilege as being grounded

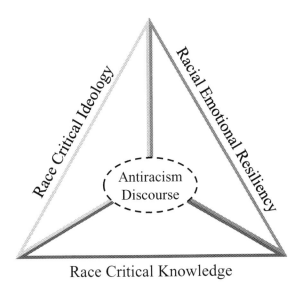

FIGURE 6.9 Visual Representation of Ideas, Beliefs, and Feelings Related to the Antiracism Discourse

in social power, being a manifestation of institutionalized superiority, being intentionally implemented, and being pervasive from the past into the present. A race critical ideology consists of three beliefs that justify a structural view of privilege while critiquing it as unjust. These beliefs are that race is socially constructed, privilege is an ordinary phenomenon that results from the normalization of Whiteness, and that privilege is knowable through the experiences of people of color. Racial emotional resiliency consists of four different feelings and ways of using emotional language that direct attention toward manifestations of privilege and fuel a desire for social change. Specifically, it involves vulnerability through the use of emotional language, along with feelings of upset, shame, anger, and determination (see Figure 6.10). They also reinforce one another in a bidirectional manner.

Moving clockwise around the triangle, ideas about privilege that center around social power anchor a belief that privilege is structural and therefore unjust. A belief that privilege is both structural and unjust serves to justify emotional language and emotional reactions that direct attention toward privilege. Emotionality that directs attention toward privilege to hold systems and individuals accountable serves as a fuel for the central notion that privilege is rooted in social power (see Figure 6.11).

Moving counterclockwise around the triangle, ideas about privilege that center around social power anchor feelings that direct attention toward privilege to hold systems and individuals accountable. Feelings that direct attention toward

182 An Iron Triangle

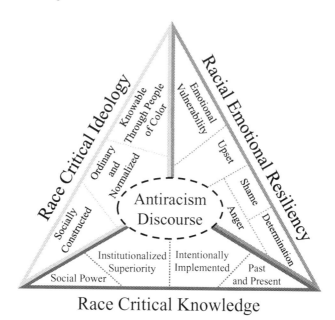

FIGURE 6.10   Visual Representation of Specific Ideas, Beliefs, and Feelings Related to the Antiracism Discourse

privilege fuel the belief that it is an unjust structural phenomenon. A belief that privilege is an unjust structural phenomenon is used to justify ideas that it is centered around the creation and maintenance of social power (see Figure 6.12).

The broader relationship between race critical knowledge, a race critical ideology, and racial emotional resiliency is visible through the specific ideas, beliefs, and feelings expressed among individuals who participate in the Antiracism Discourse. As an example, consider the remarks made about White privilege by Kirsten Gillibrand, a White female US Senator, during her presidential primary campaign in 2019. When asked about her views on White privilege, she offered the following comments:

> What [White privilege] is about is when a community has been left behind for generations because of the color of their skin. When you've been denied job, after job, after job because you're black or because you're brown. Or when you go to the emergency room to have your baby . . . and if you are a black woman you are four times more likely to die in childbirth because that healthcare provider doesn't believe you when you say I don't feel right . . . institutional racism is real . . . to fix the problems that are happening in a black community you need far more transformational efforts that [is] targeted for real racism that exists every day.[7]

An Iron Triangle 183

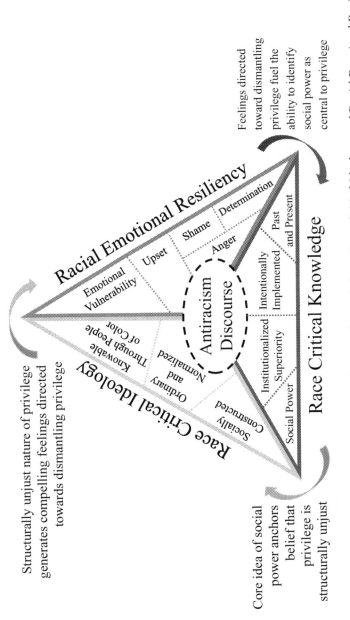

FIGURE 6.11 Clockwise Visual Representation of How Race Critical Knowledge, a Race Critical Ideology, and Racial Emotional Resiliency Reinforce One Another

184 An Iron Triangle

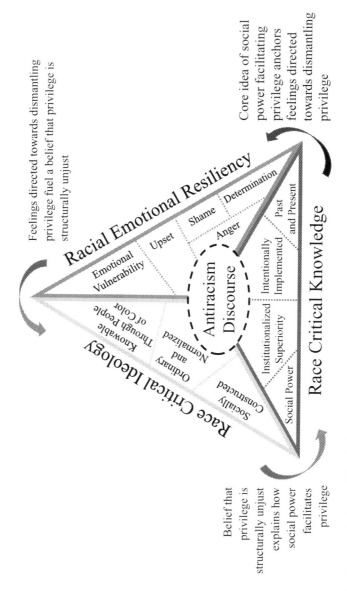

FIGURE 6.12 Counterclockwise Visual Representation of How Race Critical Knowledge, a Race Critical Ideology, and Racial Emotional Resiliency Reinforce One Another

An Iron Triangle 185

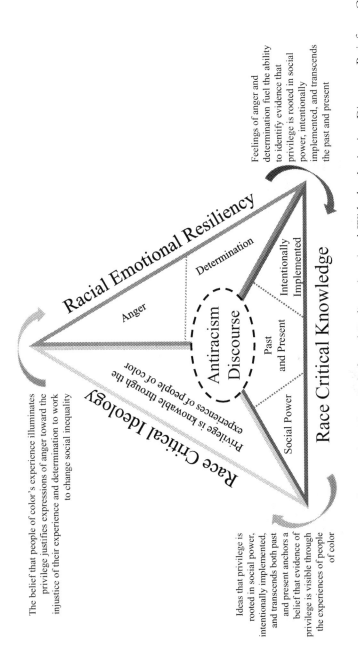

FIGURE 6.13 Visual Representation of How Select Ideas, Beliefs, and Feelings Associated With the Antiracism Discourse Reinforce One Another

Gillibrand used three specific ideas, one belief, and two feelings to advance a structural understanding of privilege. She began her comments by using the idea that privilege is based upon social power when she linked resource distribution (i.e., to one's social group membership, jobs, medical care). She used the idea that privilege persists across the past and into the present when describing the impact of privilege and oppression as occurring over "generations." She also invokes the idea that privilege is intentionally implemented by demonstrating how social power is distributed to select social groups through multiple ways (i.e., employment, medical care) and names it explicitly when stating "institutional racism is real." All of her examples tell the story of privilege that disadvantages people of color, reflecting a race critical ideology through her belief that privilege is knowable through the experiences of people of color. Her ability to quickly identify multiple examples of privilege simultaneously demonstrates muted anger at the senselessness of privilege that also drive feelings of determination to work for social change.

These three ideas, one ideological frame, and two feelings Gillibrand expressed work together to reinforce her understanding of privilege (see Figure 6.13). Her ideas that privilege is based in social power that is both intentionally implemented and persisting from the past into the present all sustain a structural view of privilege. These ideas anchor her belief that privilege is not only structural but also unjust. Her specific belief that privilege is knowable through the experiences of people of color influenced her selection of evidence of oppression faced by people of color across multiple social institutions. The broader belief that privilege is structurally unjust shaped by her specific belief that privilege is knowable through the experience of people of color shaped her emotional reaction to focus on the structural injustice of racism. Specifically, she expressed muted anger toward the insidious nature of racism and concluded with an expression of dedication for "transformational efforts" needed to redress social inequality. Her emotionally driven motivation for social change targets the realities of racism the exists in the present, fueling her ability to identify through the lens of her core ideas that privilege is intentionally implemented in the present (as connected to the past) based upon social power.

Breaking Down the Iron Triangle of Ideas, Beliefs, and Feelings: Leaning in and Leaving the Source

Ideas, beliefs, and feelings reinforce one another, creating a relatively strong defense against new information and experiences that do not fit into an individual's existing understanding. When educators solely assert new ideas against a students' existing ideas, it will likely result in a stalemate. The same is true when educators assert new beliefs and feelings against a students' existing beliefs and feelings. This standstill occurs because to each person, their respective set of ideas, beliefs, or feelings is rational. Educators who participate in the Antiracism Discourse sincerely and wholeheartedly embrace their way of understanding privilege. So do their White students who participate in the Whiteness Discourse.

A faceoff between two competing sets of ideas, beliefs, or feelings is similar to a castle siege. Imagine a White student participating in the Whiteness Discourse to be the defender of a castle while an educator participating in the Antiracism Discourse to be an incoming army. The best strategy for the defenders of a castle is to wait out any direct attack because they have the advantage of the protection of their castle walls, which must be breeched. The same is true for White students who participate in the Whiteness Discourse. When faced with new ideas, beliefs, or feelings, they have an advantage of being able to retreat into their prior knowledge to sustain their understanding.

The hardest part of any castle siege is breeching the walls. Therefore, invading armies commonly attempted to infiltrate the castle through indirect means such as sneaking inside (e.g., the famous Trojan Horse used to invade the city of Troy in *The Odyssey*) or digging tunnels to go underneath. When these methods were effectively used, they were often successful. When engaging individuals who participate in the whiteness Discourse, engaging their ideas, beliefs, and feelings and following them wherever they lead is the equivalent of "sneaking inside."

Broadly speaking, this approach uses listening and using probing questions that accepts and explores the rationality of the student's understanding. When someone participating in the Whiteness Discourse uses that idea that privilege is situational, educators can dig deeper into that idea and see how it plays out. A situational view of privilege works to individualize privilege, but there is likely a tipping point when enough "situations" share a common structural reality. When someone expresses a belief that privilege is a naturally occurring phenomenon, educators can dig deeper and apply that same belief through multiple scenarios. At some point, privilege may no longer seem "natural." When someone expresses anger when confronted with their own privilege, educators can dig deeper into the source of that feeling. Surface anger directed toward people of color may cover the hurt that people of color and White people both experience, albeit in very different ways, as a result of social inequality that may lead to anger toward systemic injustice. Accepting how the ideas, beliefs, and feelings central to participation in the Whiteness Discourse are rational creates opportunities to challenge that logic from the inside.

When educators challenge the ideas, beliefs, and feelings central to participation in the Whiteness Discourse from within, it creates an opening to further upend the remaining ideas, beliefs, and feelings that buttress one another. I can personally attest to the effectiveness of this approach when reflecting on my own experience of unlearning internalized ideas, beliefs, and feelings as a participant in the Whiteness Discourse. I entered college with an understanding of privilege as individualistic and unrelated to race. As a working-class White person, I viewed myself as a good, hardworking individual who *happened* to be White. I did not completely ignore the reality of racial differences but certainly minimized them as secondary to the individualism of every person.

Looking back at my early college experiences, I participated in the Whiteness Discourse through the same constellation of ideas, beliefs, and feelings expressed by some of the White college students in this book. I relied on the ideas that privilege was situational, grounded in choice and chance, and ahistorical. These ideas anchored my belief that privilege was not structural and was better explained by how hard we are willing to work (and thus a reflection of the choices we make as individuals). When confronted with racial privilege, I would feel uncomfortable and often remain quiet because I was a White person and therefore did not have anything to contribute to conversations about race. I also worried about saying the wrong thing and being misperceived by students of color. When I could not remain quiet because I was called into a conversation, I would express how bad *I* felt, or how sad *I* felt, and how those feelings made me feel like there was nothing *I* could do. Other times, I would express anger when others would "accuse me" of having White privilege. I would quickly and fiercely reply, "I don't have White privilege, I'm working class" to deflect attention away from my racial privilege. I honestly saw myself and the world through the lens of Whiteness.

The educators and peers who participated in the Antiracism Discourse and attempted to dissuade me from my individualistic understanding of privilege were never successful. It was only when my experience as a working-class White person was acknowledged and addressed that I begin to see privilege as structural. My "aha" moment occurred when a college instructor looked at me, acknowledged how unfair it was for working-class people to be mistreated, and then invited me to consider how my experiences were like those of people of color. This moment was the first time I recall considering the possibility that my understanding of privilege in general and racial privilege in particular, an understanding built upon years of lived experience and messages internalized from family, friends, and trusted adults, *might not* be true.

The invitation to lean into my emotional anger that was directed toward social class injustice and consider its relationship to racial injustice illuminated a thread that I continued to pull. If I was justified in feeling anger about the existence of social class oppression, that was based on my social class identity which opened the door to consider the idea that privilege was rooted in social power. Exploring the idea of privilege linked to social power lessened my attachment to the idea that privilege was situational and further prompted an exploration into my beliefs. If privilege was rooted in social power, I could neither believe that society was fair, nor social inequality the natural result of individual choices. Without the belief that society was fair, I considered the belief that privilege and social inequality must be ordinary and normalized in ways that only appear fair. These new ideas and beliefs fueled a new focus of my frustration and anger toward unjust social systems coupled with a desire to stop those systems. Furthermore, these different feelings cultivated my desire to explore new ideas further. This entire process was the result of an educator accompanying me into my prior understanding and inviting me to pull on the thread. In this way, I began to slowly unravel the tapestry of Whiteness integrated across my ideas, beliefs, and feelings.

What I described in a single paragraph did not occur in a matter of minutes, days, or even weeks. My experience of shedding ideas, beliefs, and feelings associated with participation in the Whiteness Discourse was supported by educators who explored my understanding and helped me see the seams as they helped pull it apart over months and years. It is a process that I continue to work on today because of how deeply ingrained Whiteness is as a result of our original socialization into the Whiteness Discourse. However, being around other people who actively participate in the Antiracism Discourse was equally pivotal. Realigning my relationships was critical for stemming the source of ideas, beliefs, and feelings central to Whiteness that would otherwise coax me to relapse into the familiar, and far more comfortable, understanding about privilege to which I was accustomed. The ideas, beliefs, and feelings associated with Whiteness are like water that comes from a lake and is distributed throughout a city. Water is distributed through countless pipes buried deep underground that spread into every piece of residential, commercial, and industrial land. To stop drinking tainted water, it is not enough to filter the water in your own home, as that will change only some of the water you drink. Instead, one must stop drinking water that comes from the same contaminated source. The ideas, beliefs, and feelings associated with the Whiteness Discourse are continuously supplied by other individuals who participate in the Whiteness Discourse.

Reassociating with people who participate in a different Discourse is easier said than done. At first, it may involve increasing how much time one spends with people who participate in the Antiracism Discourse. Once old ways of understanding privilege are shed and new ways of understanding begin to take root, it becomes harder to fully participate in the Whiteness Discourse. Something as small as not laughing at the same racist jokes or comments becomes noticeable because the ideas, beliefs, and feelings we express play a central role in connecting us to other people and shared social communities. Some relationships may taper off while others may end all together. Accusations of being a "race traitor" may arise because the same ideas, beliefs, and feelings once used to shift the focus away from race may be directed toward oneself as you become "another one of them." For these reasons, it is essential to understand that shedding ideas, beliefs, and feelings associated with participation in the Whiteness Discourse is an act of leaving behind both a way of understanding the world and a social community. The starkest examples of this exist among the stories of the experience of individuals who once belonged to White supremacist groups.[8]

The purpose of discussing the loss of existing relationships among individuals who work to realign themselves from the Whiteness Discourse to the Antiracism Discourse is to highlight a key way that ideas, beliefs, and feelings are sustained through social relationships. It cannot be enough to simply challenge ideas, belies, and feelings associated with Whiteness without providing social spaces and relationships to help cultivate the exploration into and growth of new ideas, beliefs, and feelings. The purpose is *not* to center the challenges of White people examining privilege as equal to or harder than the experiences of people of color who survive institutionalized oppression on a daily basis. Instead, its goal is to remind us that ideas, beliefs, and feelings reflect ways of understanding ourselves, others, and the world as directly associated with our participation in Discourses as discussed in Chapter 2.

Even when individuals successfully transition away from relationships rooted in the Whiteness Discourse and cultivate social spaces grounded in the Antiracism Discourse, these ideas, beliefs, and feelings are still ever present in our social institutions and social norms. It is for this reason that participating in the Antiracism Discourse requires constant attention and dedication. There are multiple ways in which White people can become seduced back into participating in the Whiteness Discourse. Consider the example of W. McCall Calhoun Jr., a White male lawyer from Georgia. Calhoun was an outspoken progressive who participated in antiracism efforts by advocating criminal justice reform, providing regular donations to the National Association for the Advancement of Colored People (NAACP), and calling out racism in local elections. Then, in 2019, he abruptly began participating in Whiteness though his critiques of the Black Lives Matter movement, use of racial slurs, and the possession of a Confederate flag when he participated in the armed siege of the United States Capitol in January 2021. Some local residents were baffled by what they perceived to be a stark contrast in his behaviors and views. However, others such as Rev. Mathis Kearse Wright Jr, head of the local NAACP chapter, understood the switch as unsurprising given the deeply racist history, norms, and beliefs that exist in the United States that had been cultivated during the Trump administration.[9] In other words, White people can shift their participation from the Whiteness Discourse into the Antiracism Discourse but can also shift back into the Whiteness Discourse because the ideas, beliefs, and feelings remain prevalent in our society.

Shifting Our Discourse Participation

Everyone is socialized from birth to adopt ideas, beliefs, and feelings about privilege that are central to participation in the Whiteness Discourse. Over time, individuals' internalization of White racial knowledge, a White supremacist ideology, and an emotionality of Whiteness become stronger as they reinforce one another through experience. These ideas, beliefs, and feelings about privilege collectively reinforce our understanding of privilege. Our understanding of privilege connects us to others who participate in the Whiteness Discourse. Our relationship with others who participate in the Whiteness Discourse provides sources that reinforce our adoption of these ideas, beliefs, and feelings about privilege.

When individuals have their prior knowledge about privilege challenged, they are most likely to reject new information that is contradictory to their existing understanding. Individuals use compatible ideas, beliefs, and feelings to defend their prior understanding, which is rational from their perspective. They also seek support from others who participate in the Whiteness Discourse and share their existing understanding of privilege, normalizing the rationality of their views. However, when individuals are receptive to challenging their existing ideas, beliefs, and feelings about privilege, it creates an opportunity to unravel their prior knowledge. Shedding our existing understanding of privilege is rooted in White racial knowledge, a White supremacist ideology, and an emotionality of Whiteness that (a) challenges our prior understanding, (b) creates distance between ourselves from those who participate in the Whiteness Discourse, (c) tests new ways of understanding privilege, and (d) realigns our relationships to others that participate in an Antiracism Discourse. Shifting our understanding of privilege to participate in an Antiracism Discourse necessarily requires a shift in our social spaces to sustain growth and allow opportunities to practice and master behaviors and perspectives based upon race critical knowledge, a race critical ideology, and racial emotional resiliency.

Educators who help White college students develop an accurate understanding of privilege that contributes to social change are engaging in a process larger than any single educational experience. Educational opportunities that help White college students evolve their understanding of privilege are spaces that invite these White students to reexamine their prior knowledge, existing worldview, current relationships, and broader social alignment. Existing ideas, beliefs, and feelings work hard to reinforce one another because changing our view of privilege is more effortful and impactful than simply changing our minds. Educators who understand these dynamics while being able to identify specific ideas, beliefs, and feelings associated with White racial knowledge, a White supremacist ideology, and an emotionality of Whiteness can more effectively and compassionately engage White college students in their developmental journey.

Notes

1 See Yong and Borland (2008).
2 See Centers for Disease Control and Prevention (n.d.).
3 See Live Science Staff (2004).
4 See Rodrigues (2009).
5 There are multiple aspects of Discourse participation beyond ideas, beliefs, and feelings. However, for the sake of this visual analogy other aspects are not considered here.
6 See Rico (2020).
7 See Kim (2019).
8 See Saslow (2018).
9 See Fausset and Robertson (2012).

References

Centers for Disease Control and Prevention. (n.d.). *Is what you know about smoking wrong?* [pamphlet]. www.cdc.gov/tobacco/data_statistics/sgr/2010/myths/pdfs/myths.pdf.

Fausset, R., & Robertson, C. (2012, February 18). How a hard-core liberal lawyer joined the pro-Trump mob. *The New York Times.* www.nytimes.com/2021/02/18/us/W-McCall-Calhoun-Jr-georgia-capitol-riot.html.

Kim, C. (2019, July 12). A White woman from Ohio asked Gillibrand about White privilege. Her answer was spot on. *Vox.* www.vox.com/policy-and-politics/2019/7/12/20691717/white-working-class-kirsten-gillibrand-white-privilege-institutional-racism.

Live Science Staff. (2004, October 29). Why smokers feel good. *Live Science.* www.livescience.com/53-smokers-feel-good.html.

Rico, K. (2020, June 1). Rush Limbaugh denies existence of White privilege on 'The Breakfast Club': 'That is a liberal, political construct.' *Variety.* https://variety.com/2020/tv/news/rush-limbaugh-denies-white-privilege-breakfast-club-1234622562-1234622562/.

Rodrigues, J. (2009, March 31). When smoking was cool, cheap, legal and socially acceptable. *The Guardian.* www.theguardian.com/lifeandstyle/2009/apr/01/tobacco-industry-marketing.

Saslow, E. (2018). *Rising out of hatred: The awakening of a former White nationalist.* Anchor Books.

Yong, H., & Borland, R. (2008). Functional beliefs about smoking and quitting activity among adult smokers in four countries: Findings from the international tobacco control four-country survey. *Health Psychology, 27*(3 Suppl), S216–S223.

CONCLUSION

What Have We Learned and Where Do We Go?

During a 1968 television interview with James Baldwin, he expressed frustration with the glacial pace of racial change in the United States, stating, "You always told me it takes time. It has taken my father's time, my mother's time, my uncle's time, my brothers' and my sisters' time, my nieces' and my nephews' time. How much time do you want for your 'progress'?"[1] His words remain painfully accurate today in the United States when listening to politicians and university leadership alike call for peace and patience in the face of persistent racial disparities and violence. *The Washington Post* has tracked a disturbingly consistent number of fatal police shootings of Black and Latinx people nationally. Over a 5-year period between 2016 through 2020, there were between 395 and 412 fatalities *annually*.[2] In 2018, the Centers for Disease Control and Prevention reported that the average life expectancy of Black people was nearly 4 years lower than White people.[3] In 2016, the Brookings Institution reported that the typical Black family has roughly ten times *less* wealth compared to a typical White family.[4] In 2017, the percentage of adults ages 25 and older who completed an associate, bachelor's, master's, professional, or doctoral degree was 15% lower for Black people compared to White people.[5] This evidence of privilege and social inequality persists despite universities turning to curricular and co-curricular diversity education to advance cultural competence among college students as the solution to societal inequalities.[6]

I am an ardent advocate for education as a form of intervention. However, I worry that these efforts for multiculturalism, social justice, and antiracist education are not always guided by a more systematic and empirically grounded approach. Research revealed that educators do not always use scholarship and researched best practices to develop and implement educational experiences.[7] My deep hope is that the insights discussed in this book challenge our assumptions

DOI: 10.4324/9781003082378-8

about how to effectively contribute to social justice through intentional educational practices, at the level of both the individual and the institution.

As W. E. B. Du Bois once said, "Now is the accepted time, not tomorrow, not some more convenient season. It is today that our best work can be done and not some future day or future year."[8] Indeed, the time is now to examine our educational approach and commit to enhancing our social justice education efforts. It is never too late to refine our educational expectations, curriculum, or andragogy to support student learning related to privilege. Ibram Kendi shared this view in the introduction of his popular book, *How to be an Antiracist*:

> The good news is that racist and antiracist are not fixed identities. We can be racist one minute and an antiracist the next. What we say about race, what we do about race, in each moment, determines what — now who — we are.[9]

Kendi's statement can also be applied to White students' participation in Whiteness and Antiracist Discourses. We can employ ideas, beliefs, and feelings central to the Whiteness Discourse one moment and pivot to ideas, beliefs, and feelings central to the Antiracism Discourse the next. Therefore, educators and educational institutions who are committed to an inclusive and socially just society might wish to ask themselves if they are satisfied with their students' understanding of privilege. And if they are not, how might the insights from this book be useful in their endeavor.

Summary of Insights

This book synthesized a mixture of scholarship across disciplines, empirical research, and examples from popular culture to provide insight into how White college students understand privilege. These insights have been further consolidated to see their relationship to one another more readily, along with their implications. Please refer back to earlier chapters in the book for further exploration into these insights.

Students Have Prior Knowledge About Privilege

Students are not empty buckets waiting to be filled with knowledge about privilege. Everyone begins to internalize messages about privilege after they are born. Both the existence of privilege and messages about it are deeply pervasive throughout our society. The nature of privilege is that it is rooted in social power that was intentionally implemented and leads to institutionalized superiority that stretches from the past and into the present. Therefore, the lived experience of every person in the United States is indelibly shaped by privilege, by either receiving it or being denied it. Simply living our lives shaped by our social group memberships, including the Discourses we participate in, including what we see and do not see and our interpretation of it, provides a baseline of prior knowledge about privilege.

Prior Knowledge About Privilege Entails Ideas, Beliefs, and Feelings Developed Through Socialization

Our prior knowledge about privilege specifically entails ideas, beliefs, and feelings. We internalize these ideas, beliefs, and feelings about privilege through our socialization into society, including our day-to-day interactions in the world, our relationships with others, our interactions with social institutions (e.g., educational, medical, legal, economic), and the media we consume. Our ideas about privilege influence how we receive and organize information about this phenomenon. The extent to which our existing ideas about privilege are accurate, complete, and relevant can help or hinder our ability to identify and organize new information and examples related to privilege. Our beliefs about privilege shape our explanations for how and why bits of information are, or are not, related to one another. While beliefs are used by individuals to make sense of their reality, they exist and are maintained within the Discourses into which we are socialized throughout our lives. Our feelings about privilege are a reflection about how we feel about the world, others, and ourselves that we have been socialized to adopt. We experience a range of positive and negative feelings during our lives that reinforce existing social norms and rules, including those directly and indirectly formed because of privilege.

Ideas, Beliefs, and Feelings About Privilege Are Interconnected

Our ideas, beliefs, and feelings simultaneously reinforce one another. Our ideas are the building blocks for what we believe, and our beliefs generate explanations that use and reinforce our adherence to specific ideas. Our beliefs justify how we feel about ourselves, others, and the world, and the way we feel serves as motivation for specific beliefs that we hold to be true. Our feelings direct our attention toward specific ideas, and these specific ideas fuel these same feelings.

Our ideas, beliefs, and feelings about privilege reinforce one another in the same manner. However, the nature of privilege being rooted in social power magnifies the relationship between these ideas, beliefs, and feelings. Ideas, beliefs, and feelings about privilege are not only simply about privilege as an abstract phenomenon but also influence how we understand ourselves and our entire lives, which have been impacted by privilege. The phenomenon of privilege in the abstract cannot be separated from its material reality, manifested through our association with particular Discourses. Therefore, our ideas, beliefs, and feelings may appear to be objective and distanced from ourselves; however, it is impossible to hold ideas, beliefs, and feelings about privilege that are not personal.

Ideas, Beliefs, and Feelings About Privilege Are Grounded Within Discourses

Our ideas, beliefs, and feelings about privilege are adopted through our participation in various Discourses. The variation between different ideas, beliefs, and feelings related to privilege reflect different Discourses in which individuals choose to participate. It is through our participation in any given Discourse that we adopt and replicate specific ideas, beliefs, and feelings. By adopting and replicating certain views about privilege, we reinforce their legitimacy among other individuals who participate in the same Discourses while cementing out relationships to others who choose to adopt these same views. Every Discourse sustains and replicates the ideas, beliefs, and feelings that are adopted by its participants.

The Primary Discourses Regarding Privilege Include the Whiteness Discourse and Antiracism Discourse

There exist two broad viewpoints in regard to the phenomenon of privilege. These viewpoints are related to two competing Discourses: The Antiracism Discourse and the Whiteness Discourse. The viewpoint within the Antiracism Discourse asserts that privilege is a structural phenomenon that is unfair and ought to be dismantled. Another viewpoint located within the Whiteness Discourse asserts that privilege is better understood as an individualistic phenomenon that is a natural extension of human existence. Individuals who participate in the Antiracism Discourse aspire to draw attention to privilege as a structural phenomenon to advocate for social change. Individuals who participate in the Whiteness Discourse aspire to divert attention away from privilege and toward specific individuals to obfuscate and minimize any structural aspects of privilege that are claimed to exist.

Participating in the Whiteness Discourse Involves White Racial Knowledge, a White Supremacist Ideology, and an Emotionality of Whiteness

Individuals who participate in the Whiteness Discourse adopt White racial knowledge, a White supremacist ideology, and an emotionality of Whiteness. Specific ideas, beliefs, and feelings about privilege commonly revolve around notions of individualism. The four key ideas central to White racial knowledge frame privilege as situational, occurring as the result of choice and chance, grounded in individual bias, and being ahistorical. These ideas collectively frame privilege as a variable and localized phenomenon central to specific individuals. Three specific beliefs central to a White supremacist ideology assume that everyone has equal opportunities for success, privilege is a natural extension of the human experience, and privilege is better understood as individualistic. Five specific manifestations common within an emotionality of Whiteness involve co-opting emotional language to assert counter arguments coupled with feeling bad, sad, angry, and uncomfortable to divert attention away from institutional privilege and toward individuals. These ideas, beliefs, and feelings reinforce existing social power dynamics by leveraging hegemonic views and norms. Such perspectives appear reasonable because everyone has been socialized to adopt them at some point during their lives.

Participating in the Antiracism Discourse Involves Race Critical Knowledge, a Race Critical Ideology, and Racial Emotional Resiliency

Individuals who participate in the Antiracism Discourse adopt race critical knowledge, a race critical ideology, and racial emotional resiliency. Specific ideas, beliefs, and feelings about privilege are grounded in a structural understanding of this phenomenon. The four key ideas central to race critical knowledge involve privilege being grounded in social power, being a manifestation of institutionalized superiority, being intentionally implemented, and being pervasive from the past into the present. These ideas collectively describe the structural and pervasive nature of privilege. Three specific beliefs central to a race critical ideology assume that race is a social construction, racial privilege and oppression are ordinary phenomena manifested through the normalization of Whiteness, and racial privilege and oppression are knowable through the experiences of people of color. Five specific manifestations common within racial emotional resiliency consist of vulnerability through emotional language and feeling upset, ashamed, angry, and determined that work together to hold oneself accountable and sustain efforts for social change. These ideas, beliefs, and feelings challenge existing social power dynamics by uncovering hegemonic views and norms and fueling a commitment to social action.

Ideas Within White Racial Knowledge and Race Critical Knowledge Reflect Different Views Within Similar Conceptual Categories

Separately, the specific ideas within White racial knowledge and race critical knowledge highlight an individualistic or structural view of privilege quite different from one another. When examined together, it becomes clear that these ideas reflect different stances to key questions about privilege. When and how privilege is manifested in society is answerable through the ideas about privilege being situational or rooted in social power. Who ought to be held accountable for privilege is answered used the ideas that privilege is either intentionally implemented in society or a reflection of either personal choices or random chance. Ideas about privilege resulting from institutionalized superiority versus individual bias reflect different views regarding how our perception of social identities relate to privilege. How privilege exists relative to time is answered through ideas that privilege is either ahistorical or situated in both the past and the present. Considering how these opposing ideas relate to one another reveals opportunities to influence students' conceptual understanding of privilege from individualistic to structural.

Beliefs Within a White Supremacist Ideology and Race Critical Ideology Are Based Upon Distinct Ideas to Produce Different Explanations

Beliefs and ideas are used together to provide explanations of reality. Similarly, select ideas about privilege are used to assert beliefs central to either a White supremacist ideology or a race critical ideology. The idea that privilege is situational is commonly used to buttress beliefs that everyone has equal opportunities for success, privilege is a natural extension of the human experience, and privilege is better understood as individualistic within a White supremacist ideology. Similarly, the idea that privilege is rooted in social power is commonly used to buttress beliefs that race is a social construction, racial privilege and oppression are ordinary phenomena manifested through the normalization of Whiteness, and racial privilege and oppression are knowable through the experiences of people of color within a race critical ideology. These core ideas serve as the keystones for other ideas used in these beliefs. Therefore, the rigor with which a person adheres to these beliefs is connected to their reliance upon these key ideas and vice versa.

Feelings Within an Emotionality of Whiteness and Racial Emotional Resiliency Reflect Different Approaches to Rejecting or Embracing Vulnerability and Accountability

The way we experience and express our feelings is connected to our ideas and beliefs. Participating in the Antiracism Discourse that seeks to dismantle privilege as a structural phenomenon nurtures emotionality that serves this purpose. Racial emotional resiliency cultivates feelings directed toward structural iterations of privilege. However, because individuals help reinforce these structures, it also cultivates vulnerability to allow individuals to examine themselves as part of systems and structures. Participating in the Whiteness Discourses that seeks to sustain the social power status quo nurtures emotionality that serves this purpose as well. An emotionality of Whiteness cultivates feelings directed away from structural privilege and toward other individuals as scapegoats. Relatedly, individuals turn attention inward to divert attention away from structural privilege by focusing on themselves as victims needing support and thus avoiding personal accountability themselves. Once again, the core ideas of privilege being rooted in social power versus being situational arise to sustain how these emotions are manifested. The idea of privilege being rooted in social power sustains emotional vulnerability by allowing individuals to explore their culpability as part of a larger system. The idea of privilege being situational sustains emotional defensiveness by allowing individuals to reject what is perceived as accusations of privilege that exist in other unrelated contexts.

While Everyone Is Socialized to Adopt White Racial Knowledge, a White Supremacist Ideology, and an Emotionality of Whiteness, They Can Be Unlearned

All people in the United States, including both White people and people of color alike, are socialized to participate in the Whiteness Discourse to some degree. For White people, their de facto socialization is the result of the Whiteness Discourse being the hegemonic Discourse in our institutions and "American" culture. However, it is possible to reduce our participation in the Whiteness Discourse and instead participate in the Antiracism Discourse through four equally important actions. First, reducing our participation in the Whiteness Discourse entails shedding ideas central to White racial knowledge, beliefs central to a White supremacist ideology, and the expression of feelings central to an emotionality of Whiteness. Second, altering our relationships with other individuals who participate in the Whiteness Discourse is critical to stop the flow and normativity of White racial knowledge, a White supremacist ideology, and an emotionality of Whiteness from pulling us back into the Whiteness Discourse. Third, increasing our participation in the Antiracism Discourse entails acquiring ideas central to race critical knowledge, beliefs central to a race critical ideology, and the expression of feelings central to racial emotional resiliency. Finally, increasing our social relationships with other individuals who participate in the Antiracism Discourse not only affirms and normalizes race critical knowledge, a race critical ideology, and racial emotional resiliency but also provides social spaces to practice using them to inform and change our behaviors and habits key to dismantling privilege.

Educational Recommendations

Equipped with these insights into how White college students understand privilege in general and White privilege in particular, we are left with the practical question of "What must be done?" I firmly believe that education is a critical component for realizing a vision of social justice in our society. However, I do not believe that education is the best or only medicine to cure our society from social inequality. Just as privilege is a structural phenomenon, our interventions must also be structural, including our educational interventions. Therefore, I propose the following recommendations for social justice educators to consider, not only for themselves and their individual educational practice but also when advocating about broader educational policy and practice.

Solicit, Reflect Upon, and Leverage Students' Prior Knowledge

Students' prior knowledge about privilege exists and influences future learning about privilege, regardless of our awareness of it. Because prior knowledge can help or hinder student learning, educators who actively solicit students' prior knowledge have a distinct educational advantage if they reflect upon this information and intentionally leverage it in the educational experience. Using students' prior knowledge and experience is useful to create purposeful educational experiences around the needs and realities of students and is considered a pedagogical practice consistent with the practice of social justice education.[10]

Faculty and staff who teach courses or facilitate workshops or structured conversations can solicit students' prior knowledge in multiple ways. One approach entails asking students to complete a short survey or writing prompt about their understanding and experiences related to privilege before the educational activity. Another approach could involve asking students the same question as a "teaser" or introduction to content. Yet, another approach could incorporate such questions into more intentional educational activities. For example, they could do a brainstorm around the question "what comes to mind when you think about privilege?" Or they might facilitate a "four corners" activity where students move to the corner of the room that reflects their agreement with a series of statements about privilege that reflects common ideas, beliefs, and feelings.

After collecting this information about students' prior knowledge, educators should reflect upon these views to explore how students are making sense of privilege. If soliciting insight prior to an educational experience, there is more time to reflect on students' responses and determine its implications for teaching. If soliciting insight during an educational experience, educators can use follow-up questions to invite students to make sense of what is shared. For example, if educators ask students to participate in an idea brainstorm about privilege, they can ask the students collectively reflect upon and interpret what was shared to further explore how responses fit together or are incongruent with one another.

With additional information and insight into students' understanding, educators can leverage students' prior knowledge as part of the learning experience. Educators can use their insight to create intentional educational experiences for students, such as modifying how much time is spent on privilege, or the types of activities that might be most useful to implement to address prevalent misconceptions. Educators can incorporate provocative discussion questions into their teaching that builds upon students' existing understanding and leverage different perspectives among students to encourage them to engage one another. While these approaches can be done without soliciting students' prior knowledge, educators can be more effective in their planning and implantation with this information to cultivate relevant learning opportunities for their students.

Educational institutions can also solicit students' prior knowledge about privilege on a larger level. Administrators can create questions as part of new or existing surveys to all students at the start of their college career to collect information about students' prior knowledge regarding privilege. The survey could invite students to indicate their agreement with statements such as "White privilege is a problem that needs to be addressed in society," "I believe everyone has equal opportunities to be successful if they try hard enough," or "I feel uncomfortable when discussing privilege because I worry about how others will perceive me."

In addition to collecting this information, institutions could reflect upon these insights through further analysis. Statistical correlations could be conducted to reveal if and how certain responses are likely to be related to one another. Further, breaking down the findings by race and other demographics would provide deeper insight into "who" maintains certain views. For example, breaking down the findings by race might reveal how White students view privilege relative to students of color, suggesting how conversations about privilege might play out on campus. Furthermore, breaking down findings by race and other demographics, such as federal Pell grant eligibility as a proxy for social class, could reveal how strong certain beliefs are among lower/working-class students versus middle-/upper-class White students and suggest different useful insights.

Institutions can help educators use these campus-wide insights to inform educational decisions about teaching and learning regarding privilege. Campus-wide data may support decisions to create or modify general education requirements to address privilege in particular ways. For example, should an institutional survey reveal that a large majority of students believes everyone has equal opportunities to be successful if they try hard enough, administrators may decide it is prudent to intentionally address narratives about meritocracy and rugged individualism. As a result, this topic could be addressed in a required general education course or workshop, as a theme that ought to be addressed across multiple courses, or both. Another way administrators could use campus-wide data would be to provide (required) training opportunities for faculty and staff to become more prepared to engage students around privilege. Administrators willing to use these insights to make large changes to the curriculum and educator training ensure that the institution is collectively working to promote accurate understanding about privilege as an institutional priority.

Intentionally Create Educational Experiences That Engage Students' Ideas, Beliefs, and Feelings

Students' prior knowledge consists of their ideas, beliefs, and feelings. Because ideas, beliefs, and feelings are interconnected and reinforce one another, educators would be wise to intentionally create educational experiences that engage all three elements of prior knowledge. Being prepared to engage all three elements provides educators more avenues to successfully engage students' prior knowledge to cultivate a more accurate understanding of privilege. If students are resistant to exploring and reconsidering their existing ideas, tending to their beliefs and feelings provides alternative paths for learning that can be equally useful. Integrating a focus on ideas, beliefs, and feelings can be accomplished by creating intentional learning outcomes and curating educational activities

Creating learning outcomes is a powerful way to ensure these elements are addressed in the educational experience. Learning outcomes indicate the intended goals for educational experiences that reflect our educational priorities. Doing so also satisfies another pedagogical principle of social justice education regarding addressing both the cognitive and affective elements of learning.[11] Faculty and staff could revise or create learning outcomes to intentionally cultivate student learning related to their ideas, beliefs, and feelings related to privilege.[12] Examples of such learning outcomes appropriate for courses, workshops, or structured conversations might include the following:

- Describe accurate and inaccurate ideas commonly associated with privilege.
- Explain the notion of meritocracy and how it is used to justify racial privilege in the United States.
- Identify personal feelings and associated triggers related to racial privilege.

Institutions could also create learning outcomes at the program level or university level that cultivate students' ideas, beliefs, and feelings related to privilege. When writing learning outcomes situated at a higher level, it can be tricky to ensure they are relevant to students across a range of academic experiences. However, it is possible when considering how students benefit from a robust understanding of privilege. Examples of such learning outcomes useful as university-level outcomes, standardized outcomes for required multiculturalism courses, or "common outcomes" that exist across a generation education curriculum might include the following:

- Discuss the existence and implications of racial privilege using both historical and contemporary examples within the United States.
- Examine students' personal beliefs about race and privilege and how they reinforce or challenge social power dynamics within the United States.
- Respond to evidence of privilege with emotional authenticity and vulnerability.

Curating activities within the broader educational experience to engage student learning related to ideas, beliefs, and feelings about privilege support the success of intentionally developed learning outcomes.[13] It is highly unlikely that any single activity can adequately cultivate student learning related to ideas, beliefs, and feelings about privilege. Therefore, educators should craft educational experiences that utilize multiple types of activities. Tharp and Moreano (2020) describe multiple types of activities, such as guidelines for conversations, lectures, and various task-based and discussion-based activities that can collectively address all three elements.

For example, in the context of a course, workshop, or structured conversation, an educator might use guidelines for conversations to explicitly frame how students reflect on their ideas, beliefs, and feelings, as well as normalize emotions as part of learning. A lecture could be used to introduce and frame common ideas about privilege. A simulation of privilege and oppression, a specific type of task-based activity, could be used to create an experience that purposefully unearths beliefs and feelings. Two types of discussion-based activities, discussion pairs and large-group discussions, could be used to scaffold intentional reflection about the simulation. Discussion pairs could invite students to reflect on their feelings during the simulation and what they observed. A large group discussion could then commence that poses questions to probe students' feelings and connect their observations to common beliefs about privilege more deeply. The experience could conclude with another lecture that connects these feelings and beliefs to ideas about privilege that have existed for a long time into the present day.[14]

Institutions can also consider the broader expectations they have for students and how they could engage students' ideas, beliefs, and feelings about privilege. Institutions commonly have a general education requirement that talks about diversity and difference. However, institutions could require and facilitate multiple experiences, curricular and co-curricular alike, that help students learn about privilege by engaging their ideas, beliefs, and feelings. Imagine if an institution implemented the following types of experiences across a traditional 4-year college experience:

- Curricular experiences
   - Standardized lesson plan focused around defining privilege and exploring ideas about privilege during a required first-year seminar course.
   - Writing assignment asking students to identify and reflect upon their ideas and beliefs about privilege related to their racial identity and one other social identity integrated into all required first-year student writing courses.
   - Standardized unit focused on social inequality in the past and present through the lens of race and one other social identity as part of all required multiculturism general education courses.
   - Writing assignment asking students to reflect upon their beliefs and feelings about themselves and the communities they interacted with as a required part of credit-bearing service-learning experiences.
   - Standardized writing prompt integrated into capstone project requirements that invites students to reflect upon their racial identity and associated privilege or oppression relative to their final project, approach to research, beliefs about their professional community, etc.

- Co-curricular experiences
   - Theatrical session followed with small group dialogues that focus on normalizing interracial interactions, dialogues, and feelings at college during new student orientation.

o   Required workshop on social identity and privilege focusing on beliefs and feelings in the context of the workplace to be completed within 1 month of all on-campus jobs.
o   Integrating participation in racial caucus groups that explore students' lived experiences with privilege and oppression while exploring their own ideas, beliefs, and feelings as part of leadership training programs that result in a transcript notation.

Engage Students' Ideas Related to White Racial Knowledge and Juxtapose Them With Race Critical Knowledge

Educators able to identify commonly used ideas central to White racial knowledge can more easily engage students' understanding, explore their existing ideas, and provide alternatives central to race critical knowledge to influence their understanding. Educators can use the idea categories for each of the commonly used ideas discussed in Chapter 3 to engage students' understanding and encourage deeper exploration.

When students use the idea that privilege is situational, educators can explore this idea by exploring as many "situations" of privilege as possible. Instead of challenging the idea directly, they might invite the student (or all the students together) to name as many situations where privilege exists as possible. Once students have come up with a robust list, educators could invite students to reflect upon the sheer number of "situations" that exist and consider if there might be any commonalities across them. Educators could then explicitly state the commonalities using the alternative idea that privilege is rooted in social power based upon social identity. This approach could be implemented as a facilitator technique to engage students or an intentionally developed workshop or lesson plan related to privilege.

The idea of privilege being ahistorical builds upon the idea that privilege is situational in a temporal context. Therefore, educators could engage the idea that privilege is ahistorical using a similar approach as that described previously. Educators could invite students to identify examples of privilege (and oppression) over multiple units of time (e.g., decades, generations). They could then invite students to articulate why these examples are not connected to one another or invite them to consider the ways they are interconnected.

There are other possible ways educators might engage the idea that privilege is historical as well. Educators could proactively think about making it a habit to always discuss examples of privilege in both the past and the present to reinforce the idea that privilege is pervasive over time. Another route would be to create a task or assignment that asks students to research the topic of privilege and discuss "situations" in at least two or three points of time at least 25–30 years apart. Such an assignment does not directly challenge the idea that privilege is ahistorical while inviting students to do work that might begin to soften this idea on its own. Institutions could similarly integrate expectations to explore past and present iterations of privilege as part of how it teaches students about privilege. This expectation could take the form of a learning outcome for all multiculturalism courses or could be reflected in the program design for co-curricular campus-wide celebrations (e.g., MLK celebrations, Thanksgiving events).

The idea that privilege is associated with individual bias is tricky because bias is the individualized manifestation of institutionalized supremacy, not the entire manifestation of privilege on its own. Therefore, educators could engage the idea of individual bias by exploring how, or at what point, an individual "becomes" biased. If students suggest that people are fatalistically born to be biased, similar to the Christian notion of original sin, consider exploring individuals who do *not* act out of bias. If students suggest that bias is acquired over time, consider exploring where and how it is acquired using empirical studies. Both approaches lean into the idea of individual bias by exposing ways privilege goes beyond select individuals, opening the possibility to explore institutionalized superiority. Institutions can also work to undermine ideas of individual bias by revising institutional policies, messages, and training programs that discuss or reinforce the idea that individual bias is a stand-alone phenomenon. Instead, policies, messages, and trainings could focus on institutionalized superiority that sustains and gives permission for bias. For example, some institutions shared campus-wide messages in response to the killing of eight Asian people in Atlanta spas.[15] Many of these responses reinforced the idea of individual bias by focusing on hate, bias, and bigotry that harms Asian-Americans and provided necessary resources for self-care. However, a response that focused on institutionalized superiority might have explicitly named and condemned White supremacy and its institutionalized antecedents as the cause of this contemporary violence and committed to action to hold individuals accountable for and prevent such violence from occurring would be a different, compelling response.

The ideas that privilege is explained by choice or chance are unique variations of ways to position privilege as unexplainable. When students use the idea that privilege is based upon "good" choices, educators might engage this notion by asking if students ever made good choices that did not lead to benefits or resources. Similarly, they might ask if students ever made "bad" choices that did not influence the benefits or resources they were granted by others. A broader question, "Why would anyone make choices that did not give them advantages or benefits?" could be posed to further stretch the boundaries of this idea past its breaking point and create space to consider if intentionally implemented social structures, policies, and practices might offer better insight into privilege. Should students use the idea that privilege is linked to random chance, educators might explore this idea further and ask at what point the "random chances" of the same person or group of people having privilege is no longer random and what might they have in common with one another.

Educators and institutions can avoid cultivating incomplete knowledge about privilege by actively teaching all four ideas central to race critical knowledge. The four ideas frame privilege as being grounded in social power, being a manifestation of institutionalized superiority, being intentionally implemented, and being pervasive from the past into the present and work together to provide a robust conceptual understanding. Teaching a full definition of privilege using examples across multiple social settings and institutions from the past and present could be quite compelling. Many of the same suggestions offered for engaging ideas central to White racial knowledge could work well together.

Engage Students' Beliefs Related to a White Supremacist Ideology and Juxtapose Them With a Race Critical Ideology

Educators able to identify commonly espoused beliefs central to a White supremacist ideology are similarly more likely to be successful when engaging students' existing beliefs with alternative explanations central to a race critical ideology as discussed in Chapter 4. Generally speaking, educators and institutions might be successful in facilitating experiences that focus on exploring one's own beliefs, values, and assumptions that are rooted in their social identity-based experiences. Educators might use written assignments asking students to identify their beliefs and values and how they influence their assumptions about any given discipline (e.g., finance, science, criminology, business). Institutions with global engagement requirements, such as service learning or study abroad, might integrate a similar type of exploration prior to embarking on service or a trip.[16] Another approach institutions might consider adopting is integrating self-reflection about who students are and the way their social identities influence their view of themselves and others as part of the general education curriculum. General exploration into one's own beliefs, values, and assumptions can help unearth existing beliefs regarding privilege that are more easily engaged when out in the open.

The most pervasive belief within the White supremacist ideology is that society is fair and equal opportunities already exist. This belief uses notions of meritocracy and rugged individualism to mask any acknowledgment of race and racial disparities sustained at an institutional level.[17] Engaging this belief could entail inviting students to explore a topic by finding a concrete policy that supports equality and finding evidence that supports the elimination of racial disparities since its implementation. Inviting students to explore the impact of policies they claim to be evidence of realized social equality allows them to reconsider their beliefs in a scholarly way. Educators could explore ways unfairness are normalized in ways that appear ordinary under the guise of fairness with the entire student group after students complete this assignment. Educators could alternatively engage this belief by exploring the ideas that buttress it, specifically that privilege is situational, ahistorical, and a reflection of personal choices.

Institutions could similarly infuse policy impact assignments into relevant program curriculum to help students' explore their field of study while learning about the impact of privilege in their professional industry. Another way institutions might support challenging this popular belief that society is equal by examining their own policies that reinforce this belief on campus. For example, institutions might reconsider their own admissions policies and practices to consider the underlying assumptions that they have about students based on their racialized experiences. Furthermore, they might examine the ways they feature students of color as exemplars of rugged individualism used to inspire their peers to work harder. This belief is perhaps the most pervasive of all in higher education because of the mythology that higher education is the great equalizer for upward mobility.[18] If university policies and practices reinforce the belief that society is fair and equal opportunities exist for all students who work hard enough, interventions that challenge this belief might be undermined. Students could point to the institution as evidence that anyone can succeed if they are willing to work hard enough.

The belief that privilege is an extension of the human experience is rooted in a view that people "naturally" are different and therefore experience different outcomes in society. Educators could engage this belief by exploring what is natural versus what is a social creation. Is spending time with other people "natural"? Are the codification of laws "natural"? Are the codification of laws that influence when, where, and with whom other people are allowed to spend time "natural"? Alternatively, educators could engage the ideas that privilege is linked to individual bias, situational, and based upon choices to be biased or random chance which tend to reinforce this belief. It might be quite difficult for a student to sustain this belief if they question the extent to which bias is rooted within individuals versus a learned viewpoint through social policies, practices, and norms.

Institutions could support the deconstruction of this belief by exploring where it is present through institutionalized practices and norms on campus. The generic belief that certain views or behaviors are normative or to be expected among certain social groups (e.g., "boys will be boys") should be examined. For example, institutions could conduct an internal audit of its conduct cases including the problem, the race of the students involved, and the type of sanctions or warnings that were distributed. Any observable racial discrepancies should be examined for how policies and practices are (and are not) fairly implemented based upon the false belief that certain social groups are better or worse than others as a matter of who they are. Similarly, institutions might reflect upon how they interpret racial discrepancies in general. Do university leaders view racial gaps in student retention and academic performance as problematic or a reflection of "natural" differences that "is the way it is."

Educators and institutions alike could also work to diminish the false belief that privilege (and social inequality) is a natural extension of human experience by using the race critical belief that privilege (and social inequality) is knowable, particularly by listening to the experience of people of color. Educators might commit to including more readings from scholars and authors of color (and if that is a challenge, then that may be a sign that educators need to racially diversify their reading material themselves). Institutions might require courses to assign a minimum proportion of readings or materials that were created by authors and scholars or color. Similarly, institutions could create policies that all committees must have a certain proportion of staff or faculty of color serving on them because they value pluralistic views that strengthen the life of the campus. Institutions could set caps on the number of committees any individual can serve on each calendar year to prevent the same people (or person) of color from serving.

The generic belief that privilege is generally not a structural phenomenon is harder to directly engage. However, as shared previously, leaning into the commonly associated ideas that privilege is situational and possibly ahistorical or connected to individuals' choices makes the other suggestions offered potentially useful here as well. If educators can eliminate all the "non-structural" areas where privilege is believed to exist, that belief may necessarily become extinct. Similarly, if administrators revise their polices, practices, and norms to uniformly and congruently support a structural view of social inequality, it becomes far more difficult for a generically individualist belief about privilege (and oppression) to thrive and grow. Instead, imagine how a classroom and campus might feel if educators and administrators were regularly and explicitly asserting their belief that privilege and social inequality are socially constructed products of our own creation that we are responsible for addressing.

Engage Students' Feelings and Expressions Related to an Emotionality of Whiteness With Exploration, Juxtaposing Them With Racial Emotional Resiliency, and Supporting Adult Social-Emotional Learning

The emotions and emotional language used by individuals who participate in both the Whiteness and Antiracism Discourses are very similar. It is the way these emotions and emotional language are used and who/what they are directed toward that is the primary difference. Therefore, educators should consider validating their students' emotions in honest and authentic ways.[19] When educators are purposeful in sharing of themselves, including their feelings and associated experiences, it helps minimize students' defensiveness because they experience the educator as *with* them and not *against* them.[20] This approach allows educators to examine students' feelings from a place of empathy and compassion while exploring other ways to express and direct them. For example, when a student expresses anger at being associated with privilege, an educator might join in by stating, "I can feel your anger, and I'm angry too. But I am not angry at the person who brings up privilege or says that White people like me have privilege. I feel anger toward the policies and practices that create and normalize unfair advantages for White folks and disadvantages for people of color that is the cause of so much pain and suffering for people of color and White folks alike."

Empathizing with students when they express each of the feelings central to an emotionality of Whiteness can help students refocus those feelings to work for social change. Educators can leverage the idea of choice central to White racial knowledge to facilitate these teachable moments. When students express feeling uncomfortable, educators can invite them to make a *choice* to be mindful about their feelings and how they operate. Educators can invite students to use their mindfulness to focus less on themselves and more on the reality that inequality exists in society. Furthermore, inviting students to consider being upset about systemic privilege and the idea that working for social change could help eliminate privilege and reduce future discomfort. When students express feeling sad about privilege, educators can invite them to consider ways they do not need to feel sad by instead, harnessing those feelings to examine the source of their sadness and use it as a fuel to work for social change. Students can be reminded that they have a *choice* to feel sad and paralyzed by privilege or motivated to change it and never have to face such sadness again. When students express feeling bad for themselves, educators can observe how such feelings switch the focus to themselves, which does not stop privilege and inequality. Instead, students can be invited to make the *choice* to learn from their own and other's mistakes. When students express anger toward the messenger of privilege or people of color, educators can invite them to examine the source of the anger and consider making a *choice* to redirect those feelings toward the cause of inequality versus the cause of the immediate feeling. Overall, it is useful to remember that privilege hurts everyone in very different ways.[21]

Cultivating emotional vulnerability through emotional language is successful when educators are attentive to times when students co-opt emotional language and assert their perspectives instead. Educators should listen closely to what and how students use emotional language to either *appear* emotionally expressive or to create emotional equivalencies. Upon noticing these emotional discursive maneuvers by their students, educators can call students in about both forms of expression. Educators can engage the appearance of emotional expression by explicitly naming what they observe and invite the student to try again (or perhaps invite another student to model how to express those feelings). Educators can examine false emotional equivalencies by explicitly naming what they observe and offering their own emotional experiences as a form of contradiction. For example, imagine that a student says, "I simply feel like privilege isn't real and I'm entitled to my feelings." An educator might lean in with the following response: "I appreciate that it's hard to feel privilege because privilege isn't always about how it makes us feel. I too struggled to feel privileged as a White person because I would focus on being working class, which lead to stronger feelings for me. However, just because I didn't feel privileged didn't make it disappear."

Another broad approach to cultivating racial emotional resiliency entails promoting adult social-emotional learning (SEL), the ability to understand and manage emotions that contribute to empathy and healthy relationships. Educators can support SEL by allowing emotions to be part of the learning experience. Classroom rules or workshop guidelines can explicitly welcome student emotion and provide guidance for how to appropriately express feelings in those spaces.

This approach would be particularly useful for encouraging students to express emotional vulnerability and not solely use emotional language to assert different views. As shared previously, learning outcomes can (and should) be used in learning experiences to promote the affective side of learning. Educators can also be attuned to emotional expressions and ready to engage with them and incorporate them into the learning experience.

Institutions can also promote SEL through policies, practices, and training opportunities. SEL competencies could be incorporated into performance goals and appraisal processes of faculty, staff, and student staff to normalize and validate emotional competencies that cultivate inclusive cooperation, accountability, and restoration. Administrators could examine how social norms on campus, both overall and within subunits of the institution, can be enhanced through adopting SEL practices and training opportunities. Institutions might also consider incorporating SEL learning outcomes into parts of the curricular and co-curricular experiences to further cultivate healthy social interactions across racial groups on campus.

Examine How Participation in the Whiteness Discourse Is Reinforced Through Policies, Practices, and Social Norms

Challenging students' specific ideas, beliefs, and feelings central to participation in the Whiteness Discourse is key to promoting student learning that aligns with participation in the Antiracism Discourse. However, it is equally critical to examine how educators and institutions knowingly and unknowingly reinforce this perspective, which can undermine our educational interventions. Many approaches for this suggestion have been shared previously, yet are worth repeating to highlight how such an effort can be done intentionally and systemically.

Educators can engage in purposeful reflection about themselves and their educational practice. They can systematically consider the extent to which ideas, beliefs, and feelings central to the Whiteness Discourse are present in their own lives, both personally and professionally. Additionally, educators can explore the extent to which these ideas, beliefs, and feelings are explicitly or implicitly present in their course policies, curriculum, andragogy, and assessment. Consider the following questions as a few examples of ways to audit a course syllabus:

- Are the course content and learning outcomes solely focused on conceptual knowledge, reinforcing the minimization of emotional aspects of learning?
- Is the course content solely focused on either the past or the present, reinforcing ideas that experience is better understood through ahistoricism?
- Are the assigned readings primarily written by White authors and scholars, reinforcing a belief that there is a singular superior view about the world grounded in a White perspective?
- Are course policies sufficiently flexible and conscious of the needs, experiences, and life circumstances of their students in order to maximize their ability to succeed, thus challenging the belief that society is fair and equal for all?

- Is there a statement in the syllabus that frames the course as a solely intellectual space, therefore discouraging emotional forms of knowledge and expression central to an emotionality of Whiteness?

Educators could similarly reflect upon their teaching practices. Consider the following questions as a few examples:

- Is the topic of social identity intentionally or unintentionally avoided, reinforcing the idea that a situational view of the world is preferable than one that acknowledges and embraces social identities?
- When students are invited to participate in discussion, are White students called upon more frequently, reinforcing a belief that White students are naturally superior in their knowledge?
- When students demonstrate feelings of discomfort when privilege or social inequality are discussed, is it noticed and engaged as part of the learning experience to promote racial emotional resiliency?

Institutions can also systemically review their policies, practices, and social norms to identify the presence of underlying ideas, beliefs, and feelings central to the Whiteness Discourse. While institutions might look for bias and discrimination, such an examination is only one part of this necessary review. It is equally important to explore the *lack* of policies, practices, and social norms that support equity and inclusion. The removal of explicitly discriminatory language does not equal equity. Policies for faculty and staff (traditionally established by human resources), student employees (traditionally established by student employment), and the broader student body (traditionally in the form of a code of conduct or student handbook) are places to review. Common practices, including what might be considered "de facto policies" that are not written down, should be identified, and explored as well. Hiring practices reflect a common area such ideas, beliefs, and feelings may be present. Exploring the way search committees are established and the guidelines for rating and discussing candidates are likely areas where individuals may utilize ideas, beliefs, and feelings central to Whiteness. Once again, it is equally critical to identity the presence of ideas, beliefs, and feelings central to Whiteness *and* identify where the presence of ideas, beliefs, and feelings central to Antiracism would be useful to include as part of shifting the broader institutional culture to normalize participation in an Antiracism Discourse.

Create and Support Opportunities to Practice New Habits and Behaviors Consistent With the Antiracism Discourse

White students' capacity to participate in the Antiracism Discourse relies on both the lack of opportunities to participate in a Whiteness Discourse (minimized through the aforementioned suggestions) *and* spaces to actively cultivate and practice the ideas, beliefs, and feelings central to the Antiracism Discourse. If participation in the Antiracism Discourse is not consistently nurtured, it is possible for White students to return to previous perspectives and behaviors associated with Whiteness Discourses that are familiar, comfortable, and reinforced in society overall. Therefore, educators and institutions could identify ways to bring those who participate in the Antiracism Discourse together to actively engage in these Discourses and reinforce one another's participation.

Educators could reimagine their educational spaces as places to practice participating in the Antiracism Discourses, in addition to learning central ideas, beliefs, and feelings. For example, faculty could start every class by checking in with students about their lives and current events to help center students' lives as part of the educational experience and connect course content to both current events and students' lives. Staff might also incorporate similar approaches in their work with student employees and student groups. While this time allotment may not appear to be useful for Antiracism Discourses, the opportunity to invite students to share themselves in an academic space and make sense of the world around them breaks down false barriers between "academic knowledge" and the rest of their world, which promotes systemic over situational thinking.

Faculty and staff alike might also consider incorporating personal reflection and self-examination in curricular and co-curricular experiences. The habit of introspection is critical for examining one's own ideas, beliefs, and feelings and is specifically useful for cultivating the vulnerability that is central to racial emotional resiliency. Space for introspection about students' own social location, as a part of coursework, performance evaluations, or leadership development initiatives, would also send a clear message that social identity matters and influences our lives in ways that are worthy of examination.

Institutions can also intentionally create opportunities to participate in the Antiracism Discourse through curricular and co-curricular opportunities. From a curricular perspective, multiple opportunities (e.g., activities, assignments, experiences, lesson plans) could be integrated into required coursework. For example, imagine if a students' curricular experience involved at least four opportunities through general education courses and at least two opportunities through their major courses. Such interwoven opportunities would create multiple occasions over time for students to not only practice their participation in the Antiracism Discourse but also gain feedback and hone their ideas, beliefs, and feelings over time. Furthermore, institutions with service-learning requirements could reframe these experiences to include explicit identification and analysis of systemic social inequality. Including an explicit structural analysis of social inequality could profoundly alter students' perceptions from an individualistic view of social inequality to a structural one that helps them practice articulating this type of analysis and become more comfortable experiencing and directing their feelings toward social change when faced with structural inequality.

A range of co-curricular opportunities could also be provided to students to practice participating in the Antiracism Discourse. Student involvement units could support the development of antiracism student groups on campus *in addition to* common affinity groups that exist (e.g., Black Student Union). Traditional compilations of campus-wide celebrations, such as welcome back to campus week or homecoming week, could be expanded and reframed to explicitly include antiracism programs as part of what it means to belong to the campus community. Campus-wide diversity programming could be reimagined as spaces to not only learn about but also practice using race critical knowledge, a race critical ideology, and racial emotional resiliency. For example, many institutions host keynote speakers for their annual Rev. Dr. Martin Luther King Jr. events. Consider what it would look like if institutions reimagined these events by inviting student perspectives about racial inequality and hosted peer-facilitated racial dialogues instead of having students sit quietly while invited guests talk. While all these possibilities primarily focus on spaces for students to practice participating in the Antiracism Discourse, similar spaces can, and should, be created for administrators, faculty, and staff on campus as well. Creating spaces for these folks to also practice and reinforce their participation in the Antiracism Discourse will help enlist university members to sustain these practices among the student body.

Loving Ourselves and Others to Work for Social Change

Educating White students about privilege is not a simple or easy task. Many of the recommendations posed previously require training and support for staff and faculty to successfully develop their capacity for this work. Educators must engage in necessary "self-work" coupled with developing necessary knowledge and skills to create and facilitate these experiences.[22] Even still, the most committed and competent educators begin at a severe disadvantage. Society is structured to teach and reinforce White racial knowledge, a White supremacist ideology, and an emotionality of Whiteness. Many (if not most) White students on campus arrive embodying these ways of knowing the world while actively participating in the Whiteness Discourse. Our educational institutions and practices are riddled with the ideas, beliefs, and feelings central to Whiteness that further normalize the very ways of understanding privilege that we seek to change. However, educators committed to social justice understand that we must continue to help students unlearn and relearn the ways of understanding the world to cease participating in the Whiteness Discourse and begin participating in an Antiracism Discourse.

Diane Goodman encourages educators committed to social justice to consider a powerful question, "Can we love [our students] enough to help them learn?"[23] It is easy and understandable to become frustrated with White students for not understanding privilege. This statement is particularly true for faculty and staff of color who are often expected to shoulder social justice education efforts. These individuals are often placed in the unfair position of educating White students. When White students express their conceptual, ideological, and emotional resilience, they often lash out against these educators in ways that perpetuate the harmful and violent dynamics reinforced among participation in the Whiteness Discourse. White educators can be in solidarity with their peers of color by helping support and sustain these interventions, including as social justice educators themselves. However, by reminding ourselves that White students' discursive maneuvers are a reflection of their socialization into the Whiteness Discourse that was learned and can be unlearned, we can humanize both our students and ourselves in our educational efforts.

The great Paulo Freire is often cited for his perspective on education that humanizes students, particularly those who experience oppression. Central to all his writings exists his belief that all people, students and educators alike, were constantly growing past their original conditioning reflective of our hegemonic society. It was his belief that change was possible that fueled his work as a scholar and practitioner.[24] It is from a similar place that I encourage all educators committed to social justice to ask ourselves if we are willing and able to love our students and ourselves enough to see through White students' socialization and help them embrace a new perspective and way of being that embodies participation in the Antiracism Discourse.

Education is a labor of love. Educators support student learning because they love helping students become the best versions of themselves and contribute to our society. Educators committed to social justice support student learning because they love others and themselves enough to help students understand privilege as a critical part of reimagining society and working for social change that realizes equity and inclusion. May the insights and suggestions offered here provide educators more avenues to express that love.

Notes

1. See Unaffiliated Critic (2015).
2. See Fatal Force (2021).
3. See Centers for Disease Control and Prevention (2019).
4. See McIntosh et al. (2020).
5. See Espinosa et al. (2019).
6. See Brown (2016) and Kolowich (2015).
7. See Bonilla et al. (2012).
8. See W. E. B. Du Bois Center (n.d.).
9. See Kendi (2019, p. 10).
10. See Tharp and Moreano (2020), Adams (2016).
11. See Adams (2016).
12. See Tharp and Moreano (2020).
13. While curating learning activities are not dependent upon learning outcomes, it is an educational best practice to develop activities in relationship to stated learning outcomes.
14. See chapter 10 in Tharp and Moreano (2020) for an example of a workshop that used this type of approach and set of activities.
15. See Taylor and Hauser (2021).
16. See Tharp (2013) for an example of a workshop curriculum integrated into service-learning courses.

17 See Bonilla-Silva (2014).
18 See Stevens (2007).
19 See Goodman (2015).
20 See Tharp and Moreano (2020).
21 See Goodman (2011, pp. 84–100) for a list of ways privilege groups are harmed by social inequality.
22 See Adams et al. (2015) and Tharp and Moreano (2020) for a discussion about social justice education self-work and relevant competencies.
23 See Goodman (2015).
24 See Freire (1998).

References

Adams, M. (2016). Pedagogical foundations for social justice education. In M. Adams, L. A. Bell, D. J. Goodman, & K. J. Yoshi (Eds.), *Teaching for diversity and social justice* (3rd ed., pp. 27–53. Routledge.

Adams, M., Bell, L. A., Goodman, D. J., & Joshi, K. Y. (Eds.). (2015). *Teaching for diversity and social justice* (3rd ed.). Routledge.

Bonilla, J., Lindeman, L., & Taylor, N. (2012). Educating for and assessing cultural competence. In K. N. Major & S. Gooden (Eds.), *Cultural competence for public administrators*. M. E. Sharpe.

Bonilla-Silva, E. (2014). *Racism without racists: Color-blind racism and the persistence of racial inequality in America* (4th ed.). Rowman & Littlefield Publishers.

Brown, A. (2016, January 7). Diversity courses are in high demand. Can they make a difference? *The Chronicle of Higher Education*. http://chronicle.com/article/Diversity-Courses-Are-in-High/234828.

Centers for Disease Control and Prevention. (2019). *Chartbook data tables*. www.cdc.gov/nchs/data/hus/2019/fig01-508.pdf.

Espinosa, L. L., Turk, J. M., Taylor, M., & Chessman, H. M. (2019). *Race and ethnicity in higher education: A status report*. American Council on Education.

Fatal Force. (2021, March 21). *The Washington Post*. www.washingtonpost.com/graphics/investigations/police-shootings-database/.

Freire, P. (1998). *Pedagogy of freedom*. Rowman and Littlefield Publishers, Inc.

Goodman, D. J. (2011). *Promoting diversity and social justice: Educating people from privileged groups* (2nd ed.). Routledge.

Goodman, D. J. (2015). Can you love them enough to help them learn? Reflections of a social justice educator on addressing resistance from White students to anti-racism education. *Understanding & Dismantling Privilege*, 5(1), 62–73.

Kendi, I. X. (2019). *How to be an antiracist*. One World.

Kolowich, S. (2015, November 20). Diversity training is in demand. Does it work? *The Chronicle of Higher Education*. http://chronicle.com/article/Diversity-Training-Is-in/234280.

McIntosh, K., Moss, E., Nunn, R., & Shambaugh, J. (2020, February 27). Examining the Black-White wealth gap. *The Brookings Institution*. www.brookings.edu/blog/up-front/2020/02/27/examining-the-black-white-wealth-gap/.

Stevens, M. L. (2007). *Creating a class: College admissions and the education of elites*. Harvard University Press.

Taylor, D. B., & Hauser, C. (2021, March 17). What to know about the Atlanta spa shootings. *The New York Times*. www.nytimes.com/2021/03/17/us/atlanta-spa-shootings.html.

Tharp, D. S. (2013). A proposed workshop curriculum for students to responsibly engage in cultural conflict in community-based service learning. *Journal of Transformative Education, 10*, 177–194.

Tharp, D. S., & Moreano, R. A. (2020). *Doing social justice education: A practitioner's guide for workshops and structured conversations*. Stylus.

Unaffiliated Critic. (2015, April 28). James Baldwin: How much time do you want for your "progress?". [Video]. *YouTube*. www.youtube.com/watch?v=OCUlE5ldPvM&t=1s.

W. E. B. Du Bois Center. (n.d.). *Du Bois Quotes*. http://duboiscenter.library.umass.edu/du-bois-quotes/.

INDEX

Note: Page numbers in *italics* indicate a figure and page numbers in **bold** indicate a table on the corresponding page. Page numbers followed by "n" indicate a note.

2019 Pew Research Center survey 8, 13

adult social-emotional learning 208–210
affirmative action 120
ahistorical privilege 86–90
American Dream, The (political cartoon) 14, 87–89, 111–115, 119–122, 132–135, 138–139, 150, 151, 153, 154, 156–158
anger 136–140, 152–157
antiracism 10–12; college students' views on privilege 12–14; race critical ideology 11; race critical knowledge 10–11; racial emotional resiliency 11; Whiteness and 12; *see also* Antiracism Discourse
Antiracism Discourse 50, 67–68, 99, 196; colonization 72–74; critical knowledge, critical ideology and emotional resiliency reinforcement on one another *183*, *184*; institutionalized superiority 70–72, 75, 77; intentional implementation of privilege 72–74, 77; iron triangle of ideas, beliefs, and feelings 180–186, *181*, *182*; new habits and behaviors practice 211–213; participants and participation in 54–58; participating in 180–186, *181–185*; privilege and social inequality 56–57; privilege situated in past and present 75–78; racial emotional resiliency 56–57; social power 68–70, 76–77; superiority complexes 72–74; Whiteness Discourse and 57–58; White privilege 58–61
Arbery, A. 15
Aristotle 31
Association of American Colleges and Universities 1, 16n1
awkwardness 157

Baldwin, J. 193
Beck, G. 53
beliefs 98–99, 124–125, 126n, 127n; about privilege 31–34; accurate 99–101; accurate beliefs and ideas 101–103; acknowledging and engaging beliefs and ideas 118–122; affirmative action 120; collective memory 30; cultural racism 32; Discourses 196; emotionality and 165–166; ideas and feelings interconnected 195; ideology 29–31; inaccurate 103–115; individualistic 110–115; information about privilege and belief in equality 33; information about privilege and belief in superiority 33; racialized ideologies 31–32; racial privilege and oppression 102, 126n5, 126n6; social construction of race 102, 126n4; socialization 195; society

126n9; structural refutation 111–112; Whiteness and Antiracism Discourses 122–124; *see also* inaccurate beliefs about privilege; iron triangle of ideas, beliefs, and feelings
Bennett, M. J. 45
"big D" Discourse 46–47
Black chattel slavery 3–4, 55
Black Discourse 49
Black Lives Matter (BLM) 1, 9, 24, 103, 108, 129, 190
Black oppression 3, 11, 108
Black people 2–4, 8, 9, 31, 33, 37, 38, 49, 53, 72, 84, 85, 87–89, 101, 113–115, 193; *see also* people of color
Black privileges 113, 114, 148
BLM *see* Black Lives Matter (BLM)
Bonilla-Silva, E. 4, 32, 99
Boone, A. 161
Breakfast Club, The 176

Calhoun, W. M. 190
Carlson, T. 52, 53
Cisgender Discourses 48–49
Cisgender Feminine Discourse 48–49
Cisgender Masculine Discourse 48
collective memory 30
colonization 72–74
color-blind equality 107–109, 116
color-blindness 4, 13, 32, 37, 92, 99, 104
communicative practices 46–48, 50, 54, 58
community 30; Black 11, 137, 182; White race 31, 38
conceptual knowledge: as coordinating class 27–28; described 26–27
Cooper, A. 38
Copernican Revolution (1500s) 98
core ideas about privilege: affirmative action 78–79; as ahistorical 86–90; Antiracism Discourse 68–76; choice and chance 81–83, 90; different ideas and common categories 92, 92–94; Discourse 92–94; home ownership 93–94; individual bias 83–86, 90; institutionalized superiority 70–72, 75, 77, 93; intentionally implemented 72–74, 77; past and present 75–78; race consciousness 92; race critical knowledge 77, 78–79; situational view 79–81, 90–91, 96; social power 68–70, 76–77; time and privilege relationship between 93; Whiteness Discourse 79–91

critical race theory 11, 52, 53, 55
Crow, J. 55, 60
Cruz, T. 161
cultural racism 32
culture 45
cycle of liberation 8, 10
cycle of socialization 7, 8, 10, 35, 45–46

Daily Show, The 57–61
Daniel Tiger's Neighborhood 22
Dear White People 13, 49
de facto policies 211
Delgado, R. 99
determination: expressions of 141; for social change 140–141
DiAngelo, R. 145
discomfort 157–159
Discourses 94, 196; antiracism 54–61; "big D" 46–47; Black 49; Cisgender 48–49; Cisgender Feminine 48–49; Cisgender Masculine 48; exploring college students' understanding of privilege 61–64; "little d" 46, 47; Non-Smoking 170; Parenting 47; Professional 50; Racial 49, 50; Smoking 170, 173; social groups and 46–50; *see also* Antiracism Discourse; iron triangle of ideas, beliefs, and feelings; Medical Doctor Discourse; Whiteness Discourse
diSessa, A. A. 27
discrimination 68; *see also* reverse discrimination
diversity education 1
Dora the Explorer 22
Du Bois, W. E. B. 194

emotionality 131; beliefs and 165–166; privilege 166–167; racial emotional resiliency and 131, 162–165; social inequality 167; *see also* emotionality of Whiteness; feelings
emotionality of Whiteness 144–146, 167n3, 196–197; anger toward others 152–157; co-opting emotional expression to assert dominance 146–149; discomfort 157–159; feeling bad 151–152; racial emotional resiliency and 167n4, 198–199, 208–210; sadness 149–150; *see also* feelings
emotions: cycle of socialization 7, 8, 10, 35, 45–46; co-opting emotional expression to assert dominance 146–149; described 34; and emotional

responses 35; negative 5; socialization process 37; vulnerability 131–133; White emotionality 37–39; Whiteness Discourse 51; *see also* emotionality; emotionality of Whiteness; feelings

family social group 45
fan days 43
Feagin, J. R. 3
feelings 26, 34–40, 129–130, 166–167; anger 136–140, 152–157; bad 145, 151–152; beliefs about privilege 39; beliefs and ideas interconnected 195; color-blind 37–38; connecting emotionality to beliefs 165–166; determination 140–141; discomfort 157–159; Discourses 196; emotionality of Whiteness 144–159, 198–199, 208–210; facilitating social change 141–144; frustration 153–154; gendered expressions of sadness 36–37; guilt and shame 39; happiness and pride 35; racial emotional resiliency 130–141, 198–199, 208–210; relationship between ideas, beliefs, and 39–40; resisting social change 144–161; sadness 36–37, 149–150; shame 35, 39, 136, 151–152; similarities and differences 162–165; social change 141–161; socialization 35–37, 195; upset 133–135; White emotionality 37–39; *see also* anger; guilt; iron triangle of ideas, beliefs, and feelings; *specific feelings*
Floyd, G. 15, 38, 56, 176
Freire, P. 214
frustration 153–154

Gee, J. P. 14, 46
Gillibrand, K. 182, 186
Goodman, D. J. 213
Greene, M. T. 117
guilt 38, 39, 59, 136, 151–152, 176, 180

Halbwachs, M. 30
Harro, B. 7, 8, 35, 45, 131
home ownership 93–94
How to be an Antiracist 194
Hunger Games, The 49

ideas: beliefs and feelings interconnected 195; Discourses 196; socialization 195; *see also* core ideas about privilege; iron triangle of ideas, beliefs, and feelings

ideology 29–30; community 30, 31; individuals 30, 31; material impact of 30–31; social groups 30, 31; *see also* race critical ideology; White supremacy ideology
inaccurate beliefs about privilege 104–105; color-blind equality 107–109; ideas and 115–118; individualistic phenomenon 110–115; meritocracy 104–107; social inequality 109–110; society is fair 104–109
individual bias 83–86, 90
inequality 121
institutionalized superiority 70–72, 75, 77, 93
iron triangle of ideas, beliefs, and feelings 170–171; Antiracism Discourse 180–186, *181–185*; breaking down 186–190; clockwise visual representation 172–173, *173*; Discourse 171–172, *172*; reinforcement of one another 171–186; shifting our Discourse participation 190–191; Smoking Discourse 172–174; Whiteness Discourse 174–180, *175, 179*
irritation 152–154

Jim Crow laws 78, 87, 88, 121–122

Kaepernick, C. 161
Kelly, M. 160
Kendall, F. E. 4
Kendi, I. X. 11, 12, 194
kneeling controversy 161

Latinx people 2, 7, 84, 85, 193
Leonardo, Z. 3, 8
Limbaugh, R. 176, 180
"little d" discourse 46, 47

Matias, C. E. 37, 144
McIntosh, P. 2
Medical Doctor Discourse 47–48
meritocracy 104–107
Monday, R. 161
Moreano, R. A. 202
Mullin, M. 118
Mulvaney, M. 117
musical instruments 141–142

narcissism of Whiteness 144–145
National Association for the Advancement of Colored People (NAACP) 190

negative emotions 5
New York Times 142
nominal identity 107
Non-Smoking Discourse 170

Obama, B. 4, 129
oppression: described 2–3; whiteness as racialized lens for 3–6
O'Reilly, B. 58–60, 122
Outburst! 67
Owens, C. 53

Parenting Discourse 47
people of color 3–9, 17n13, 37–38, 51–53, 69–72, 93, 100–103, 155–159, 186–190, 197–199, 208
political cartoon *see American Dream, The* (political cartoon)
post–civil rights movement 31
prior knowledge 40
prison system 101
privilege 58–59; ahistorical 86–90; Antiracism Discourse 196, 197; Black 113, 114, 148; college students' views 12–14; defined 2; educational recommendations 199–213; emotional intensity about 59; emotionality 166–167; exploring college students' understanding relative to discourses 61–64; guilt and 59; ideas, beliefs, and feelings interconnected 195; individualistic or structural 59; oppression and 2–3; organized around hard work *29*; organized around social power *28*; social change 213–214; social identity and 60; social inequality and 162–165; students prior knowledge about 194–195, 200–201; White 2, 52, 58–61, 182; whiteness as racialized lens for 3–6; Whiteness Discourse 196–197; *see also* beliefs; core ideas about privilege; inaccurate beliefs about privilege; racial privilege
Professional Discourses 50

race consciousness 92
race critical ideology 125n2, 126n3, 197, 198, 206–208; *see also* beliefs
race critical knowledge 77, 78–79, 197; relationship between white 90; White racial knowledge and 197–198, 204–206; *see also* Antiracism Discourse
Racial Discourses 49, 50

racial emotional resiliency 130, 163–165, *183*, *184*, 197–199, 208–210; anger 136–140; described 130; emotionality and 131, 162–165; emotionality of Whiteness and 198–199, 208–210; feeling determination 140–141; shame or guilt 136; upset 133–135; vulnerability through emotional expression 131–133; waking up process 131
racial inferiority 69–70
racial privilege: anger and 137; described 2; and oppression 30, 87, 99, 102, 114, 126, 197, 198; and social inequality 50; *see also* antiracism; Whiteness
racial superiority 69–70
Ramsey, F. 56, 57
reverse discrimination 146
Roediger, D. 3

sadness 36–37, 149–150
sexism 141
shame 35, 39, 136, 151–152
Shapiro, B. 94–96, 122
Sherin, B. 27
sincere fictions 4
slavery 88, 101
smoking 170–174; *see also* iron triangle of ideas, beliefs, and feelings
Smoking Discourse 170, 173
social change 213–214; anger 152–157; co-opting emotional expression to assert dominance 144–149; discomfort 157–159; feeling bad 151–152; feelings facilitating social change working together 141–144; feelings resisting 144–161; sadness 149–150
social-emotional learning (SEL) 209–210
social groups 30, 43–44; communicative practices 46–48; culture defined 45; Discourses 45; family 45; learning to belong 44–46; socialization 44–46; superiority of 70–72
social identity: groups 7, 27, 31, 32, 35, 36, 38, 83–85, 93, 101, 111; privilege and 60
social inequality 100, 109–110, 116; emotionality 167; privilege and 162–165; Whiteness Discourse 51–52
socialization 40, 44–45, 195, 199; cycle of 45–46; described 45
social power 68–70, 76–77
sociocultural learning theory 6

South Park 13
Stefancic, J. 99
Stewart, J. 57–60
Strayed, C. 142, 143
student learning 22–23; beliefs and 29–34; conceptual knowledge 26–28; feelings and 34–40; ideas and 26–29; prior knowledge and experience 24–26; socialization and 6–10; teaching 23
students: educational recommendations 199–213; prior knowledge about privilege 194–195, 200–201; *see also* student learning
superiority complexes 62, 70–74, 100, 138

Talbert, S. 38
Taylor, B. 15, 38
teaching 23
Tharp, D. S. 202
time and privilege 93
Trump, D. 1, 4, 37, 117, 129, 161, 190

upset feelings 133–135

vulnerability 131–133
Vygotsky, L. S. 6

"waking up" movement 9, 10, 131
Warren, E. 57
Washington Post, The 193
White emotionality 4–5, 37–39
White fragility 145
White insurrectionists 103, 117, 118
White like Me 143–144
Whiteness 8; described 3; narcissism of 144–145; racial emotional resiliency *vs.* emotionality 162–165; White emotionality 4–5; White racial knowledge 3–5; White supremacy 4, 5; *see also* Whiteness Discourse
Whiteness begets Whiteness 3
Whiteness Discourse 50–54, 67, 89–91, 196; ahistorical view of privilege 86–90; choice and chance 81–83, 90; described 50; emotions and emotional displays 51–52; individual bias 83–86, 90; iron triangle of ideas, beliefs, and feelings 174–180, *175, 179*; knowledge, supremacist ideology and emotionality reinforcement on one another *177, 178*; participation in 50–54, 174–180, *175, 177–179*, 210–211; privilege 52–53; relationship between white racial knowledge ideas *90*; situational view of privilege 79–81, 90–91; social inequality 51–52; White racial knowledge used 95–96
White people 121
White privilege 2, 52, 58–61, 182
White Puritans 31
White racial community 31, 38
White racial knowledge 3–5, 95–96, 174, *175, 177–179*, 196–197, 199, 204–206; ideas about privilege 89–91, *90*; race critical knowledge and 197–198, 204–206; *see also* beliefs
White supremacist ideology 1, 99, 115, 126, 165, 174, 176–178, 190, 191, 196–199, 206–208, 213
White supremacy ideology 4, 5, 104, 116, 118–120, 122–125, 126n, 135; *see also* beliefs
White women's tears 38, 145
Wise, T. 143, 144
Wright, M. K. 190

Young Americans for Freedom 95–96

Zucker, J. 52, 53

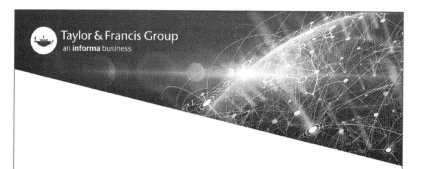

Taylor & Francis eBooks

www.taylorfrancis.com

A single destination for eBooks from Taylor & Francis with increased functionality and an improved user experience to meet the needs of our customers.

90,000+ eBooks of award-winning academic content in Humanities, Social Science, Science, Technology, Engineering, and Medical written by a global network of editors and authors.

TAYLOR & FRANCIS EBOOKS OFFERS:

- A streamlined experience for our library customers
- A single point of discovery for all of our eBook content
- Improved search and discovery of content at both book and chapter level

REQUEST A FREE TRIAL
support@taylorfrancis.com

Printed in the United States
by Baker & Taylor Publisher Services